CRIME
and
THE LIFE
COURSE

An Introduction

Michael L. Benson

University of Cincinnati

Roxbury Publishing Company
Los Angeles, California

Library of Congress Cataloging-in-Publication Data

Benson, Michael L.
Crime and the life course: an introduction / Michael L. Benson.
   p. cm.
Includes bibliographical references and index.
ISBN 1-891487-78-7
1. Criminology. 2. Developmental psychology. 3. Life cycle, Human. I.
   Title.
HV6030.B45 2002   364–dc21
   2001019795   CIP

CRIME AND THE LIFE COURSE: AN INTRODUCTION

Publisher: Claude Teweles
Managing Editor: Dawn VanDercreek
Production Editor: Jim Ballinger
Copyeditor: Pauline Piekarz
Proofreaders: Roger Mensink, David Marion
Indexing: Evergreen Valley Indexing Service, IndexArts
Typography: Synergistic Data Systems
Cover Design: Marnie Kenney

Printed on acid-free paper in the United States of America. This book meets the standards for recycling of the Environmental Protection Agency.

ISBN 1-891487-78-7

Roxbury Publishing Company
P.O. Box 491044
Los Angeles, California 90049-9044
Tel.: (310) 473-3312 • Fax: (310) 473-4490
E-mail: roxbury@roxbury.net
Website: www.roxbury.net

The Roxbury Series in Crime, Justice, and Law

Series Coeditors:

Ronald L. Akers, University of Florida

Gary F. Jensen, Vanderbilt University

This new series features concisely and cogently written books on an array of important topics, including specific types of crime and central or emerging issues in criminology, justice, and law.

The books in this series are designed and written specifically for classroom use in criminology, sociology, deviance, delinquency, criminal justice, and related classes. The intent of the series is to provide both an introduction to the issues and the latest knowledge available—at a level accessible to undergraduate students. ✦

Contents

Acknowledgements

Special thanks to Claude Teweles who contacted me several years ago about writing a book for Roxbury. I appreciate his willingness to let me take on the topic of crime and the life course, especially since most of my published work is in the area of white-collar crime. It was something of a gamble on his part to turn me loose on this foreign territory, one that I hope has turned out to be useful.

Several friends and colleagues have in one way or another enriched my thinking about criminology and the life course perspective. Sally Simpson read and offered many helpful comments on chapter 5 and white-collar crime. I greatly appreciate her willingness to help out. I am also indebted to Frank Cullen and Greer Fox for many stimulating conversations about criminology, families, and the life course approach. For her encouragement, support, understanding, and friendship, I am grateful to Diana K. Harris. Finally, thanks to Donald "Chip" Hastings who read and provided numerous insightful suggestions on an early version of the manuscript. Of course, none of these individuals bears any responsibility for my interpretations and conclusions.

It is a pleasure to acknowledge my debt to the many colleagues who graciously agreed to review the manuscript for Roxbury. Their guidance and suggestions proved to be very useful: Ronald L. Akers (*University of Florida*), Thomas Bernard (*Pennsylvania State University*), Mathieu Deflem (*Purdue University*), Ineke Haen Marshall (*University of Nebraska at Omaha*), Robert E. Stanfield (*University of Vermont*), Christopher Uggen (*University of Minnesota*), Jeffrey T. Ulmer (*Pennsylvania State University*), and Richard A. Wright (*Chicago State University*).

And finally, thanks to Shelley and Christopher, who have made my life course more interesting, more fun, and much richer than I deserve. ✦

Chapter 1

An Overview of Life Course Theory and Research

On life's vast ocean diversely we sail.

—Alexander Pope

four Million Babies

E very year close to 4 million babies are born in the United States. In 1999, according to the U.S. National Center for Health Statistics, the exact number was 3,959,417. A little over half (51 percent) are boys, and the rest, obviously, are girls. At birth, the average life expectancy of this cohort of newborns is about 73 years for males and 79 years for females. In the three-quarters of a century that most of these children will live, they will do many things and many things will happen to them. If current trends continue, approximately 1.25 million of these children will be born out of wedlock—that is, to unmarried mothers. Half of the children will grow up in stable two-parent households with their biological parents. The other half will live in households with only one parent at least some of the time before they are 18 years old. Almost all of the children will go to school, and of those who graduate from high school nearly two-thirds (62 percent)

1

will attend college. After finishing their schooling, they will get jobs, lose jobs, and eventually retire from the workforce. Nearly 90 percent will get married at least once during their lives, but over half of the marriages (51 percent) will end in divorce.[1] Many of these children eventually will have children of their own.

In addition to the normal and expected activities of going to school, marrying, and working, these individuals will also engage in a variety of other activities as they age. Some of these activities will not be "normal" in the sense of being normatively expected and approved by society. Rather, they will be defined as abnormal or deviant or criminal. There is a difference, though, between moral and statistical deviance. Self-report studies indicate that virtually all of the boys will commit some kind of minor delinquency some time during their teenage years, and so will a substantial proportion of the girls (Short and Nye 1958; Gold 1966; Hindelang 1973). Indeed, minor delinquency is so common that it is statistically "normal" in the sense that the vast majority of kids do it (Moffitt 1997). A small percentage of the boys, anywhere from 3 to 6 percent, will engage in forms of delinquency that are not normal in either the statistical or moral sense of the word. They will repeatedly commit serious personal and property offenses (Wolfgang, Figlio, and Sellin 1972; West and Farrington 1977; Shannon 1982). They stand a good chance of becoming career criminals and spending large parts of their lives in jail or prison, or they will die early in life.

From the viewpoint of each individual child, the procession of events between birth and death will make up a life, a life that will feel to the individual as though it is filled with unique, one-of-a-kind experiences. Everyone knows, of course, that other people go to school, get jobs, marry, have children, and break the law. Only an astonishingly unaware and self-centered person would not recognize that these events and activities are commonplace. Nevertheless, as they travel along the paths of their lives, each individual will have experiences and emotions that will feel unique to her or him. And in a sense, they are. The accidents of time and place, for example, that bring two people together to marry are unique to the individuals involved, just as are the intimate disagreements and fights that may cause them to divorce. Likewise, the combination of peer pressure and the dumb luck of being in the wrong place at the wrong time that leads a teenager to vandalize his high school some Saturday night will, from the perspective of the teenager, appear as a unique set of circumstances.

Because each of us has a unique inner emotional experience of the events that make up our life, it is difficult for us to step back and look at the broader patterns of common experience. Yet, stripped of their singular details of time, place, and personality, the events of our lives form a limited number of patterns, and many people experience similar patterns. For example, in the United States most people enter the workforce full time sometime in their twenties and work more or less continuously until they retire at age 65. There are, of course, variations and exceptions to this general pattern, and a certain amount of disorder in the life course is not uncommon (Rindfuss, Swicegood, and Rosenfeld 1987). Some people switch careers and jobs frequently; others stay put for decades. Some people become disabled and have to stop working early, or they may experience prolonged unemployment for other reasons, or they may strike it rich with an Internet startup company and retire early. Nevertheless, a substantial proportion of the population follows the general pattern of full-time work until age 65.

The study of patterns and variations in people's experiences as they age is the subject of life course theory. This book explores how the life course approach may be used to better understand crime in society and patterns in the involvement of individuals in crime.

The Life Course Perspective

The life course perspective is a broad multidisciplinary intellectual movement. It encompasses ideas and empirical observations from a variety of disciplines, including history, biology, psychology, and sociology, to name a few. It is not an explicit theory of anything, but rather a new way of thinking about and studying human lives and development; it is an emerging paradigm (Elder 1996).

In its simplest sense, the life course may be defined as the "duration of a person's existence" (Riley 1986). The duration of a person's existence, however, does not simply consist of a continuous flux of undifferentiated time and experience. Life is more structured than that. Our lives consist of a sequence of phases that are socially constructed and that are recognized by individuals and society as being different from one and another. The different phases typically are separated from each other by normatively defined transitions and tend to be ordered in the sense that certain events are expected to precede or follow other events most of the time (Mayer and Muller 1986). For example, from a normative point of view getting married is expected to proceed to having children, even though the ordering of these two events often is reversed in practice.

Glen H. Elder, Jr., a leading figure in life course research, defines the life course as the interconnected trajectories that a person has as he or she ages through life (Elder 1985). A trajectory is a sequence of linked states within a conceptually defined range of behavior or experience. It is a career or pathway over the life span. For example, we can speak of a person's educational trajectory, which is a series of linked states related to education. To illustrate, for many people the standard educational trajectory consists of passage through elementary school, junior high school, high school, and college, leading eventually to a college degree and cessation of the formal educational trajectory around age 22 or 23. As people move through this trajectory, they graduate from one level of schooling to another. Each graduation marks a change in state that is called a transition. Entering college marks a transition from one state to another in an educational trajectory. Transitions are always embedded in trajectories, and the states that make up a trajectory are always linked to one another by transitions (Elder 1996).

According to Elder (1985), the life course perspective is based on four central premises, which can be summarized as the following:

(1) Aging and developmental change must be viewed as continuous processes that occur throughout life.

(2) Trajectories in different realms of life are interconnected and have reciprocal effects on one another.

(3) Human development is influenced by social and historical conditions.

(4) Efforts to optimize human development through preventive or corrective interventions will be most effective if they are sensitive to the developmental needs and capabilities of particular age periods in the life span.

Although we typically think of development and growth primarily in regard to children or adolescents, the life course perspective holds that "aging is not simply growing old beyond some arbitrary point in the life course" (Riley 1986). Rather, aging and development are continuous processes. Adulthood is not a static unchanging condition. As adults age, they undergo continuous biological, psychological, and social changes, though perhaps at slower rates than children and adolescents. Aging and development go on continuously from the moment of one's conception in the womb to one's last breath. From beginning to end, we change and develop biologically, psychologically, and socially.

Life course researchers typically conceive of trajectories in three different domains of human behavior and functioning—biological, psychological, and social. According to the second premise of the life course perspective, trajectories in these different realms are intimately connected and have reciprocal effects on each other. Biological developments can influence our psychological and social trajectories. For example, as biological beings, we are born without the ability to reproduce. We develop reproductive capacity when we go through puberty. Puberty is an important biological transition that has important implications for psychological and social trajectories. When young women go through puberty, they often experience profound changes in their psychological makeup, such as reduced self-esteem. Thus, puberty may lead to a transition in psychological trajectories of young women, which may in turn affect how they perform in school and hence have the potential to alter their educational trajectories. Indeed, researchers have found that in some settings girls who reach menarche at age 11 or younger are more likely to exhibit multiple forms of behavioral deviancy than girls who mature later (Magnusson and Cairns 1996). Thus, a transition in a biological trajectory can have ramifications for psychological and social trajectories. In turn, social events also may influence psychological and even biological trajectories. Trajectories across and within the different domains of human behavior and functioning have mutual interactive effects on one another.

The third premise of the life course perspective is more complex than the first two and requires a more extended discussion. The premise is that human development is multidetermined and influenced by social and historical conditions and changes (Magnusson and Cairns 1996). As we develop over the life course, we are shaped by a multitude of factors and experiences. Some of these factors and experiences are close, personal, and very direct in their effects upon us. For example, the type of family we grow up in, our relationships with our parents, whether we have older or younger siblings, all of these idiosyncratic circumstances that characterize our personal histories can dramatically shape our development and the trajectories we follow in life. Our individual lives are linked to the lives of others in the sense that changes in the lives of persons around us can have an impact on our own trajectories (Elder 1996). Consider, for instance, how a 10-year-old daughter would be affected if her mother were convicted of a crime and sentenced to prison. In this case, an event in the mother's life would undoubtedly have a strong, and most likely negative, impact on the child's psychological and social development. The way in which we are linked to others influences who we are and who we become (Elder 1996).

Even though families and other significant individuals help shape the life course, they represent only one source of influence on our lives. Broader social conditions and changes also influence the life course. Our lives carry the imprint of what happens in our particular social worlds (Elder 1995). If our social world undergoes rapid change, it can disrupt our lives and change the timing and direction of important social events, such as marriage, having children, or pursuing an occupational career. For example, during the Cultural Revolution in China in the late 1960s and early 1970s, the Chinese government implemented a policy of "sending-down" urban youths to live and work in rural areas. Being sent-down affected the youths' educational, family, and occupational trajectories. The longer the duration of the send-down experience, the more likely that marriage and childbearing would be delayed (Zhou and Hou 1999). For a generation of urban youth, the send-down policy radically changed the life course. The Cultural Revolution and the send-down policy are dramatic examples of rapid social change. Wars and economic depressions are other examples. The Great Depression of the 1930s had profound effects on children raised during that period, and the nature of the effects varied, depending upon how old a child was when the depression began (Elder 1974).

Events such as the Cultural Revolution, the Great Depression, and world wars are the social equivalents of a large comet striking the earth. They shake things up dramatically, visibly, and quickly. Other social changes occur incrementally and work their effects more slowly, less visibly, but just as profoundly nevertheless.

Over the course of the past century and a half, American society has shifted from a farm-based rural society to a highly industrialized urban society. This change has taken place over several generations. Coinciding with the change from a rural to an urban society has been a change in the nature of work that has sharply altered the adolescent phase of the typical life course. Work has become less manual and more technical, requiring specialized skills, training, and education. In the nineteenth century, by the time a young man reached the age of 16, he was more or less fully equipped to play a productive role in society and the economy. Most of the available work was farm-related manual labor. It did not require special skills but rather strength, agility, and endurance, traits that teenagers and young adults have in abundance. Thus, young people between the ages of 16 and 20 were ready to assume adult roles in society. People tended to marry early and to start families early. The transitions from child to adult to parent occurred over a shorter duration than they do now, and there was a closer connection between physical and social maturity.

In the late twentieth and early twenty-first centuries in advanced societies, manual labor is becoming increasingly rare and increasingly poorly remunerated. Work requires technical skills and advanced education. As a result, young people are no longer able to assume productive roles in the adult economy. They must delay entry into the adult world of work and marriage in order to have time to pursue the education necessary to perform today's complex information-based work. A gap has opened between the age at which people become physically mature and the age at which they become socially mature. By socially mature, I mean able to assume a productive role in society. This gap, sometimes called the *maturity gap*, represents a major change in the duration of the adolescent life stage and in the timing of important transitions. The widening of the maturity gap that has occurred throughout the twentieth century is an important factor in the rise and changing patterns of youth crime (Moffitt 1997; Felson 1998).

The life course perspective holds that human lives can be better understood if they are viewed in their changing worlds. We can call this the *principle of contextualism*, which holds that human development cannot be separated from the context in which it occurs (Dannefer 1984). People cannot be separated from their time and place in history. Perhaps at no other time has the connection between biography and history been more telling than in the twentieth century. Throughout the past century, monumental changes—two world wars, a profound economic depression, the rise and fall of communism, and technological advances in transportation and communication that were practically unimaginable at the beginning of the century—filled the historical record. All of these changes undoubtedly affected the lives of those who lived through them. Human development in the twentieth century cannot be understood in isolation from this ever-changing social environment. To ignore social and historical change is to engage in a perverse and blinding form of tunnel vision.

Related to the principle of contextualism is the *life stage principle*, which holds that the way that individual and social events affect life patterns is influenced by how old people are when events occur (Elder 1994). The same event may have dramatically different effects, depending on the age of the person experiencing it. For example, a declaration of war will affect the lives of young children much differently than it will the lives of adult men (Elder 1985).

As a criminological example of the life stage principle, consider how an arrest for illegal drug use may have different effects on the life course, depending on the age of the person who is arrested. If you were arrested at age 11 for such a crime, it would be a serious matter that probably would have profound consequences for your future life course. There is a good chance that you would be labeled a trouble-maker and have difficulty completing school on time. Poor school performance, in turn, would reduce your future occupational opportunities. On the other hand, if you were able to avoid arrest until age 23, after you had a college degree in hand, the effects of this event would likely be less damaging. Granted, being arrested at any age is not a good thing and is bound to reflect poorly on you. But in the years between ages 11 and 23 you would have had the opportunity to acquire human capital and presumably a track record of conforming behavior. You could call upon these assets to overcome the stigma and embarrassment of the arrest. Being arrested for the first time at age 11 is likely to be a life-changing event. Being arrested for the first time at age 23 is more likely to be an inconvenience. Thus, an arrest is an event in the life course (Hagan 1994). As with all events, its effects depend on the life stage at which it is experienced.

The fourth and final premise of the life course perspective follows from the other three. This premise is that efforts to optimize human development through preventive or corrective interventions will benefit if they are undertaken with sensitivity to the "particular age period in the framework of the entire life span" (Sorensen, Weinert, and Sherrod 1986). This premise simply alerts us that people are or can be influenced by different things at different stages of the life course, and it reflects another aspect of the life stage principle. The timing of events and interventions is crucial to their effect. What may be an effective intervention strategy for an adult criminal may not work as well or at all for a troubled adolescent on the way toward becoming a juvenile delinquent. For example, recent research suggests that providing employment opportunities reduces recidivism among older criminals but has little effect on criminals in their teens or early twenties (Uggen 2000). Thus, the principle of timing relates to the effects of both unplanned events and planned interventions that occur in the life course.

Criminal Careers, Career Criminals, and the Rise of Life Course Criminology

As with all theoretical developments in the social sciences, the life course approach to crime did not spring sui generis from the heads of contemporary criminologists. Rather, it evolved out of a theoretical context. This context is rooted most directly in the early twentieth century, when sociologists at the University of Chicago began conducting studies of problems confronting American society. These studies adopted what was essentially a life course perspective (Thomas and Znaniecki 1974). In *The Polish Peasant in Europe and America,* William I. Thomas and Florian Znaniecki used self-reported narratives of life histories from their subjects to trace patterns in experiences across generations. At approximately the same time, two longitudinal studies that focused on children born in the 1920s in California—the Oakland Growth Study and the Berkeley Guidance and Growth Studies (Eichorn, Clausen, Haan, Honzik, and Mussen 1981)—were initiated. These studies eventually collected data well into the 1980s and have been used to study variations in patterns of development and outcomes over a large segment of the life course (Caspi, Elder, and Bem 1987).

American criminologists were not far behind sociologists in recognizing the potential insights that longitudinal studies might provide into their subject matter. By the 1930s, two important longitudinal studies of delinquents—the Crime Causation Study (Glueck and Glueck 1950) and the Cambridge-Somerville Youth Study (Powers and Witmer 1951)—were underway. These studies are described in greater detail later in this chapter. But for now, we note that they were important developments in the history of criminology. In both studies, data were collected on the subjects over the course of several decades. They serve as theoretical and empirical exemplars for contemporary longitudinal research on careers in crime.

An important turning point in criminological research in the United States took place in Philadelphia in the 1960s, when a seminal birth cohort study was undertaken by Marvin Wolfgang, Robert Figlio, and Thorsten Sellin (1972). In this study, data were collected on a cohort of approximately 10,000 boys who were born in Philadelphia in 1945 and who lived there from the time they were 10 until they were at least 18. It is important because of the very detailed information it provided on the longitudinal sequencing of offenses in the cohort.

In 1986, the National Academy of Sciences published an influential two-volume report on career criminals and criminal careers (Blumstein, Cohen, Roth, and Visher 1986). This report laid the groundwork for contemporary research on criminal careers and crime over the life course. The criminal career approach focuses on the activity of individuals who commit criminal offenses (Blumstein et al. 1986, 1), and the criminal career is defined as the "longitudinal sequence of crimes committed by an individual offender" (Blumstein et al. 1986, 12). Criminal careers are characterized by four key dimensions. The dimension of *participation* distinguishes those who engage in crime at least once in their lifetimes from those who never engage in crime. *Current participation* refers to those who engage in crime during a particular period in time from those who do not engage in crime during that period. The first time a person engages in crime, which is referred to as the *age of onset*, marks the beginning of a criminal career. *Desistance* is the term typically used to describe the end point of a criminal career. For life course researchers, age of onset is an important feature of the criminal career because it appears to be associated with the three other key dimensions of careers—*frequency, seriousness*, and *career length*.

Frequency refers to an individual's rate of criminal activity, that is, to the number of offenses that the individual commits during a certain period of time. This rate is called lambda λ. Individual offending frequencies vary dramatically among offenders, with some having very high rates and others very low ones (Chaiken and Chaiken 1982). Offending rates also may vary over time throughout an individual's criminal career. Differences in λ are associated with demographic characteristics such as age, race, and sex, and with other factors, such as age of onset and drug use (Blumstein et al. 1986, 4–5). Individuals who begin their criminal careers at younger ages generally have higher values for λ than those who begin later. Active offenders who use drugs often commit offenses at relatively high rates. For life course researchers, an important question is what events or features of the life course influence individual offending rates. How does the life course of a high-rate offender differ from that of a low-rate offender? What factors are associated with increases or decreases in offending frequency?

Offenders also may vary in the *seriousness* of the offenses they commit. In regard to the dimension of seriousness, criminal career and life course researchers have invested considerable effort in trying to determine whether there are distinct types of criminal careers based on distinct patterns in offending seriousness (Nagin and Land 1993). Do some offenders escalate in the seriousness of the offenses they commit as their careers progress, and if so, what factors distinguish those who escalate from those who do not? To what extent are minor and serious offenses randomly intermixed throughout the duration of the typical criminal career? As offenders near the end of their criminal careers, do their offenses *de-escalate* in seriousness or do their offenses remain the same throughout their careers until desistance? Do individual offenders tend to specialize in particular types of offenses or are they *generalists* (that is, willing to engage in a wide variety of offense types)? These are some of the important questions criminal career and life course researchers continue to investigate.

Finally, researchers have focused closely on *duration*, or *career length*, as an important dimension of criminal careers. The research on duration consistently finds that criminal careers tend to be short, typically starting in the mid-teenage years and ending in the late teens or early 20s (Steffensmeier and Allan 2000). But some individuals who initiate criminal careers as teenagers continue to commit offenses well into their 30s and beyond (Tracy, Wolfgang, and Figlio 1990). Thus, it is important to understand the factors that distinguish offenders with long careers from those with short careers. Likewise, life course researchers want to understand the relationship between duration and the other dimensions of criminal careers—frequency and seriousness. Do offenders with long careers tend to commit more serious offenses at higher rates than offenders with short careers, or are duration, frequency, and seriousness unrelated to one another?

What the life course perspective takes from the criminal career tradition is the idea that it is important to focus on the longitudinal sequencing of offenses and a recognition that the dimensions of criminal careers vary among individuals. What the life course perspective adds to the criminal career tradition is greater recognition of the reciprocal, mutually interacting connections between trajectories in crime and trajectories in other domains of life. The life course perspective assumes that trajectories in crime represent only one limited part of individual life courses. It assumes that trajectories in crime can be better understood if they are viewed within the total context of the individual's life and development. Even the most serious high-rate repeat offenders engage in crime only for a relatively small part of each day. The rest of the time they are doing other things. The life course perspective also is more attuned to the role of history and macrosociological factors in shaping criminal careers and individual life courses.

Research on criminal careers has led to many important theoretical and policy-related findings in criminology. Nevertheless, like all research paradigms, it has its limitations. Because the life course perspective has been so closely connected to and shaped by the criminal career paradigm, it is imperative to be aware of those limitations. One significant limitation involves the conceptualization of crime. In the United States, the vast majority of criminological research and theory focuses on ordinary street crime and on offenders who commit ordinary street crimes, that is, the index crimes that are tracked in the Federal Bureau of Investigation's annual Uniform Crime Report. Our image of criminal careers and career criminals is based almost entirely on data collected from persons who have been arrested or incarcerated for index crimes. And it is probably fair to say that for most people the term "career criminal" brings to mind the image of an unrepentant, lifelong, "superpredator," as some commentators so vividly describe them (Bennett, DiluLio, and Walters 1996). The stereotypical career criminal is a male who started offending early, commits serious crimes often, and spends much of his life incarcerated or running from the law.

By focusing so strongly on offenders who commit street crimes and on samples of persons who have been arrested or incarcerated, however, the career criminal approach ignores offenders who do not often appear in official statistics, such as those who commit white-collar crimes. It presents an image of criminal careers that is incomplete and based on class-biased samples of offenders and offenses. It may accurately describe the criminal careers of individuals who grow up in disadvantaged circumstances and who run afoul of the law early in life, but it tells us little or nothing about the criminal careers of individuals who commit white-collar crimes. Recent evidence suggests that careers in white-collar crime differ substantially from careers in street crime (Weisburd, Chayet, and Waring 1990; Benson and Kerley 2000; Weisburd, Waring, and Chayet 2001). This issue is treated at length in chapter 5. For now, we note that the life course perspective suffers from the same class-biased conceptualization of crime as the criminal career tradition. The factors that have been identified by life course researchers as important determinants of trajectories in street crime may not apply to those who commit white-collar crimes.

Important Theoretical Concepts and Issues

Like their counterparts in other theoretical traditions, life course researchers rely upon a set of concepts that guide their investigations and orient the theoretical issues they address. To help familiarize you with the specialized vocabulary of life course research, I explicate the more important concepts here. Trajectory and transition were briefly introduced earlier, but they require a more formal treatment. So I begin with an expanded discussion of these two important concepts.

Trajectories and transitions. Recall that a trajectory is a sequence of linked states within a conceptually defined realm of behavior or experience. Trajectories are characterized by a number of dimensions that have consequences for how individuals develop. Three important dimensions are *entrance, success,* and *timing* (Thornberry 1997). In regard to entrance, individuals can be described according to those trajectories they enter and those they do not. Not everyone has children; thus, not everyone has a parenthood trajectory. Once individuals enter a particular trajectory, they can have varying levels of success in completing the typical tasks or activities that constitute that trajectory. For example, some people do well in school. At every level of their educational trajectories they stand out as overachievers. Others perform poorly. They may drop out of high school and never even get to college. Of special importance with respect to development over the life course is the matter of timing in trajectories. In every society, there are normatively defined correct times for individuals to enter or leave certain trajectories and to make transitions within trajectories.

In other words, trajectories are age graded. Transitions that are made at the right time are considered to be "age appropriate," whereas those that are made abnormally early or late are considered to be "off age" (Thornberry 1997). For example, in America it is age appropriate for children to leave their parental homes and to establish their own households sometime in their late teens or early 20s. Children who leave when they are much younger or who wait until they are in their 30s before leaving are making this transition at off-age times. Timing is important because transitions that are made off-age often have harmful consequences for other behavioral trajectories. For example, a child who leaves his or her parental home at a young age is at great risk of failing to complete schooling and may end up homeless and living on the street (Hagan and McCarthy 1997).

Transitions also are important because they can represent turning points or change in the life course. For example, a juvenile delinquent who finds a good job as he enters adulthood and who desists from crime as a result of having stable employment has undergone an important turning point in the life course. His trajectory in crime exhibits change in behavior. On the other hand, some delinquents do not desist from crime as they enter adulthood. Their crime trajectories are characterized by continuity throughout the life course. A trademark of life course studies is the dual focus on continuity and change. Life course researchers attempt to understand how childhood or adolescent experiences are linked to adult outcomes and how transitions or turning points may lead to change in life course trajectories.

Cumulative continuity and self-selection. A particularly important issue in the life course perspective involves the distinction between *cumulative continuity* and *self-selection*. Cumulative continuity refers to the way in which behavior at one point in life influences opportunities and behavior later in life. For example, a young boy who is arrested early in life may be labeled a troublemaker by the police, teachers, and other adults. Because he has been labeled a troublemaker, the boy may be prevented from associating with the "good" kids in his neighborhood and forced to find companionship with other known troublemakers. Hanging around with other troublemakers leads naturally to more trouble and more run-ins with the police. In this case, the boy's early arrest leads to subsequent arrests and eventually to the accumulation of an extensive criminal record. Another example of cumulative continuity might involve doing poorly in high school, which closes off educational and occupational opportunities, leading to unemployment later in life.

In regard to crime, cumulative continuity refers to a dynamic process in which delinquent behavior at one point in time has consequences that increase the likelihood of continued delinquent behavior at later points in time. For example, two well-known life course researchers, Robert J. Sampson and John Laub (1993), argue that the most important consequence of delinquent behavior is that it may block the individual's opportunity to develop adult social bonds. Serious delinquency may lead to a "knifing off" of future opportunities (Caspi, Lynam, Moffitt, and Silva 1993). The process of cumulative continuity leads eventually to *cumulative disadvantage*, a piling up of negative experiences and failures that make it difficult for a person to succeed in life (Hagan 1997).

Cumulative continuity is different from *self-selection*. Self-selection refers to the tendency of individuals to select experiences that are consistent with internal traits or dispositions that are established early in life. For example, an antisocial child becomes an antisocial adult whose antisocial nature leads to marital and occupational instability as well as unsuccessful performance in other life domains (Sampson and Laub 1993). Statistically, self-selection means that correlations between adult crime and other adult behaviors (e.g., job instability) are spurious and will disappear if controls for prior individual-level differences in internal traits are used. Statistically, self-selection also means that the correlation between delinquent behavior at one point in time and delinquent behavior at a later point in time is spurious or not causal. Both early and late offenses are caused by the internal traits of the individual. Early offenses do not independently increase the likelihood of later offenses through the process of cumulative continuity.

The distinction between self-selection and cumulative continuity is the same as the distinction between *state dependence* and *population heterogeneity* (Nagin and Paternoster 1991). If participation in delinquency at Time 1 has a behavioral impact on the future conduct of the individual, that is state dependence. State dependence could explain the well-known positive correlation between past and future delinquency. On the other hand, population heterogeneity might also account for the association. Population heterogeneity refers to an unmeasured propensity toward delinquency over time. People high in this propensity will commit crimes at every stage of the life course, whereas people low in propensity will not commit crime. Over time, crime or delinquency at Time 1 will be positively correlated with crime or delinquency at Time 2.

Ontogenesis and the ontogenetic fallacy. Because the life course perspective incorporates the biological dimension, it is important to understand the terms *ontogenesis* and *ontogenetic fallacy*. Ontogenesis refers to the origin and development of an individual and to the way in which personal biologically based traits influence this process. The ontogenetic fallacy is the "fallacy of attributing developmental outcomes solely to the unfolding of personal traits and ignoring that it is the interaction between traits and the environment that produces the outcome" (Dannefer 1984). For example, to say that a person succeeded in college solely because he or she was born with a high IQ is to commit the ontogenetic fallacy, because in reality this outcome—academic success—results from the interaction of the person's IQ with a host of other factors, such as his or her social class origins and parents' wishes.

Cohorts and age. A *cohort* is defined as a group of individuals who experience the "same event within the same time interval" (Ryder 1965). Typically, the defining event is birth. For example, in the Philadelphia study, Wolfgang, Figlio, and Sellin (1972, 4–5) studied a birth cohort whose members were all boys born in 1945. Although cohorts are most often defined by age, the sharing of some other common characteristic can identify them. For example, a cohort may be defined in terms of year of marriage or year of entering college (Ryder 1965). Life course researchers depend heavily on longitudinal studies that are designed to gather data on cohorts of individuals that are followed over time. Recent cohort studies have been based on cohorts defined by relatively narrow age ranges of between one to three years, but sometimes larger age ranges are used.

Different age cohorts may be compared with one another to observe what are known as *cohort effects*. A cohort effect is said to be present when members of different cohorts vary significantly in some characteristic. For example, a cohort effect appeared to be present when the 1945 Philadelphia cohort was compared to a cohort of Philadelphia children born in 1958 (Wolfgang et al. 1972; Tracy, Wolfgang, and Figlio 1990). The 1958 cohort had much higher levels of violent crime when they were teenagers than the 1945 cohort did at the same age. A cohort effect might also arise if cohorts respond differently to an historical event. For example, the impact of a dramatic event such as a war or a depression may affect individuals differently, depending on their age when the event occurred. War has a different meaning and is a different experience for a 10-year-old boy than it is for a 20-year-old young man. This difference is a cohort effect. Cohort effects are important for the life course perspective, because they signal the likely presence of macrohistorical influences on the structure of the life course.

Bound up with the concepts of cohort and cohort effect are the twin concepts of *social age* and *historical age*. Social age refers to the norms and expectations that impinge upon people at different ages. There are normatively defined "right" times to experience or accomplish major events and transitions, such as getting married, having children, getting a job, and finishing school. Making a transition out of sequence or at an unusual time has normative and demographic consequences (Elder 1985, 26). Historical age relates to one's cohort. Age may have different meanings, depending on cohort or historical position. Being 16 in 1998 is different from being 16 in 1898. Historical age and social age are connected in that the meaning or implications of events and transitions may vary depending on when they are experienced historically. Elder (1985, 26–27) gives the example of young children experiencing divorce during periods of low versus rapidly rising divorce rates. Divorce is likely to be a more traumatizing and stigmatizing event for a child during periods when it is uncommon than in periods when many of the child's friends have divorced parents. The meaning of social age thus may change over historical periods, which would influence the impact of events on life patterns.

Research designs. The life course perspective assumes that events that happen at one time in life affect events at later times. The concept of trajectory implies momentum and continuity in behavior, psychological functioning, and biological development over time. Methodological consequences follow from these theoretical assumptions. The most important of these consequences is that life course research must be carried out using longitudinal research designs. Hence, it is important to understand the features and types of longitudinal research designs. There are two basic types of longitudinal research designs that have often been used in life course research: *prospective* and *retrospective*. Each has strengths and weaknesses (for an extensive discussion of methodological issues in longitudinal research, see Farrington 1979).

Prospective designs follow a sample, usually a cohort of similarly aged individuals, over time. At the start of the study, baseline data is collected on the sample subjects. At periodic intervals thereafter, the researchers collect new data on the subjects. Thus, for example, a sample of children aged 10 may be selected and followed for a 10-year period until they reach age 20, with data collected every two years. In criminological life course research, data typically come from interviews with the subjects, but data may also be collected from parents and teachers as well as from official records of schools and law enforcement agencies.

The primary advantage of prospective designs is that information on events can be collected relatively soon after they happen, before they have been distorted by the subject's retrospective reinterpretation. A boy interviewed at age 16 would probably be able to provide a more accurate self-report of his criminal activity at age 15 than he would if the interview was delayed until he reached age 25.

The disadvantage of prospective studies for criminological research is that they may be uneconomical for serious crimes, depending on how the sample is drawn. Samples may be drawn from the general population, and these are known as *normal* or *population samples*; alternatively, samples may be drawn from *high-risk* or *clinical populations*. Because prospective studies generally start with samples of relatively young children, it is not known in advance how many of the sample subjects will engage in serious crimes during the course of the study. The prevalence of serious index-type crimes, such as murder, robbery, rape, and aggravated assault, is relatively low in the general population. If researchers simply draw a random sample of, say, 400 children, they may find that none or only a very few of the children will engage in serious crimes over the course of the study. The small number of serious offenders reduces statistical power and makes it more difficult for researchers to draw conclusions about the factors that distinguish serious from nonserious offenders. One way around this problem is to draw large samples, but that is expensive. The other solution is to draw what are known as *high-risk samples,* that is, samples in which the subjects come from social backgrounds that tend to have higher rates of criminal offending than normal. For example, rather than taking a random sample of children in a school system, researchers may restrict their sample to children who reside in disadvantaged neighborhoods, where crime is common. This strategy increases the likelihood that a sufficiently large number of individuals who will engage in serious crime will be included in the sample. Both normal and high-risk sampling designs may be combined in a single study. Researchers may, for example, take a random sample of the general population and then another sample of similar size from a high-risk population. Through the use of statistical weighting procedures the two samples may be combined.

In a *retrospective longitudinal design*, the sample subjects are typically older and are selected because they meet some criteria established by the study. After the sample is selected, the researchers gather data from various sources on the subjects' past experiences. For example, researchers might select a sample of adult prison inmates and interview them about their family backgrounds and criminal activities when they were younger. The obvious disadvantages of retrospective interviews are the problems of forgetfulness and reinterpretation of events. As time passes, most of us forget things, and we have a tendency to distort or selectively reinterpret past events in order to make sense of our present situation. Researchers using retrospective designs try to correct for these problems by using a special interviewing technique known as a *life history calendar* (Freedman et al. 1988). A life history calendar is a large grid-shaped chart. On the left side of the grid are listed details of behavioral patterns that are being investigated, such as types of crimes. The top side is divided into time units for which behavior patterns can be recorded. For example, a life history calendar might be constructed to gather data on the timing of delinquent acts by a juvenile and events in his or her family life. The life history calendar helps improve the quality of retrospective data because it permits the respondent to relate the timing of events both visually and mentally (Freedman et al. 1988). Researchers may also supplement interviews by checking official records to reconstruct the subjects' trajectories in crime. But official records have their shortcomings, too. They only include acts that come to the attention of authorities. Furthermore, official records are compiled to meet the needs of bureaucracies, not researchers. They often do not contain information on concepts and issues relevant to researchers. For criminological research, the main advantage of retrospective designs is that they permit researchers to draw samples that meet the needs of their research questions. For example, they can draw samples that include adequate numbers of serious offenders for statistical analysis.

Major Developmental Studies

The number of well-designed longitudinal studies suitable for life course criminological research probably does not yet number in the hundreds, but it is growing at a steady pace. The chapters that follow will refer repeatedly to several of the most important studies, many of which are ongoing. These studies have served as the basis for literally hundreds, if not thousands, of publications on issues related to crime and the life course. In some cases, the original collectors of the data have made them available for use by other researchers. To help familiarize you with the methodological details of the major studies in life course criminology, I identify and briefly describe them here. The studies are presented roughly in the chronological order of when data collection was initiated.

Deviant Children Grown Up

This famous study was conducted by Lee Robins and Patricia O'Neal. It attempted to describe the natural histories of subjects who displayed antisocial personalities and behavior. Data collection began in 1924. It is a complex study that involves three different cohorts. The first cohort included 524 white subjects under the age of 18, selected from the patients of a municipal child-guidance clinic in St. Louis, Missouri. The second cohort was designed to serve as a control for the first. It included 100 white elementary-school students of the same-age and sex distribution as the first cohort and from the same census tracts. For cohorts 1 and 2, data were collected in two waves. Wave 1 lasted from 1924 to 1929, and wave 2 lasted from 1955 to 1960. In the second wave, the subjects ranged in age from 30 to 55. The third cohort consisted of the sons of cohorts 1 and 2 (N = 67). Data were collected from a variety of sources, including personal interviews, official police and court records, school records, and mental health agency records (Robins 1966).

Cambridge-Somerville Youth Study

The Cambridge-Somerville Youth Study was the brainchild of Dr. Richard Clarke Cabot, a physician and social philosopher who believed that delinquency could be prevented if potential delinquents had an opportunity to form a strong bond with an understanding adult early in life (McCord and McCord, with Zola 1959). Beginning in 1937, Dr. Cabot initiated a study that eventually involved 650 high-risk and low-risk boys from disadvantaged neighborhoods in Cambridge, Massachusetts. Boys randomly selected from high-risk and low-risk pools were paired by age, background, and personality. Half the boys were placed in a treatment group and half in a control group. The treatment group was supposed to receive treatment in the form of a close, intimate friendship with a counselor, but in most cases the treatment did not achieve this ideal (McCord et al. 1959). The idea was to determine whether the treated boys fared better than the control group in avoiding delinquency (Powers and Witmer 1951). The sample was 95 percent white and mostly from poor or working-class backgrounds. Sample ages ranged from 4 to 11 at the start of study. A full range of data was collected on life history variables and criminal history. Three waves of data were collected in 1936–37, 1939–45, and 1975–76. In the final wave, subjects were between the ages of 43 and 50.

Crime Causation Study: Unraveling Juvenile Delinquency

Sheldon and Eleanor Glueck were pioneers in the use of longitudinal research designs in criminology. During their long tenure at Harvard University, they conducted several longitudinal studies of delinquents and nondelinquents in Massachusetts. Their most well-known investigation, the Crime Causation Study: Unraveling Juvenile Delinquency (UJD), was the basis for several books (Glueck and Glueck 1950; Glueck and Glueck 1952; Glueck and Glueck 1956; Glueck and Glueck 1968). This study began in 1939 with a sample of 1,000 boys aged 10 to 17 from disadvantaged neighborhoods in Boston. A unique feature of the UJD study was its matching design. Half of the sample, 500 boys, were officially defined delinquents, selected from the rosters of two facilities for juvenile delinquents in Boston. The other half of the sample consisted of 500 nondelinquent boys who were matched with the delinquents on age, race and ethnicity, and intelligence (Sampson and Laub 1993, 27). All of the boys were white.

Between 1939 and 1948, detailed information on the delinquents and nondelinquents was collected. The data covered social, psychological, and biological characteristics, family life, school performance, work experience, delinquent behavior, and other life events (Sampson and Laub 1993, 28). A great strength of the Gluecks' data-collection procedures was the use of multiple respondents and multiple data sources. Information about the boys and their families was gathered through interviews with the boys themselves and with their parents, teachers, neighbors, and criminal justice officials. Measures of delinquency came from self-reports, parent reports, and teacher reports and were supplemented with checks of official records.

Between 1949 and 1963, the Gluecks conducted follow-ups on the original sample at age 25 and again at age 32. Thus, data are available from childhood through young adulthood. The retention rate for the follow-ups was extraordinarily good. Sampson and Laub (1993, 29) calculate that the follow-up success rate is approximately 92 percent, adjusted for mortality. Data from all three age periods are available for 438 of the 500 delinquents and 442 of the nondelinquent controls.

After lying dormant in Harvard Law School Library for nearly two decades, the UJD data were rediscovered by Robert Sampson and John Laub (1993, 1). They undertook to recode and computerize the original paper case files, an exceedingly complicated and daunting task. After several years, they succeeded in reconstructing the data and eventually used them as the major source of information for their book *Crime in the Making: Pathways and Turning Points Through Life,* arguably the most important work yet published on crime from the life course perspective.

Philadelphia Cohort Studies

There are two Philadelphia cohort studies (Wolfgang et al. 1972; Tracy et al. 1990). The first, and most famous, of the pair of studies followed an unselected cohort of 9,945 boys who were born in 1945 and who resided in Philadelphia between their 10th and 18th birthdays (1955 to 1963). The researchers collected data on the boys from official police records and from schools and other governmental agencies. In the original study, interviews were not conducted with the members of the cohort. However, in a later extension of the study, interviews were conducted with a 10 percent random sample of the original cohort, approximately 975 men. The interviews took place when the subjects were age 26 and collected detailed information on their marital, educational, and occupational histories, as well as information on criminal behavior and victimization experiences (Wolfgang, Thornberry, and Figlio 1987).

The second of the Philadelphia studies followed a larger cohort of over 27,000 individuals born in Philadelphia in 1958. Girls were included in this cohort. Data were collected from police and district attorney records, personal interviews, and self-enumerated questionnaires. The sample was followed up to 1988, when they were 30 years of age. Information is available on offenses committed while the members of the cohort were juveniles and while they were adults (Tracy et al. 1990).

Juvenile Delinquency and Adult Crime in Racine, Wisconsin

Designed and conducted by Lyle Shannon, this study contains data on juvenile delinquency and adult crime for three birth cohorts born in 1942, 1949, and 1955 in Racine, Wisconsin (Shannon 1982; Shannon 1988). Shannon used personal interviews and police and court records to gather data on the cohorts. The sample sizes for 1942, 1949, and 1955 are 1,352, 2,099, and 2,676, respectively. A unique feature of this study is the availability of ecological data on the neighborhoods in which the members of each cohort resided in Racine. Shannon supplemented the individual-level data with census data for each city block in Racine for 1950, 1960, and 1970. In addition, other ecological data were gathered from land-use maps and city directories.

The Cambridge Study in Delinquent Development

The Cambridge Study in Delinquent Development is an important long-term prospective study of crime and delinquency among 411 inner-city males who were born around 1953. At the time they were selected for inclusion in the study, all were living in a working-class area of London (Farrington and West 1990). The study was originally directed by Donald J. West and is now under the direction of David P. Farrington. Analyses of data collected during this study have resulted in four books and over 60 articles (West and Farrington 1973; West and Farrington 1977; Farrington 1977; Farrington 1983).

Throughout the Cambridge study, data have been collected from multiple sources, including the subjects, their parents, teachers, peers, and official sources (Farrington and West 1990, 117). As of 1990, eight personal interviews had been conducted with the subjects from age 8 to age 32. The attrition rate for the study has been very low. Up through age 32, the researchers have been able to keep in touch with 94 percent of the original sample. Information has been collected on a very wide array of theoretical dimensions, such as intelligence, personality, parent-child relationship, delinquency of peers, school performance, marital stability, and employment histories.

National Youth Survey

The National Youth Survey (NYS) began in 1976. It is a prospective longitudinal study of a representative sample of 1,725 youths aged 11 to 17 at the start of the study (Elliott 1994). Thus, it includes seven birth cohorts (1959–65) (Elliott, Huizinga, and Ageton 1985). As of 1994, nine waves of data had been collected. Interviews with the sample subjects are supplemented with official record data. Official record data are also available for the parents or primary caretakers of the subjects (Elliott and Huizinga 1983; Elliott, Huizinga, and Ageton 1985).

The NYS was designed to provide a "comprehensive description of the prevalence and incidence of delinquent behavior and drug use in the American youth population" (Elliott et al. 1985, 91). It contains extensive and detailed measures of concepts drawn from strain and control theories, and has been used to construct and evaluate an integrated theoretical model of delinquent behavior (Elliott et al. 1985, 91). A great strength of the NYS is that it is based on a national probability sample of American youth. Hence, results based on the NYS can be generalized to the population of American youth (Elliott 1994). Many other longitudinal studies are based on samples drawn from high-risk populations, making it difficult to use them to draw firm conclusions about youth in general.

Dunedin Multidisciplinary Health and Development Study

The Multidisciplinary Health and Development Study is set in Dunedin, New Zealand. It is a prospective longitudinal cohort study of an unselected population. The cohort consists of all children born at the only maternity hospital in Dunedin between April 1, 1972, and March 31, 1973, who were still living in the local province when the study began three years later, in 1975. At that time, 1,139 of the children were eligible for the study and 1,037 participated. The sample has been assessed every two years since 1975 with an extensive array of psychological, medical, and sociological measures. Interviews are conducted with the subjects, their parents, and their teachers. Official record data also are collected (Klein 1987; Moffitt and Silva 1988; Moffitt 1990; Henry, Caspi, Moffitt, and Silva 1996).

Understanding and Prediction of Delinquent Child Behavior

This study is based on a relatively small sample of 206 males in Eugene, Oregon. Data collection began in 1984, when males from high-risk, fourth-grade classrooms were selected. At the start of the study, subjects were 9 to 11 years old. Most of the subjects are white and from poor or working-class families. Data were collected annually from 1984 to 1989. The distinguishing feature of this study is the detailed collection of measures of family processes. The researchers have constructed a theory of family processes as they relate to delinquency that has been highly influential in the life course perspective (Patterson, Reid, and Dishion 1992).

Program of Research on the Causes and Correlates of Delinquency

The Causes and Correlates of Delinquency Program encompasses three federally funded longitudinal research projects located in three cities—Denver, Colorado, Pittsburgh, Pennsylvania, and Rochester, New York. The program was initiated in 1986 by the U.S. Department of Justice's Office of Juvenile Justice and Delinquency Prevention. Different teams of researchers conduct the projects at the three sites, but there is extensive communication and coordination of research activities among the research teams.

All the projects use a similar research design that consists of a longitudinal investigation of high-risk inner-city youth during their developmental years. In each project, the researchers have conducted regular face-to-face interviews with the research subjects. The interviews with the youths are supplemented by interviews with parents or other caretakers and with teachers. Official data from police, courts, schools, and social service agencies on each subject are also collected. A unique feature of the Causes and Correlates of Delinquency Program is the use of common measures of important concepts such as self-reported delinquency, drug use, community and neighborhood characteristics, a host of youth, family, and peer variables, and arrest and judicial-processing histories. At all three sites, researchers have maintained high sample retention rates (Browning, Huizinga, Loeber, and Thornberry 1999).

The Denver Youth Survey sample includes 806 boys and 721 girls who were selected from randomly chosen households in disadvantaged neighborhoods. Data collection began in 1987, when the children were 7, 9, 11, 13, or 15 years old. Between 1988 and 1992, the youths and their caretakers were interviewed annually. Annual interviews were also conducted from 1995 up to 1999 (Huizinga, Weiher, Menard, Espiritu, and Esbensen 1998).

The Pittsburgh Youth Study sample was assembled in stages (Peeples and Loeber 1994; Wikstrom and Loeber 2000). First, the researchers selected and screened a random sample of boys in the first, fourth, and seventh grades of the Pittsburgh public school system. Based on the initial screening, the researchers identified the 30 percent of boys with the most disruptive behavior. These boys were included in the final study sample along with a random sample of the remaining 70 percent of boys. This procedure resulted in a total sample of 1,517 boys, with approximately 500 coming from each grade level. Subjects and their caretakers were interviewed at six-month intervals for the first five years of the study. Teachers were also asked to rate the subjects. After seven assessments, the researchers stopped collecting data on the middle sample (fourth grade). Interviews with the two other samples have continued on an annual basis.

The Rochester Youth Development Study involves 1,000 students (729 boys and 271 girls) randomly selected from students in the seventh and eighth grades of the Rochester public schools in spring 1988 (Thornberry, Krohn, Lizotte, Smith, and Perter 1998; Smith et al. 2000). Subjects and their caretakers were interviewed at six-month intervals from 1988 to 1992 and annually from 1994 to 1996.

Project on Human Development in Chicago Neighborhoods

The Project on Human Development in Chicago Neighborhoods (PHDCN) is a mammoth research effort jointly funded by the

National Institute of Justice, National Institute of Mental Health, U.S. Department of Education, and the John D. and Catherine T. MacArthur Foundation. There are two major parts to the study. One part of the study, which focuses on Chicago's neighborhoods, is divided into three components (Sampson, Raudenbush, and Earls 1997). The first component of the neighborhood study includes in-person interviews with a randomly selected sample of more than 8,700 residents of all Chicago neighborhoods. The interviews covered a variety of community-related issues, such as perceived violence and neighborhood decline. For the second component of the neighborhood study, 80 neighborhoods were selected for systematic social observation. Researchers videotape blocks in the 80 neighborhoods to record "life and behavior in each neighborhood" (Sampson et al. 1997, 2). The final component of the neighborhood study is a survey of neighborhood leaders and experts.

For life course researchers, the second part of the study may be more interesting than the community study. The second part of the PHDCN is a longitudinal cohort study of 7,000 individuals ranging in age from birth to 18. The cohort sample will be drawn from the 80 neighborhoods undergoing systematic social observation. In the cohort study, equal numbers of males and females in seven age cohorts (birth, 3, 6, 9, 12, 15, 18) are being selected from African-American, Hispanic, white, and mixed-ethnic communities. All social classes are included. Each cohort will be assessed annually for eight years via interviews with the subjects (for those old enough) and their caretakers.

Because it includes data on both individuals and communities, the PHDCN is potentially an extremely important study. Researchers will be able to investigate in more detail than ever before possible the links between individuals, families, and communities in shaping developmental trajectories. Several articles have been published from the community design phase of the study (Sampson et al. 1997; Sampson and Raudenbush 1999; Sampson, Morenoff, and Earls 1999). No results have yet been published from the cohort study.

Other Federal Studies

U.S. government agencies support a number of longitudinal studies of different segments of the U.S. population. Some of these studies include subjects and measures useful for life course research on criminological issues. Two important studies that have been used for criminological research are the National Longitudinal Survey of Labor Market Experiences (Monk-Turner 1989) and the National Longitudinal Survey of Youth (Tanner, Davies, and O'Grady 1999). The main advantage of these studies is that they are based on large unselected or normal samples of the population. Thus, unlike some criminological research projects that rely on high-risk samples, these studies permit researchers to investigate criminological and life course issues in samples with a broad range of variation in class-linked variables. A weakness of these studies for criminological research is that the measures of criminality are often not detailed. In addition, data usually are collected only from the sample subjects. Other persons related to the subjects, such as parents and teachers, are not contacted. As a result, measurement error and data validity are more problematic.

Plan of the Book

As a way of organizing my presentation, I have divided the life course into three stages: (1) prenatal and early childhood, (2) early adolescence and young adulthood, and (3) adulthood and old age. Separate chapters are devoted to each of these stages. The prenatal and early childhood life stage encompasses the time from conception through age 10. During this stage, biology and family are the most important factors. For some children, signs of future trouble begin to appear very early during this period. The second stage begins around age 10 and continues through the teenage years to approximately age 20. During this period of the life course, we will witness an explosion of criminal, deviant, and antisocial behavior. Involvement in delinquent behavior typically peaks sometime between the ages of 15 and 17. After the late teenage years, crime and deviance start to decline rapidly. The adult stage begins around age 21. During this stage, involvement in criminal and antisocial activity continues to decline, but the consequences of earlier criminality begin to manifest themselves more profoundly in other life trajectories, most notably family and occupation. In the latter stages of life, intensive involvement in crime becomes rare. Those who were most active in the earlier stages are by now either serving long terms of incarceration, or are physically debilitated from long years of drug and alcohol abuse, or dead.

Crime is both a dependent and an independent variable, a cause as well as an effect. Just as there are social causes of crime, crime itself has causal effects on other domains of life. Thus, as we move through the three stages, we will trace the factors that influence trajectories in crime and explore the consequences of following particular crime trajectories on other domains in life. Among the factors that shape trajectories in crime are social class, race, gender, family, and neighborhood context. Among the potential consequences of involvement in crime are reduced opportunities for a good family life and a worthwhile occupational career.

After we have finished tracing crime across the span of the life course, two final chapters will be devoted to two issues not often addressed by criminologists working in the life course perspective. The first is white-collar crime and the life course. Like most criminologists, those working in the life course tradition have almost completely ignored white-collar crime and white-collar criminals. In chapter 5, we review some recent work on the criminal careers of white-collar offenders and consider how the life course perspective might be applied to this type of offending. Finally, in chapter 6, we will consider social change and state policies as influences on crime and the life course. Although the life course perspective is based on the assumption that historical context and social change are major influences on developmental trajectories, criminologists working in the life course tradition have not often considered the historical dimension in their investigations. Thus, in the concluding chapter, we will reflect on how social change and state policies over the past century may have influenced trajectories in crime.

Note

1. The statistics cited in this paragraph come from various reports published by the U.S. National Center for Health Statistics. They are also available via the Internet at the Center's homepage, <www.cdc.gov/nchs/default.htm>. ✦

Chapter 2

Biology and the Family

Initial Trajectories

The events of the opening years do start an infant down a particular path, but it is a path with an extraordinarily large number of intersections.

—Jerome Kagan

Prediction is hard, especially when it's about the future.

—Neils Bohr

Overview

In this chapter, we focus on biological precursors of crime and on early childhood as a stage in the life course. We begin by reviewing evidence on the genetic bases of behavior, including criminal behavior. Your genetic makeup influences how you look, think, and act. Next, we turn to early childhood. Developmentally, the importance of early childhood can hardly be overstated. In the first few years of life, we learn language, develop personality, and establish patterns of behavior that may persist throughout our lives. If we are lucky, we form strong emotional bonds to our parents and siblings, which may also last a lifetime. This stage in the life course sets our initial trajectories.

31

With respect to trajectories in crime, early childhood is important because behavioral patterns established during this stage are linked to behavior later in life (Loeber and Dishion 1983). Numerous longitudinal studies have shown that children who display antisocial behavior early in life go on to exhibit delinquent behavior later, when they become teenagers (Farrington 1978). For example, in the Cambridge study, teachers and peers were asked to rate the boys in the study on "troublesomeness." Those who were rated high on troublesomeness between the ages of 8 and 10 were more likely to have official court records by the time they were 17 than their less-troublesome counterparts (West and Farrington 1973). Other investigators have asked parents to evaluate their own children on problem behaviors, such as destructiveness, wandering, lying, and stealing (Mitchell and Rosa 1981). Fifteen years later, boys who rated highly on these problem behaviors were more likely to have criminal records than boys who scored lower. Some children appear to establish behavioral trajectories directed toward crime and delinquency very early in life.

Although many children who engage in maladaptive behavior when they are young continue to exhibit behavior problems as they grow older, many others do not. In a careful review of longitudinal studies, Loeber and Dishion (1983) found that a majority of children who display behavior problems early in life ultimately improve and do not end up with criminal records. According to their review, anywhere from 57 to 70 percent of children rated as having behavior problems early in life did not display such problems later in life. Likewise, it is not uncommon for children who behave normally early in life to start displaying behavior problems years later. In some studies, as many as one-quarter of children who are initially regarded as problem-free go on to become members of the criminal group later. Although they are undeniably important, early life trajectories are always subject to change and modification as we age. As Jerome Kagan puts it, there are "many intersections" on the road of life.

Starting Behind the Starting Line: Biology and Crime

The idea that criminal behavior has biological causes is not new. Over 100 years ago, the Italian physician Cesare Lombroso proposed his influential atavistic theory of crime (Lombroso 1887). An atavism is the recurrence in an organism of a characteristic or trait that is supposed to have been possessed in the past by the organism's ancient ancestors. According to this theory, some criminals are biological anomalies. They are evolutionary throwbacks, literally primitive humans. These individuals are born with the traits of our evolutionary ancestors. In a sense, they are not fully developed humans, but rather part human and part ape. They reflect a reversion to what is assumed to have been the brutish and apish past of the human race. In Lombroso's eyes, they displayed apish stigmata or physical signs of their degeneracy, such as greater skull thickness, relatively long arms, large jaws, and low and narrow foreheads (Gould 1981). These stigmata indicated that the germs of our ancestral past had come to life in these unfortunate individuals. Thus, Lombroso reasoned, their violent criminal behavior only reproduced the "ferocious instincts of primitive humanity and the inferior animals" (Taylor, Walton, and Young 1973). Criminal behavior for them was a natural outgrowth of their biological makeup. They were literally "born criminals."

In fairness to Lombroso, it is important to note that he did not think that all criminals were biological throwbacks. Neither did he believe that biology was the sole cause of criminality. Indeed, as Michael Gottfredson and Travis Hirschi (1990) have noted, in Lombroso's most famous work, *Crime: Its Causes and Remedies,* he advances a sophisticated multicausal explanation of crime. He never claimed that all criminals are driven by hereditary compulsion, only about 40 percent. Other criminal acts resulted from passion, rage, or desperation (Gould 1981).

Lombroso's theories and those of his many followers have long since been discredited. But the idea that there are biological and hereditary components to crime continues to thrive and is an important part of the life course approach. From the perspective of the life course and individual development, biology is not destiny; it does not endow us with "ferocious instincts" over which we have no control, as Lombroso thought. Rather, our biological makeup is one source of influence on our development.

Behavioral Genetics

Behavioral genetics focuses on understanding genetic influences on human behavior, abilities, and traits (Walsh 2000). This field of research is revolutionizing the way that the social and life sciences understand human development and the connection between genes and the environment. Behavioral genetics has shown that the age-old dichotomy between nature and nurture is a false one. In regard to human development, genes and the environment are inextricably connected, and it makes no sense to think that genetic influences and environmental influences on human behavior can be divided into separable ingredients. The idea that genes solely determine anatomical and psychological traits is outmoded. Genes are but one part of a hierarchically organized system of factors located at different levels that mutually and reciprocally affect individual development. The different levels range from genes through cells, organ systems, and organisms up to the individual's social and cultural environment. How genes express themselves is affected by events that occur at higher levels, including events in our physical environment, and by our own behavior (Gottlieb 1996).

A simple example illustrates how genetic expression can be influenced by environmental conditions. Phenylketonuria (PKU) is a recessive, single-gene disease that causes mental retardation if it is not properly treated. Babies with PKU cannot produce enough of a certain enzyme needed to break down phenylalanine, a common substance in our diets. If phenylalanine builds up in a baby's body, it damages the child's developing brain, leading eventually to severe retardation. Fortunately, PKU can be detected as soon as a baby is born and can be treated by simply restricting the amount of phenylalanine in the child's diet until the early school years. By the time the child is in school, the brain has developed enough that excess phenylalanine will not hurt it (Plomin, Chipuer, and Loehlin 1990). In the case of the gene for PKU, its devastating expression can be completely eliminated if the proper environmental conditions exist.

Gregory Carey (2000) suggests a way of thinking about the connection between genes and the environment that illustrates how the two cannot be separated. He uses the analogy of lemonade. Suppose someone asked you this question: "Is lemonade lemons, water, or sugar?" You might respond that the question is phenomenally stupid and does not make any sense. Lemonade is not any one of these things; by definition, it is a combination of the three. Genes and the environment are linked like lemonade. It makes no sense to ask if your behavior or your personality is genetically or environmentally determined. By definition, both factors are involved.

Because our genetic makeup influences how we develop over the life course and because genes are the first, though not necessarily the most important, source of influence to appear on the scene, it is an appropriate starting point for our investigation of crime and the life course. We need to understand to what extent children inherit personality traits and behavioral tendencies from their parents. Further, we need to understand just how biologically based traits may influence behavior. For example, if it is possible to inherit an aggressive temperament or a taste for risky behavior, this suggests that some individuals may be biologically predisposed to behave in ways often defined as deviant or criminal by society at large. This is not to say that someone born with an aggressive temperament inevitably will engage in criminally violent acts or that a taste for risky behavior will always be manifested as criminal behavior. It depends on the environmental influences present during the child's development. In interactions with particular environmental influences, aggressive males can become football players rather than murderers, and a risk lover may find his thrills in the stock market rather than in reckless driving and drug use (Shah and Roth 1974). Nevertheless, possession of these traits may increase the likelihood that certain behavioral trajectories will be followed rather than others.

To fashion a metaphor, we might say that your genetic makeup forms a part of your personal launching pad into life. The angle at which a launch pad is fixed determines the initial direction of the trajectory that a projectile will follow. However, just as the initial trajectory of a projectile can be changed if a strong wind is blowing, our individual trajectories through life can be affected by a myriad of other factors that begin to operate after we leave our initial starting point. Of course, this metaphor is not perfect. A real launching pad ceases to affect the path of a projectile after the projectile is launched, but our genes continue to operate throughout our lives. In addition, we must not forget that genes alone do not determine the angle of our launch pad. Another important component of the launch pad is the family you are born into, but we will get to the family later. For now, we turn to a consideration of the links between genetics, personality, and behavior.

Insofar as genetic researchers have been able to determine, it appears that all of our individual traits are influenced to some degree by heredity, that is, by the genes that we receive from our parents (Carey 2000). Height, weight, body type, eye color, hair color, and facial appearance are some of the more obvious physical traits for which it often is easy to see physical resemblances between parents and their offspring. In addition to these gross anatomical characteristics, we also inherit psychological characteristics and behavioral tendencies from our parents (Plomin et al. 1990). For example, aggressive parents are more likely to have aggressive children than nonaggressive parents (Huesmann, Eron, Lefkowitz, and Walder 1984). Some of these inherited personality characteristics and behavioral tendencies may be implicated in criminal behavior in the sense that people who possess them may be more likely than average to engage in antisocial behavior. Antisocial refers to behavior that "intentionally hurts or harms a fellow group member" (Ellis 1990). For obvious reasons, social groups often criminalize such behavior. Indeed, physical assault on others epitomizes antisocial behavior. What children may inherit from their parents is not a "crime gene," but rather a tendency toward antisocial behavior.

Although antisocial behavior and criminal behavior may be related, it is important to keep in mind that they are not identical. Young children may engage in behavior that we recognize as antisocial without it being criminal. It is also important to note that just as antisocial behavior is not always criminal, neither is criminal behavior always antisocial. Breaking the law does not always equate with psychopathology (Rutter 1996). Sometimes people deliberately disobey the law out of a sense of duty and principle, as many people did, for example, during the civil rights protests of the 1960s in the United States. Some forms of lawbreaking are also completely acceptable or normal in subgroups of society. Among my fellow college students in the 1960s, recreational use of marijuana was entirely normal.

Investigating Genetics and Antisocial Behavior: Twin and Adoption Studies

Parents shape the behavior of their children in more ways than just by passing on their genes. They also raise their children, teach them, and interact with them for many years. Parents create an external environment for their children, which we usually call the family environment. The family environment may also include siblings and other people who affect how a child develops. However, to keep things from getting too complicated, we will ignore other aspects of the family environment for now and focus on the similarities and differences between parents and children. Because both genes and the family environment are sources of influence on the development of children, how do we know that the similarities between parents and children are not caused by the family environment rather than by genetic transmission? This question is the subject of developmental behavioral genetics. Behavioral geneticists collect and analyze data that come from "pairs of people who share all, some, or none of their genes, and who did or did not grow up in the same home" (Harris 1995).

Assessing the causal role of genetic factors on behavior is complicated because it is difficult to disentangle hereditary influences from environmental influences, especially the family environment. Hereditary influences refer to genetically caused similarities between parents and their offspring. The family environment refers to the effects that the parents' behavior, especially their interactional style and child-rearing practices, may have on the child. Because a parent's own behavior is influenced by his or her genetic makeup, the parent's genes may have both hereditary and environmental effects on the child. The parent's genes are passed on to the child, resulting in a hereditary effect on the child's behavior. In addition, by influencing how the parent behaves and interacts with the child, the parent's genetic endowment may also have an environmental effect on the child's behavior.

To disentangle hereditary from environmental effects, developmental behavioral geneticists study twins and adoptees. Although the basic ideas behind twin and adoption studies are relatively simple, the statistics are often complex. Here we will try to give an overview of the methodology without delving too far into the underlying statistical subtleties.

Twins provide the best, though not perfect, data for identifying genetic influences on variation in human characteristics. There are two types of twins, identical (called MZ, for monozygotic) and fraternal (called DZ, for dizygotic). Because they develop from a single fertilized egg that splits into two embryos, identical twins share all of their genes. Fraternal twins develop from two fertilized eggs and hence share only about half of their genes, the same as ordinary brothers and sisters. Identical twins are always of the same sex, but the sex of fraternal twins may be the same or different.

To estimate the extent of genetic involvement in a trait, behavioral geneticists compare the degree of similarity between identical and same-sex fraternal twins regarding a particular trait. The comparison approximates a kind of naturally occurring controlled experiment (Wilson and Herrnstein 1985). Because twins experience the same prenatal environment and the same family environment, the effects of these environments can be considered controlled. That is, in theory, they can be ignored when we compare identical and fraternal twins. Because identical twins share all of their genes, whereas fraternal twins share only about half, greater similarity between identical twins than fraternal twins regarding any given trait is evidence for a genetic factor. Using statistical procedures, behavioral geneticists can produce various numerical estimates of the contribution that genes make in regard to a trait.

Behavioral geneticists argue that this strategy of comparing identical and fraternal twins can be used to estimate genetic effects on more than just obvious physical traits, such as height, weight, eye color, and hair color. It can also be applied to psychological traits, such as self-esteem, happiness, or intelligence. Further, it can be used to measure genetic contributions to behavior, including criminal behavior. For example, one could compare twins in the area of arrest records. If there are genetic contributions to criminal behavior, then identical twins should show greater similarity in arrest records than fraternal twins.

One way to estimate the heritability of criminality is to calculate the *pairwise concordance rate* among twin pairs on some measure of criminality. This concordance rate is defined as the ratio of concordant pairs (that is, pairs in which both twins are criminal) to all criminal pairs. A criminal pair is any pair of twins in which at least one member is defined as a criminal. Thus, the formula for the pairwise concordance rate is $PwCR = C / C + D$, where C is the number of concordant pairs and D is the number of discordant pairs (that is, pairs in which only one twin has a criminal record). If criminality were entirely heritable, then identical twins would be identical in the area of criminality, whereas fraternal twins would be only as similar as ordinary siblings. If criminality is not at all heritable, then identical twins will be no more alike in that area than fraternal twins. The difference in the pairwise concordance rate between identical twins and fraternal twins indicates the amount of genetic contribution to the trait.

In a large study of 3,586 twin pairs selected from the Danish Twin Registry, Karl O. Christiansen investigated criminality among twins. All of the twins studied were born in Denmark between 1881 and 1910 and survived at least until the age of 15 (Christiansen 1977). To measure criminality, Christiansen searched the National Police Register and the Penal Register of Denmark. Of the 7,172 individuals under study, 926 individuals belonging to 799 twin pairs were found in one or both of these registers. After dividing the twin pairs by sex and zygosity, Christiansen found that the identical twins had a higher pairwise concordance rate than the fraternal twins for both male and female twin pairs. Male identical twins had a concordance rate of .35 compared to .13 for male fraternal twins. Thus, male identical twins were about two and a half times more likely to be concordant than male fraternal twins. For females, the relative difference in concordance rates between identical and fraternal twins was of about the same magnitude. Christiansen's results and those found in other smaller studies provide suggestive evidence that there is a genetic contribution to criminality (Christiansen 1977).

Like all empirical methods, however, the twin method has its weaknesses. One particularly important weakness involves the family environment. The twin method assumes that all twins share a common environment, but this assumption may not be correct in all cases (Christiansen 1977). For example, if the parents of identical twins dress their children in identical outfits, give them identical toys, and otherwise treat them as if they are supposed to be exactly the same more often than do the parents of fraternal twins, then it would not be surprising that the former act more alike than the latter. In this case, some of the similarity between identical twins would reflect contamination by the environment. Any analysis that did not take into account this environmental contamination would overestimate the genetic contribution to the trait. There are statistical techniques to correct for environmental contamination, but they have generally not been used in twin studies of criminality (Wilson and Herrnstein 1985).

As with twin studies, adoption studies involve comparisons between pairs of people and can be used to assess genetic influences on traits. In adoption studies, adopted children are compared to their biological and adoptive relatives (e.g., their parents and siblings). The basic question is simple: Are adopted children more likely to grow up resembling their biological relatives or their adoptive relatives? The extent to which adopted children grow up to resemble their biological relatives more than their adoptive relatives is evidence of genetic influence. The extent to which they resemble their adoptive relatives is evidence of environmental influence. For example, suppose a child is born to parents who are atheists, but the child is adopted as a baby and raised by a family that attends church every week. If the child grows up and attends church regularly, this would be evidence that religious practice is not influenced by genetics. Rather, it is learned behavior.

If we lived in a world run only for scientific purposes, adoption studies would be easy to design and carry out. Children would be randomly separated from their biological parents at birth and randomly placed with other parents. Only the scientists would know which children were being switched, and only they would know which children really belonged to which parents. The random assignment of children to parents would constitute a true randomized experimental design for investigating genetic influences.

Thankfully and properly, scientists do not run the world and adoptions are not conducted like scientific experiments. Children are adopted at different ages, and adoptive parents are not a random selection of parents. Adoption agencies try to match children to adoptive parents. Parents may behave differently toward children whom they adopt than they do to children who are their true biological offspring. The emotional connection between parent and child may be strongly conditioned by whether their relationship is adoptive or biological. For all of these reasons, adoption studies are not controlled experiments. Like twin studies, they have inherent weaknesses.

The largest and most well-known adoption study to explore genetic influences on the etiology of criminal behavior was conducted in Denmark (Mednick, Gabrielli, and Hutchings 1987). It was based on nonfamilial adoptions that occurred between 1924 and 1947. The original sample included 14,427 male and female adoptees and their biological and adoptive parents. After cases were excluded for missing data, the sample comprised 13,194 adoptees and over 10,000 parents. Criminal court convictions were used as the measure of criminal behavior.

To investigate the connection between the criminal behavior of parents and children, the researchers divided the male adoptees into four groups, depending on whether or not their biological or adoptive parents had been convicted. The rates of court convictions among adoptees were then calculated. Among male adoptees whose biological and adoptive parents had no court convictions, the conviction rate was 13.5 percent. This can be considered the base rate for court convictions in this population. If only the adoptive parents had been convicted, the conviction rate for the adopted boys was slightly higher, 14.7 percent. In contrast, in cases where a boy's biological parents had been convicted but the adoptive parents had not, the conviction rate was 20.0 percent. Among adoptees whose biological and adoptive parents both had been convicted, the conviction rate was the highest, 24.5 percent. These results have been interpreted as favoring a "partial genetic etiology," which means that criminal behavior may be at least partially heritable.

The investigators also examined the relationship between the degree of parental criminality and children's criminality. As the number of convictions of the biological parents increased, the likelihood that their sons would also have a conviction went up. Among sons of biological parents who had no convictions, 13 percent had convictions themselves. For sons who came from biological parents with three or more convictions, the rate nearly doubled to 25 percent.

Although there appears to be a connection between parents' criminal behavior and that of their sons, the relationship, clearly, is not perfect. Indeed, it may not be very strong at all (Gottfredson and Hirschi 1990). The vast majority of the children (a full 80 percent) whose biological parents had been convicted had no court convictions themselves. Even among parents with three or more convictions, 75 percent of their sons did not have court convictions. Thus, most of the children born to convicted parents did not go on to have court convictions themselves.

Gottfredson and Hirschi (1990) provide a suggestive illustration of just how weak the connection between parental criminality and the criminality of their offspring may be. Assume that the correlation between a father's genetic makeup and his son's genetic makeup is .50 (see Figure 2.1). Further assume that the correlation between each individual's genetic makeup and his criminal behavior is .25. To calculate the correlation between a father's criminal behavior and his son's criminal behavior, we multiply all the coefficients between father's and son's criminal behavior (e.g., .25 x .50 x .25). This produces a correlation coefficient of only .031.

Figure 2.1

Correlations Necessary to Produce an Observed Correlation of .03 Between the Criminal Behavior of Father and Son

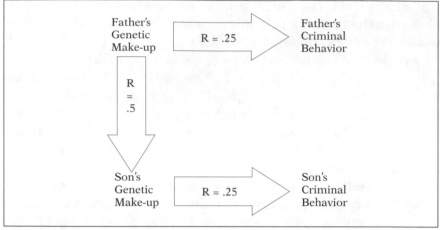

Michael R. Gottfredson and Travis Hirschi, (1990). *A General Theory of Crime*, p. 60. Copyright © 1990 by the Board of Trustees of the Leland Stanford Junior University. Reprinted with permission of Stanford University Press, www.sup.org.

Regardless of whether the Danish study provides suggestive evidence of a genetic component to crime or not, it does not help us assess the relative importance of genetic versus environmental explanations. As the Danish investigators recognize, the analyses do not provide a fair comparison between genetic and environmental influences (Mednick et al. 1987). Simply knowing that an adoptive parent had been convicted is not a very good indicator of how criminogenic the adoptive home environment is. Adoption agencies do not simply hand children over to parents who are obviously criminal. They go to great lengths to find upstanding parents. In this study, agency rules required parents to be free of convictions for five years prior to adopting, and the adoptive parents had a lower rate of repeat convictions than the biological parents (Mednick et al. 1987). In statistical terms this means that there was probably little variation in home environments for the adoptees, making it extremely difficult to identify environmental effects. Thus, the Danish study reveals next to nothing about the influence of home environment on criminal behavior.

This study is frequently cited as evidence that there is a moderate genetic contribution to criminality. Other smaller adoption studies have reached a similar conclusion. For example, Crowe (1972) studied 52 children of female felons in Iowa who were put up for adoption. The arrest records for the adopted children of the felons were compared to a control sample of children adopted from noncriminal mothers and matched in age, sex, race, and approximate time of adoption. The controls were significantly less likely to have an arrest record than were the children adopted from felons (4 percent to 15 percent, respectively). Yet, an adoption study in Sweden failed to replicate the Danish adoption study results, finding little correlation between parental and child criminality (Carey 1994). In this study, the correlation between adoptee conviction and biological parent conviction was not significant for male adoptees. Of 258 adoptees whose biological parents had been convicted, 13.2 percent were convicted, compared to 10.4 percent of 604 adoptees whose biological parents had not been convicted.

Although behavioral genetic studies of criminality have produced weak and sometimes inconsistent results, there is stronger evidence linking genetics to personality characteristics that may be associated with criminality. Indeed, the heritability of criminality is consistently found to be less than the heritability of personality traits that are associated with it, such as aggressiveness (Walsh 2000). For example, except for one study by Plomin (1981), twin studies of aggressiveness consistently find higher correlations between identical (MZ) twins than fraternal (DZ) twins (Carey 1994, 26–30). Similarly, adoption studies find stronger correlations between the aggressiveness of adopted children and their biological parents than between adopted children and their adoptive parents (Carey 1994). That personality traits appear to be more heritable than criminality suggests that genetic effects on crime may work through these traits (Rutter 1996). Through their influence on personality traits, genetic endowments may contribute to stability in antisocial behavior and criminality across the life course.

Genetic Expression and the Environment

Up to this point, we have focused on the connection between genes and behavior without paying too much attention to the role of the environment in this process. But the environment is crucial, because the way in which genetic influences express themselves is always shaped by environmental conditions. Some of the most interesting and important findings produced by behavioral genetics involve the interaction between genes and environment. Just how the interaction of genes and environment works is an enormously complicated subject and not well understood. Despite the preliminary nature of much of what is known, however, two aspects of the gene-environment relationship deserve discussion because they may turn out to be vitally important for the life course approach to criminology. These aspects include the influence of environment on the heritability of traits and the power of individuals to shape their environment.

Heritability estimates for traits are not the same across populations, and they may fluctuate within a population as it experiences different environments (Walsh 2000). For example, numerous studies have shown that IQ scores are heritable. (We refer to "IQ scores" rather than simply "IQ" or "intelligence" to avoid getting bogged down in the complicated debate over what IQ is and whether IQ tests really measure intelligence.) But the degree to which IQ scores are heritable varies across populations. Two studies found dramatic differences in the heritability of IQ scores, depending on the social class of the population under investigation. In one study of African-American twins, the heritability coefficient of IQ scores was estimated to be .34 among twins of low socioeconomic status (SES), but among African-American twins of high SES, the heritability coefficient was .72 (Scarr-Salapatak 1971). A study in Sweden found virtually identical heritability coefficients for low and high SES white twins (.30 and .70, respectively) (Fischbein 1980). So, do genes affect IQ scores? Yes. How much? Well, that depends.

The general point to be drawn from this example is that genetic effects are not stable across different environments. Genetic effects on a trait may be strong in one environment and weak in another. If a trait is strongly influenced by genetic factors in one environment, this does not preclude the possibility that we could create another environment in which the degree of influence would be different. In other words, by modifying the environment we can influence how genetic effects are expressed. The example used at the beginning of this chapter about PKU illustrates perfectly how a modification in environment (diet, in this case) can prevent the expression of undesirable genetic effects.

Genetic effects on criminality also fluctuate across environments. Anthony Walsh (2000) theorizes that in environments where there are many opportunities for crime and where there is little social resistance to crime, genetic effects will be low. But in environments where there are few opportunities for crime and where there is strong social resistance, genetic effects will be high (Walsh 2000). For example, low tonic heart rate is a heritable trait thought to be associated with antisocial behavior and criminality. One study found that among high SES children, low tonic heart rate was a significant predictor of antisocial behavior, but among low SES children it was not (Venables 1987). Cognitive problems significantly predict violent delinquency in advantaged environments but not in disadvantaged ones (Walsh 2000). What these studies suggest is that in disadvantaged environments, environmental causes of crime may overwhelm genetic causes (Walsh 2000). They further suggest that in disadvantaged environments well-adjusted or "good" kids are at an increased risk of becoming adolescent delinquents (Wikstrom and Loeber 2000).

The second aspect of the gene-environment relationship that deserves attention involves the power of individuals to shape their environment in ways that may influence how genes express themselves. In addition to responding to the environment in different ways, depending on their personalities and abilities, people shape and select their environments (Rutter 1996; Walsh 2000). By shaping the environment, we mean that individuals behave in ways that provoke certain responses from the environment, which then act back upon the individual, influencing his or her behavior and development. For example, a child who is bad tempered and who has a lot of tantrums may provoke parents to use more coercive forms of discipline than would a child who is easygoing and even tempered. Sampson and Laub, for example, found that childhood temper tantrums and difficultness predicted the use of harsh and erratic discipline by both mothers and fathers (1993, 88–91).

A recent study of adopted children provides another illustration of how children may create their environments (O'Connor, Deater-Deckard, Fulker, Rutter, and Plomin 1998). In this study, the mothers of children who would eventually be adopted were asked to self-report about their own antisocial behavior. After the children were born, they were classified as being either at genetic risk or not at genetic risk for antisocial behavior, according to the self-report data collected from their mothers earlier. The children were then followed over a period of time in their adopted homes. From ages 7 to 12, the children who were rated as being at genetic risk for antisocial behavior received more negative parenting from their adoptive parents than did the children who were not at risk. Poor behavior from children appeared to evoke negative parenting.

Individuals may also select their environments, or engage in what is called "niche-picking" (Scarr and McCartney 1983). Twin studies show that regardless of whether they are reared together or apart, identical twins often construct or end up in similar environments, and their environments are more similar than those of fraternal twins (Rowe 1994). This is not surprising. It makes sense that to the extent that they can control their lives, people will seek out environments in which they feel comfortable. Some people are "party animals." They like to get hammered and rowdy on weekends. Others are more introverted and would prefer to stay home and read a book. These individual preferences are driven by our genetic makeup, but as with all aspects of genetic expression, niche-picking is only influenced—not determined—by our genetic makeup.

The unavoidable reality of the gene-environment relationship raises complex and interrelated substantive and methodological issues for the life course perspective on crime. Substantively, it means that correlations between external environmental factors, such as employment or marital status, and criminality must always be interpreted with caution. Both cross-sectional and longitudinal correlations between environmental factors and measures of crime are likely to reflect processes of self-selection and should not be interpreted solely as casual connections. Based on their temperaments, talents, and traits, people will sort themselves into different employment and marital statuses. Thus, these preexisting differences between people influence both their employment status and their involvement in crime. In order to avoid misinterpreting these sorts of correlations, it is essential to control for preexisting differences in temperament and behavioral dispositions between people.

The gene-environment relationship also means that we must be careful in how we interpret correlations over time between internal factors, such as temperament and antisocial behavior. We must be careful to avoid the ontogenetic fallacy because longitudinal correlations between temperament and antisocial behavior are always specific to particular environments. For example, if we find in a sample of children from low-income families that temper tantrums at age 3 are strongly correlated with delinquency at age 15, we should not jump to the conclusion that some kids are just born bad and that the genetic factors that make children prone to temper tantrums will later cause them to develop into juvenile delinquents. If the same children had been born into high-income families, the correlation between early temper tantrums and later delinquency would be different. Avoiding the ontogenetic fallacy requires that we examine longitudinal correlations between individual level traits and measures of antisocial behavior in a variety of different contexts and environments.

The Biological Bases of Delinquent Behavior

If our personalities and behavioral tendencies, including tendencies toward antisocial behavior, are at least partially controlled by genetic conditions present at birth, just how does this influence work? One answer is that genetic conditions influence what are known as brain-functioning variables, that is, neurological and neurochemical conditions and processes in the brain (Ellis 1990). These neurological and neurochemical conditions shape how we behave, think, learn, perceive, and feel (Rowe 1990).

Some people learn more quickly and easily than others. They are born with psychological traits that equip them to achieve success in life relatively easily. Other people have difficulty learning or are born with personalities that make it difficult for them to conform to society's rules or to get along with others. These traits do not guarantee success or failure in life, but they do affect the odds. For example, all other things being equal, it is probably safe to assume that someone who is intelligent, persistent, and adaptable has a better chance of achieving success in life than someone who is unintelligent, impulsive, and intractable (Caspi, Elder, and Bem 1987). The latter individual is more likely to engage in behavior that will be defined by others as deviant or criminal than the former. To the extent that these traits are genetically based, biology is one source of influence on individual behavioral trajectories through the life course.

Numerous studies have found that delinquents perform less well than nondelinquents on tests designed to measure neuropsychological processes (Buikhuisen 1987). As a group, delinquents appear less able than nondelinquents to comprehend and use conceptual material (Yeudall, Fromm-Auch, and Davies 1982). They also perform relatively poorly on tasks that require sequencing skills or perceptual organization (Yeudall et al. 1982; Pontius and Yudowitz 1980). Delinquents appear to have shorter attention spans, lesser powers of concentration, and worse memories than nondelinquents (Yeudall et al. 1982; Voorhees 1981). Finally, as a group, delinquents appear to do less well than nondelinquents in processing visual information (Slavin 1978). These findings coincide with tests showing that delinquents score significantly lower than nondelinquents on intelligence tests, especially in regard to verbal reasoning abilities (Wilson and Herrnstein 1985).

The observed neuropsychological differences between delinquents and nondelinquents involve particular areas of the brain, specifically the frontal and temporal lobes. These areas of the brain control certain functions related to behavior and emotions that have potentially intriguing links to crime and delinquency. For example, the frontal lobe is involved in regulating and initiating behavior. It plays an important role in formulating plans, assessing consequences, learning from experience, and modifying a course of action on the basis of feedback from the environment (Buikhuisen 1987). Persons who suffer frontal lobe deficits are less able than most to form plans and evaluate potential consequences. They are apt to act impulsively without having a clear idea of what the likely outcome of their actions will be, and they do not profit much from experience. Thus, frontal lobe deficits may encourage the sort of impulsive, poorly thought out crimes that are characteristic of many criminals (Shover 1996).

The temporal lobe of the brain is involved in the subjective consciousness, emotional life, and instinctive feelings of the individual. Some research suggests that delinquents may perceive and react to negatively emotionally charged stimuli differently than nondelinquents (Buikhuisen 1987). For example, delinquents may be less able to experience fear than nondelinquents and hence less likely to learn from experience and the threat of sanction. For a sanction threat to work, it must be capable of invoking a subjective feeling of fear and subsequently a desire to avoid the threatened consequence that causes fear. This is called avoidance learning, and it is fear-motivated behavior. Failure to experience fear means avoidance learning is unlikely to occur. This may explain why some individuals appear to be less responsive to punishment than others and why some delinquents continue to engage in troublesome behavior despite their having been caught and punished before.

In effect, both frontal and temporal lobe dysfunctions reduce the individual's ability to adapt to environmental contingencies. To adapt to one's environment requires the capacity to perceive, comprehend, recall, and process information accurately. It requires the capacity to experience emotions such as fear and to learn from those experiences. To the extent that these capacities are deficient in a person, that person is at a disadvantage in adapting successfully to the environment. Thus, babies born with these sorts of cerebral dysfunctions may be predisposed to conduct problems unless their parents make special efforts to overcome these problems. In effect, such babies start behind the starting line; they are handicapped from the beginning.

Families: Structure, Support, and Discipline

It goes without saying that the first and most important nongenetic or prenatal influence on a child's development is the family, especially parents. Some children, of course, are raised and cared for by someone other than their biological parents, but the point remains the same. Whoever plays the role of caregiver early in an infant's life will have a profound effect on how the infant develops. Besides providing the basic objective necessities of life—food, shelter, and clothing—parents begin socializing and emotionally nurturing their children as soon as they are born. Parents (and siblings, if present) continue to serve as the most important socializers of children for years. The dominant role of the family lasts at least until children begin to form friendships with age peers. Because the family exerts its strongest influence during the period when the child is undergoing rapid growth and development, the family plays an extremely important role in determining the direction of many of the child's initial trajectories in life. Trajectories in crime and deviance are no exception.

A large body of research indicates that delinquent, aggressive, and criminal behaviors are rooted in the family (Loeber and Stouthamer-Loeber 1986). We need to learn more about what family factors are related to the development of offending over time. What goes wrong in some families to produce children who display conduct problems early and who go on to become juvenile delinquents and serious criminals?

One way to approach the question of what goes wrong in some families is to consider what goes right in most others. With respect to raising a child, what should families do? Ideally, the family socializes and prepares the child to live in society in such a way that he or she is not a threat or a burden to others. If all goes well, the family helps the child learn to behave in ways that are socially appropriate, that is, to respect the feelings, rights, and property of others. The family also helps the child to prepare to become a productive, self-supporting member of society. Good families accomplish these twin goals by providing a robust and ever-shifting balance of support and control (Cullen 1994).

Parents can help their children undertake successful trajectories in life by providing both expressive and instrumental support. In the context of the family, expressive support refers to how well parents meet the needs of their children for love, affection, self-esteem, and a sense of belonging and being needed. Parents who provide expressive support spend time with their children talking about feelings, hopes, and dreams. They help children vent frustrations and deal with the difficult problems of growing up (Vaux 1988). Instrumental support includes not only providing the basic material necessities of life, such as food, shelter, and clothing, but also information and guidance (Lin 1986). Parents who help their children with their projects by working with them, or getting them the supplies they need, or taking them where they need to go are providing instrumental support. These simple activities are important in building strong bonds between children and their parents, and strong bonds help prevent involvement in crime and delinquency.

Francis Cullen argues persuasively that expressive support from parents diminishes the risk of criminal involvement for children (1994). A long line of research supports this view. Over 50 years ago, the Gluecks noted that compared to delinquents, nondelinquents had "warmer" relations with their parents. The families of nondelinquents were more likely to engage in family activities and to support one another emotionally. In nondelinquent families, both parents and children seemed to care more about each other (Glueck and Glueck 1950). The Gluecks are not alone in noting emotional differences between the families of delinquents and nondelinquents. In a comprehensive review of research on families and crime, Loeber and Stouthamer-Loeber concluded that there is a clear relationship between how involved parents are with a child and the child's risk of becoming delinquent. Children lucky enough to have parents who spend time with them in intimate communication and sharing activities are less likely to become delinquent than the children whose parents reject and ignore them and who display little love or affection (Loeber and Stouthamer-Loeber 1986). Children who avoid early involvement in delinquent activities appear to be raised in families that are systematically different from those of children who begin delinquent trajectories early.

It certainly would simplify things if there were only two types of families: good and bad. If that were the case, it would be easy to see how often bad kids came from bad families. But reality is not that simple. Families cannot be neatly divided into good or bad. Families that appear to function differently may nonetheless produce children who behave similarly, whereas those that appear the same may produce very different sorts of children. With respect to conduct problems and juvenile delinquency, it is likely that several different developmental paths may lead to the same outcome (Loeber and Stouthamer-Loeber 1986).

Loeber and Stouthamer-Loeber (1986) have proposed four heuristic paradigms of family functioning—neglect, conflict, deviancy, and disruption. These paradigms refer to different patterns of behavior and interaction involving parents and children. Research indicates that children raised in families displaying one or more of these functioning patterns are at greater risk of exhibiting conduct problems and delinquency than children fortunate enough to be raised in more well-functioning families.

Neglect occurs when parents spend insufficient time with their children and when they are unaware of their children's misconduct. Children in neglectful families have more freedom to do as they please, with little or no parental guidance, than children with parents who pay close attention. As a result, the early signs of behavioral problems in children are unlikely to be noticed or corrected. The neglect paradigm does not assume that it is only the parents who withdraw from the child; the lack of involvement may be mutual. Parents may withdraw from children who are difficult to handle, or over time they may become more permissive of their children's misbehavior simply out of exhaustion (Lykken 1995, 205). For example, Sampson and Laub (1993) found that mothers of children who had a lot of temper tantrums were less likely to supervise their children closely than mothers of more easygoing children. Regardless of who withdraws, the parents' lack of time and limited awareness restricts their opportunities to discipline misbehavior and to reward good behavior.

The *conflict* paradigm describes families in which children and parents continually conflict with one another. Frequently, the source of the conflict is the child's chronic misbehavior, which the parents do not respond to appropriately. Confronted with disobedience or misbehavior, the parents are unable to discipline the child in a consistent but nonaggressive manner. Instead, they either nag the child without ever really imposing discipline or they use harsh but erratic physical punishment. In their study of boys and families in Eugene, Oregon, Patterson and colleagues identified a particularly destructive pattern of parent-child interaction that they called the "three-step dance." The parent makes a demand of the child ("Stop hitting the cat"), the child responds with a temper tantrum or an argument ("But Johnny gets to hit his cat"), and the parent backs off ("Oh, let the cat take care of itself") (Patterson, Reid, and Dishion 1992, 11). These episodes reinforce the child's defiant behavior, which leads to more misbehavior. This style of disciplining tends to be ineffective in curtailing problem behavior, leading to further conflicts between the parents and the child. Over time, the continual conflict may cause parents and children to regard each other as enemies and to reject each other.

The distinguishing feature of the *deviancy* paradigm is its focus on what parents teach their children rather than on how they relate to them. The neglect and conflict paradigms describe styles of family functioning in which the quantity or style of interaction between the parent and child is inadequate or misguided. The parents either ignore the child's behavior or else they respond to it inappropriately. In these families, there is something wrong with the way parents and children relate to one another. Instead of focusing on the way in which parents relate to their children, the deviancy paradigm focuses on the content of the parent-child interaction. According to this paradigm, parents may provoke conduct problems and delinquency in their children in several ways. Parents themselves may engage in deviancy, which the children may witness or learn about and then imitate. Or parents may transmit deviant attitudes and values to their children. For example, parents may encourage their children to be tough and to use force in their disputes with other children (Anderson 1990).

The last of the four paradigms of family functioning is the *disruption* paradigm. Disruption occurs when parents are continually in conflict with one another or when they separate or divorce. In the case of separation and divorce, the stressful period that precedes the breakup of the marriage, as well as the breakup itself, can directly and indirectly affect a child's behavior. Strain and conflict between parents may cause them to be irritable and to behave aggressively toward each other and the children. The children in turn may respond by getting upset or by learning to avoid the cranky parents. As a result, children and parents spend less positive time together, and parents are less likely to deal effectively with the problem behaviors of their children.

Although it is useful for analytical purposes to separate the four paradigms, in reality, families may often experience several disadvantages concurrently. For example, disruption may lead to neglect of the child or to conflict between the parents and the child. Parents who are going through a divorce may become so preoccupied with their own problems that they fail to attend sufficiently to their children. Or, they may increase their use of coercive discipline, which may lead to greater conflict with their children. Troubled families often have many troubles.

The empirical connection between family background and delinquency is well established. Cross-sectional, prospective, and retrospective research designs consistently find differences between the families of delinquents and nondelinquents. For example, in their reanalysis of the Gluecks' data, Sampson and Laub (1993) explored the family context of juvenile delinquency. They examined the effects of both family structure variables and family process variables on juvenile delinquency. Family structure variables include factors such as the size of the family, overcrowding in the home, the socioeconomic status of the family, whether the mother is employed outside the home, and whether the family has been disrupted by divorce or separation, as well as other conditions. In Sampson's and Laub's theory, the structural variables set the context in which the parents relate to their children. The family process variables include the use of harsh or erratic discipline by the parents, the degree of supervision by the mother, the degree of parental rejection of the child, and the child's attachment to the parents. The process variables influence how the parents and child relate to one another, how closely the parents attempt to control the child's behavior, and the strength of the emotional bond between the child and parents.

Using sophisticated statistical analysis, Sampson and Laub show that the family process variables exert a strong effect on both official and unofficial measures of delinquency. Children whose parents reject them and who use harsh and erratic discipline engage in more delinquency than children whose parents do not reject them and who use more consistent and gentle forms of discipline. Mothers who supervise their children closely reduce their involvement in delinquency, and children who are strongly attached to their parents are less involved in delinquency than those who are less attached to their parents. These results coincide with those observed by many other researchers and point to the general conclusion that what matters most are those aspects of family functioning that involve direct contacts between the parent and child (Loeber and Stouthamer-Loeber 1986).

Family structure does not appear to be as important as family functioning in directly influencing delinquency. Only three of the family structure variables examined by Sampson and Laub—family size, overcrowding, and residential mobility—have significant effects on delinquency, and the size of their effects is small (Sampson and Laub 1993, 94). Nevertheless, family structure cannot be ignored as a factor in delinquency because structure is associated with functioning. Sampson and Laub found that the processes that directly affect delinquency are more likely to appear in some families than others (80). Poverty, residential mobility, and family disruption are all significantly related to parental rejection of their children and to children's attachment to their parents. Children born into families that are poor, disrupted, or that move often are more likely to experience emotional rejection from their parents and less likely to develop strong emotional bonds to their parents. Family structure is also related to how discipline and supervision are exercised in families. The use of harsh and erratic discipline by both mothers and fathers is more likely in large, overcrowded families and in families that are poor. Mothers in large poor families also appear to supervise their children less strictly than mothers in smaller, more well-off families. Family structure influences family functioning.

Sampson and Laub (1993) theorized that the family process variables influence the extent to which children become involved in delinquency. However, because of the potential problem of self-selection, they recognized the possibility that the behavior of the child may influence the family process variables first. It is possible that children may actually cause important family processes, such as parental rejection or the use of harsh discipline, if they happen to be particularly difficult. By virtue of their difficult behavior, children may in a sense "select" bad parents. In this case, later delinquency would be merely a new form of expression of difficult behavior by the child, and the correlation between family process and delinquency would be spurious.

Sampson and Laub investigated this self-selection hypothesis. The Gluecks' data contain measures of early behavior problems such as temper tantrums by the child. Sampson and Laub found that early behavior problems do exert significant effects on the family process variables, but family structure remains important in predicting family process. Further, when all three sets of variables—early behavior problems, family structure, and family process—are used to predict delinquency, the results show that both early behavior and family process have significant effects. Sampson and Laub conclude that child effects on delinquency do exist, but they are not as important as family socialization processes.

Impressive as the study by Sampson and Laub is, it is still, nevertheless, just one study. It is based on a sample drawn at a particular time and in a particular place. What about children and families at other times and in other places? Would the results be the same?

The Cambridge Study by West and Farrington (1973) suggests that the answer is yes. In their study, parental attitudes toward their children, parental disciplinary styles, and parental conflict were all related to delinquency. Boys whose parents displayed "cruel, passive, or neglectful" attitudes toward them were significantly more likely to become delinquent than boys whose parents were warm and loving (West and Farrington 1973, 49–50). Boys whose parents used "very strict or erratic" discipline were also more likely to engage in delinquency than were the sons of parents who used other disciplinary methods (51–52). Finally, boys raised in homes in which there was a noticeable degree of conflict between the parents were more likely to be delinquent than their counterparts who experienced less marital disharmony (53–54).

The Glueck study, which was conducted in Boston, Massachusetts, began in 1939. The Cambridge study started in Cambridge, England, about 20 years later. More recent research indicates that troubled families are still an important source of delinquency. Researchers in the Program on the Causes and Correlates of Delinquency have observed similar relationships between family life and delinquency in their studies in Pittsburgh, Denver, and Rochester. In these prospective studies, which began in the late 1980s, young children were more likely to develop into juvenile delinquents if they were raised in families characterized by the use of physical punishment, poor parent-child communication, and weak attachment between parents and children (Loeber, Farrington, Stouthamer-

Loeber, Moffitt, and Caspi 1998; Huizinga, Weiher, Menard, Espiritu, and Esbensen 1998; Thornberry, Krohn, Lizotte, Smith, and Perter 1998). Thus, the families of delinquents raised in different countries and at widely different times appear quite similar. They are families in which the parents have negative, rejecting attitudes toward their children. Children in these families do not have strong, warm attachments to their parents. The parents in these families use erratic, harsh discipline.

The descriptive slogans used by quantitative researchers, such as "negative, rejecting attitudes" and "erratic, harsh discipline," do not convey the emotional and physical brutality of some of these families. Nor do they do justice to the explosive climate that may permeate the homes of delinquents. In their important *Mean Streets* study, John Hagan and Bill McCarthy shed light on just how bad the families of delinquents can be. They interviewed homeless youths in Toronto and Vancouver, Canada (Hagan and McCarthy 1997). These youths are textbook examples of what it means to be "at risk." For them, involvement in crime, delinquency, drug use, and sexual deviance is normal. Many of the youths took to the streets to escape violent families, as one young woman, Brenda, describing her decision to leave, explained:

> I was tired of going, um, I was tired of walking home and getting to the door and crying and, you know, not knowing if I was going to get killed that night or not, kinda thing . . . I didn't like having to, just, kind of, walk on eggshells twenty-four hours a day . . . And I was going mental. And it was either me or them. I was either going to kill myself or kill my parents, and my parents aren't worth going to jail for. (Hagan and McCarthy 1997, 110)

Two boys in the study were more succinct than Brenda, but their reasons for leaving sound much the same (Hagan and McCarthy 1997, 110). When asked why he left, a boy named Barry simply responded, "Um, my dad beat the piss out of me," and the circumstances that led Ryan to leave strongly resemble Barry's:

> I was tired of always gettin' hit and shit like this, so I just said, forget it, I don't need that kind of bullshit, you know. No one needs that kind of shit, you know.

Hagan and McCarthy (111–112) are aware of the self-selection problem, and they are careful to note that the climate of the delinquent's home life is not solely the fault of the parents. The youths in their study bear some responsibility for the conflict. In the interviews, these youths do not come across as compliant and easygoing children but rather as difficult and, in some instances, prone to violence themselves. In other words, their problems may have ontogenetic as well as sociogenic roots. The case of Derek illustrates how violence in a home can be reciprocal and can be initiated by the youth rather than the parent. He described the incident that preceded his being thrown out of his house this way:

> I kicked in the door. I think that had a lot to do with it, considering he [the father] was standing behind it. He got injured when he grabbed me and threw me up against the wall. First instinct, you know. You know, like you gotta swing if someone puts you up against the wall. I hit him, and then, he like, kicked me in the ribs and threw me out. (Hagan and McCarthy 1997, 111–112)

Derek himself, then, appears to be partly responsible for ending up on the street, and his case illustrates the phenomenon of self-selection. The experiences of other homeless youths who were troublemakers before they left home also appear to be examples of self-selection in that their behavior provoked responses from their parents that led to their living on the street. Tyrone is a case in point:

> Um, when I first got the boot? Um, let's see . . . skipping out of school too much, getting kicked out of school too much. Um, selling narcotics, fighting with siblings, stealing money from relatives and friends. I seemed to be becoming a little bit of an embarrassment in the neighborhood for my mom. And, so her friends kept going, 'Kick him out, kick him out—maybe he'll learn.' (Hagan and McCarthy 1997, 112)

The stories of Derek and Tyrone and the other youths in the *Mean Streets* study illustrate the complex process by which individuals self-select an environment—in this case, homelessness. They also illustrate how ontogenetic (individual temperament) and sociogenic (family environment) factors combine to influence delinquent trajectories. It is probably safe to say that despite their troublesomeness these youths would have followed different trajectories had their parents been more caring and understanding. Some research finds that strong social bonds between parents and children can moderate the effects of ontogenetic factors on delinquent trajectories (Long and Witte 1981; Wright, Caspi, Moffitt, and Silva 1999; Wright, Caspi, Moffitt, and Silva 2000). It is probably also true that if these children had been more easygoing and compliant, they would eventually have emerged from these homes more or less ready to follow conventional lives. But we don't really know for sure. We don't know enough about families to say with absolute certainty what parents can do to prevent kids like Derek and Tyrone from ending up on urban streets. Neither do we know what sorts of kids, if any, could survive undamaged in homes like these.

The fundamental processes that seem to be present in successful families and missing in unsuccessful ones are attachment and control. Attachment refers to an emotional connection between parent and child, in which the child has feelings of love, respect, and admiration toward the parent and the parent feels similarly toward the child. It is a reciprocal process, involving both parent and child, but it starts with the parent. By giving love and expressive support early on, parents can foster a sense of attachment in their children. Children who develop strong attachments to their parents care about their parents' feelings and opinions. They are aware of and sensitive to the impact that their behavior can have on their parents. They understand that if they are caught doing something wrong, it will embarrass and disappoint their parents, and they don't want that to happen. Rather, they want their parents to be proud of them. The emotional connection functions as a sort of internal monitor of the child's behavior when parents are not present. Parents who work at developing a strong sense of attachment in their children when they are young are rewarded for their efforts when their children enter adolescence in reduced levels of delinquency.

Showering children with love and affection when they are young in the hopes of developing a strong sense of attachment, however, is not enough in and of itself to prevent delinquency. Francis Cullen (1994) is right when he affirms that expressive support is crucial, but parents who want to keep their children out of trouble must also invoke the other fundamental process of successful families—control. Control involves consistently monitoring the child's behavior, recognizing deviance when it occurs, and correcting misbehavior when it happens (Gottfredson and Hirschi 1990). Parents must pay attention to their children and be aware of what they are doing. This is the first step in effective child rearing. Parents must also recognize deviance when it occurs. Surprising as it may seem, not all parents do this. Research by Patterson and colleagues found that the parents of children who steal don't "track," that is, they don't interpret stealing as deviant and they don't correct their children when they steal (Patterson 1980, 88–89). By monitoring their children, recognizing deviance, and correcting misbehavior, parents can foster the development of self-control in their children and help start them off on trajectories aimed away from serious delinquency (Gottfredson and Hirschi 1990).

As we will see in following chapters, the locus of attachment and control changes over the life course. Parents and families are most important in the early years. As we age out of early childhood, peers, schools, spouses, and employers rise in salience.

How Early Can Trouble Start?

As any parent, teacher, daycare worker, or baby-sitter can tell you, all young children have their moments when they are difficult to handle, when they definitely fall short of what we would call civilized behavior. Much of this misbehavior is completely normal and appropriate for children, depending on their age. For example, it is normal for 2- and 3-year-olds to occasionally defy their parents and to be aggressive with siblings and playmates (Loeber and Hay 1994). Over time, aggression and oppositional behavior decrease between ages 3 and 6 as children learn prosocial skills. They learn how to deal with conflict and how to express their needs verbally.

Some toddlers and preschoolers, however, distinguish themselves from the norm by initiating hostile conflict instead of reacting when provoked. They commit acts of intense aggression and are regarded by their parents as having a difficult temperament, or as prone to throwing temper tantrums. These early signs of conduct problems often signal trouble in the future. For example, in a study of 205 boys aged 10 to 16, researchers asked the mothers to recall how easy or difficult it had been to get along with their sons when they were 1 to 5 years old. Five years later, when the boys were 15 to 21 years old, those who had been characterized by their mothers as "difficult" were twice as likely to have an official record of delinquency as those rated "easy." The difficult boys also self-reported committing delinquent acts at a higher rate than the easy boys (Loeber, Stouthamer-Loeber, and Green 1991). In a careful study using the Dunedin, New Zealand, data, White et al. (1990) found considerable continuity in antisocial and delinquent behavior from age 3 through the early teen years. Children who scored high on measures of disobedient and aggressive behavior at age 3 were more likely to exhibit other conduct disorders later in childhood and to be arrested by the police in their early teen years than children who scored low in disobedience and aggression (White et al. 1990). The fact that some children begin to show signs of abnormal conduct so early in life suggests that some forms of antisocial behavior reflect a general temperament (White et al. 1990). This study provides impressive evidence for continuity in antisocial behavior because it is a prospective study of a normal population.

Retrospective studies are apt to find even more continuity between early child and adult antisocial behavior. Retrospective studies find that, virtually without exception, antisocial adults are antisocial children grown up (Wilson and Herrnstein 1985). In her 30-year study of 526 white children, Robins found no case of adult sociopathy that was not preceded by evidence of antisocial behavior before age 18. Over half of the sociopathic males in her sample showed conduct disorders and behavioral problems before age 8 (Robins 1966).

Evidence for continuity in antisocial behavior is plentiful, but it must be interpreted carefully. Too often, commentators tell us that conduct problems at a young age predict delinquency in the teenage years without revealing that the success rate of these predictions is not very good. Most antisocial preschoolers do not go on to become antisocial adults or even antisocial juveniles. In the Dunedin study, for example, there was a high false-positive rate when antisocial behavior at age 3 alone was used as a predictor of antisocial behavior at age 11. The researchers note: "Of the 209 children predicted to have antisocial outcomes at age 11, 84.7 percent did not develop stable and pervasive antisocial behavior" (White et al. 1990, 521). In addition, a number of children who did not display antisocial behavior in middle childhood emerged later as delinquents. These children had other conduct problems, such as attention deficit disorder or hyperactivity.

The search for early predictors of future conduct disorders is certainly a project worth pursuing. If truly reliable and accurate predictors could ever be identified, it might become possible to design intensive early intervention efforts that would save many children from a lifetime of conflict and failure. At present, however, the usefulness of preschool behavioral predictors for identifying children who would benefit from early interventions is limited (White et al. 1990). Some preschool predictors are strong in the statistical sense that they have highly significant statistical relationships with later antisocial outcomes, but their predictive efficiency is low. They lead to an unacceptably high rate of false positives. False negatives also emerge with regularity.

Is this situation likely to improve in the future? It is hard to say. The number of well-designed prospective studies is still small, and the research conducted on these data so far suffers from a number of shortcomings. Most studies focus on only one or two domains of risk factors as predictors, such as behavioral problems or cognitive disorders, and ignore other potential risk factors, such as family interaction patterns or family socioeconomic status, which might improve predictive accuracy (Loeber and Dishion 1983). Perhaps we simply have not yet discovered the right variable or combination of variables. Perhaps future research will eventually yield more useful results.

It is always possible that future research will lead to the discovery of some sort of magic lens through which we will be able to peer into the future of the young child and predict his or her path through life. Yet, seductive as this goal is, it is important to remember the ontogenetic fallacy, that is, the fallacy of attributing developmental outcomes solely to maturational processes. The search for early childhood predictors of criminality assumes that teenage crime and delinquency represent the natural outgrowth of characteristics that are either present at birth or develop very shortly thereafter in some individuals. This assumption is questionable for both empirical and theoretical reasons. Empirically, prospective predictions of teenage antisocial behavior made from variables measured in early childhood are not very accurate. The rate of false positives in studies is well over 50 percent.

Theoretically, the assumption that adult behavior can be predicted in early childhood flows against the central premises of the life course approach. The life course approach is based on the premises that development is an ongoing process that unfolds over the entire lifespan, and development involves interactions between the individual and the environment. It is not easy to reconcile the assumption of strong early predictors with the assumption that development is a continuous process influenced by events that occur in the individual's environment. Predicting the life course of an individual based only on factors present at an early age ignores all of the causal factors that come into play later. It is like trying to predict the course that Columbus took to the New World based only on the strength and direction of the wind and water currents at the time that his boat left the dock.

The great physicist Neils Bohr was right: "Prediction is hard, especially when it's about the future."

Summary

In the early stages of life, children begin to develop ways of behaving and interacting with others that over time evolve into different trajectories through life. Both genetic endowments and family socialization experiences influence the direction of early trajectories, including trajectories in crime. Children born to parents who have criminal backgrounds are at greater risk of becoming criminals themselves than children born to parents without such backgrounds (Rowe and Farrington 1997). Evidence suggests that the connection between the criminality of parents and that of their children is in part genetically based, and that it most likely operates through certain personality characteristics. Exactly how strong the genetic components of crime and personality are remains to be determined. It also remains to be determined how susceptible genetic influences are to treatment.

In addition to genetic endowments, experiences in the family also matter. How parents relate to their children—how they supervise and discipline them—strongly influences the likelihood of delinquency. Parents who relate warmly and supportively to their children, who supervise them closely, and who exercise consistent but mild discipline stand a good chance of seeing their children grow up to become happy, productive members of society. In contrast, parents who reject their children, who feel cold or passive toward them, who respond harshly or erratically or not at all when they misbehave are likely to have children who often get into trouble. These children are at great risk of developing into serious juvenile delinquents and perhaps even into adult career criminals.

Policy Implications

How do we prevent this risk from becoming a reality? It's a difficult question, one for which we do not yet have a clear unequivocal answer. Nevertheless, if the research reviewed in this chapter tells us anything, it is that crime prevention should start early and should focus on children and the family. And there is some evidence that some family-based prevention programs do work.

Starting with families is not going to be easy. Historically, many Americans have considered families to be sacrosanct, absolutely the last place that government should be permitted to intrude. Coupled with a historical distrust of government-sponsored family-planning programs is a widespread belief that such programs are at best examples of misguided but irrelevant "do-gooderism" and at worst nothing more than political "pork" (Currie 1998). Ideological and political resistance to the idea of trying to prevent crime by helping families is not insignificant in America. Despite the mantra that most politicians recite about the importance of family values, the United States provides little in the way of support to families compared to other developed countries (Messner and Rosenfeld 1997).

Of course, we should not expect too much from government-sponsored family support, and it is easy to overstate the case for the effectiveness of prevention programs. There is no shortage of programs that have been dismal failures, and conservative critics make a good point when they say that a lot of money has been wasted on poorly conceived and ineffective interventions. Even the programs that do work are not panaceas. As Elliott Currie (1998, 81) notes, liberals who support the idea of crime prevention often have been blissfully naive in the "uncritical belief that small-scale, modestly financed social programs will, by themselves, magically transform violence-ridden communities and rescue poor children from lives of crime." Even good programs can be overwhelmed by deteriorating social conditions, and we have to recognize the current limits to our ability to predict, let alone change, human development. Thus, it is important to be realistic about crime prevention. The problem is complicated.

Nevertheless, given what we have learned about families and crime and about crime prevention in recent years, three priorities seem especially critical: preventing child abuse and neglect, helping at-risk children with intensive preschool programs, and reducing teenage pregnancies. These may not be the only programs that will work, but they are the ones that seem to offer the most convincing evidence of their effectiveness. They also correspond with our growing understanding of the roots of delinquency and violent crime (Currie 1998, 82).

A top priority should be to reduce child abuse and neglect. Child abuse itself is a tragic violent crime. It leads directly to the deaths of 5,000 children per year and to well over 150,000 serious injuries to children annually (Currie 1998, 82). And the effects of child abuse radiate far beyond the individual children who suffer from it. The evidence is compelling that much of the violent crime that terrifies us has its roots in abusive families. For example, the Rochester Youth Development Study found that youths who had been abused—as measured by an official report to the county child-protective agency—were twice as likely to be arrested as were youths who did not have an official report. The former also reported twice as many violent crimes as the latter (Smith and Thornberry 1995).

One way to reduce child abuse that is gaining increasing interest and that appears to work is actually an old-fashioned approach—home visiting. Home visiting involves sending a public-health professional or even just a caring and informed layperson to visit young women who are pregnant and families with young children. The home visitors can provide information about nutrition, health, and child-rearing to disadvantaged families. They can link young families with other support services and, most importantly, build a long-term supportive relationship with mothers whose problems would ordinarily be ignored. Simple as the idea of home visits may sound, it appears to work. Evaluations of programs in New York, Maryland, and Hawaii all found reductions in child abuse and neglect in families that had received home visits (Currie 1998, 83–91). The program in Elmira, New York, is particularly important because it includes a long term follow-up of the children in the treatment and control group. The follow-up assessed not only the rate of child abuse in the two groups, but also the children's own behavior. At age 15, the children of the mothers in the treatment group who had received home visits were less likely to have problems with alcohol or drugs and far less likely to be arrested than the children of mothers in the control group who had not received home visits (Currie 1998, 86).

The next crime prevention priority should be to increase and improve early intervention for children who are at risk for impaired cognitive development and behavior problems. Cognitive and behavior problems often show up early in life, sometimes even before children enter kindergarten, and it is clear that they often lead to early failure in school and to delinquency. Because these problems emerge so early, it is easy to assume that some children are simply born losers and that nothing can be done to improve their chances in life. Yet, the success of some early-childhood programs offers a different, and much more encouraging, prospect (Currie 1998, 91).

Early intervention programs come in different shapes and sizes, but they usually involve providing preschool, medical services, and home visits for children from disadvantaged environments. A number of programs designed along these lines have been carefully evaluated by comparing follow-up rates of behavior problems, delinquency, and other developmental outcomes between treatment and control groups. The results are encouraging. The children who receive early treatment consistently display fewer behavior problems later in life. They are less likely to become delinquents and more likely to succeed in school than children in the control groups (Currie 1998, 90–98). It is not yet clear exactly why some programs work and others do not, but the more successful programs seem to share the strategy of targeting parents as well as children.

Finally, programs to reduce the number of teenage pregnancies are needed. The problem of teenage pregnancy is threefold. First, children born to teenagers are more likely to receive poor prenatal care, have low birthweights, and suffer from other medical problems. Second, evidence suggests that teenagers are sometimes not very good at parenting. The risk of exposure to child abuse and neglect is highest for children born to poor, teenage, single mothers (Gelles 1992). Third, the children of teenage parents are much more likely to grow up in disadvantaged and criminogenic environments than are the children of older married parents. They are more likely to be poor themselves and to be raised in poverty-stricken neighborhoods (Coulton, Pandey, and Chow 1990; Coulton and Pandey 1992). Thus, teenage pregnancy increases the likelihood that three very potent sets of developmental risk factors will converge: biological deficiencies, poor parenting, and criminogenic neighborhoods. It is not surprising that comparatively many of the children raised in these circumstances go on to become serious delinquents in adolescence, the next stage in the life course. ✦

Chapter 3

Adolescence and Crime

Continuity and Change

> *Our choices were few.*
> *So, the thought never hit*
> *that the one road we traveled*
> *would ever shatter or split.*
>
> —from *Bob Dylan's Dream*

Overview

Age 13 heralds the start of a time of trouble for many parents. During the teenage years, there is a rapid, almost explosive, increase in the prevalence of offending. Indeed, involvement in minor forms of delinquency is so widespread among teenagers that it is statistically normal (Moffitt 1997). It may seem odd and certainly goes against the wishes of most parents, but a child who never does anything wrong is out of step with peers and actually a cause for concern. For criminologists, the teenage years are where the action is.

The age of onset—that is, the age at which a person commits his or her first offense—appears to peak between 15 and 17 (Farrington 1994; Steffensmeier and Allan 2000). Regardless of whether offending is measured by self-reports or official statistics such as arrest rates, a large proportion of young people become involved in delinquent behavior during this period.

From the perspective of life course theory, this two-year period is especially important because it is when most people start their trajectories in crime and delinquency. Luckily for society, these trajectories tend to be short-lived and characterized by relatively minor offenses (Farrington, Ohlin, and Wilson 1986). After a brief teenage walk on the wild side, the average person settles down to a life of more or less consistent conformity. But this pattern is not universal. Some individuals follow trajectories of much longer duration, involving much more serious types of offenses. Thus, as we will see, the teenage years are marked by both continuity and discontinuity in behavior. For life course criminology, the teenage years encompass two important turning points: onset of offending and desistance from offending.

Although there is near-universal consensus on the general shape of the age-crime curve, scholars still debate a number of important details about the relationship between age and crime (Steffensmeier and Allan 2000; Gottfredson and Hirschi 1990). One particularly important matter concerns the theoretical interpretation of the relationship between age and crime. What causes or underlies the rapid increase in the prevalence of offending during the early teenage years? Equally important, what causes the almost equally rapid decline in offending near the end of the teenage years? A second important issue concerns the universality or invariance of the age-crime relationship. Is the relationship between age and crime the same in all societies and among all groups of people, or does it vary over time, place, demographic category, and type of crime? Do some individuals follow trajectories that do not coincide with the general trend? To put it another way, are there different types of trajectories in crime and deviance? And if so, how many types are there, what are their characteristics, and why do some people follow these alternative trajectories?

We begin this chapter by returning to the subject of biology. Recent research indicates that during the teenage years a number of important biological developments take place besides the well-known onset of puberty. These developments, which involve the teenage brain, are implicated in the distinctive behavior patterns of teenagers. After a brief review of this new research, we move on to the issue of age and crime, looking first at societal patterns as revealed by official statistics and self-report surveys. Next, we delve more deeply into the details of the relationship between age and crime to investigate how age-crime patterns may vary across cultures, over time, and by race. Then, we turn to the investigation of individual patterns in crime over time. At this point, the issue of the theoretical interpretation of the age-crime curve becomes entangled with the issue of different types of trajectories. If there are different types of trajectories in crime, as the evidence tends to suggest, then it becomes important to identify the factors that may account for these differences. Thus, we review the contributions of a number of life course theorists who have proposed accounts of the different types of criminal careers that become apparent during the teenage years. Finally, we conclude with some policy recommendations relevant to this stage of the life course.

Back to Biology: Inside the Teenage Brain

Biological developments in the early teen years, most notably the hormonal surges and rapid increase in physical strength and endurance associated with puberty, have long been considered important factors in teenage rebelliousness, misbehavior, and delinquency (Steffensmeier et al. 1989). Raging hormones seem well-suited to explain the emotional turmoil of teenagers, their moodiness, and their propensity to take offense easily. Also, as they get bigger, faster, and stronger, teenagers become physically able to take more risks than they could as young children. Hence, their greater involvement in violence and other physically demanding forms of delinquency is not surprising.

Until recently, most scientists believed that the biological developments that took place during the teenage years did not involve changes in the brain. Maximum brain growth was assumed to have occurred by age 6, and the brain was assumed to be fully developed by the time children reached puberty (Kowalski 2000; Brownlee et al. 1999). Thus, most people thought that teenagers had all the intellectual equipment they needed to reason and make judgments like adults. They just lacked the necessary education and experience.

New research, however, has changed this view. Rather than being a fully formed cognitive machine, the teenage brain is a work in progress, and it does not function like an adult's brain (Brownlee et al. 1999; Begley 2000). The different parts of the brain continue to develop and change at varying rates into the early 20s. One of the last parts to mature is the prefrontal cortex, which is in charge of making sound judgments. On the other hand, the limbic system, where deep emotions such as fear and manic elation are generated, matures earlier (Brownlee et al. 1999). In adults, the prefrontal cortex manages and interprets the raw emotions produced by the limbic system. In teenagers the prefrontal cortex is less able to modulate emotional reactions, and thus, teenage emotions come through loud and clear. These developmental changes in the brain contribute to teenagers' emotional volatility and maddening penchant for making bad decisions.

Neuropsychologists have also discovered that teenagers are not as good as adults at reading facial expressions. In one experiment, adults and teenagers were shown pictures of people's faces contorted with fear and asked what they thought the person in the picture was feeling. Many of the teenagers could not correctly identify the expression. Adults, on the other hand, almost always got it right (Brownlee et al. 1999). Investigating further with magnetic resonance imaging, a technology that can take a picture of the brain and identify what parts are being used, the researchers found that when adults looked at the pictures, the limbic area and the prefrontal cortex lit up. When teenagers looked, these parts of the brain were dark. They were less able than adults to correctly interpret people's facial expressions. Hence, teenagers may be less able than adults to perceive the feelings and emotions of others.

It is not a long leap from this new research to the idea that the teenage brain has a lot to do with teenage delinquency. When it comes to managing their behavior, teenagers lack more than just experience and education; they also lack some of the mental equipment necessary to make sound judgments and to act responsibly. At the outset of the teenage years, our emotional inner life takes on a vividness that we have never experienced before and that our brain is not yet fully ready to handle. From a developmental perspective, the misperceptions, bad decisions, and emotional overreactions of teenagers are to a certain degree biologically programmed. Conformity is simply more difficult for teenagers than adults.

Societal Age-Crime Patterns

Our picture of the age-crime curve is based primarily on two data sources: arrest statistics and self-report surveys used to assess the relationship between age and crime. Arrest statistics are the most common indicator of criminal behavior. The standard technique for examining arrests and age is to calculate age-adjusted arrest rates for a given time period, type of offense, and locality. An age-adjusted arrest rate is the rate at which persons of a particular age are arrested. Rates are usually expressed as the number of arrests per constant, such as 1,000. For example, using data from the 1999 Uniform Crime Report and estimated population data from the U.S. Census, we can calculate age-adjusted arrest rates for all offenses for selected age groups, as shown in Figure 3.1. These data are approximate, but they give us a feel for the relationship between age and crime. The graph describes an inverted *j* pattern (Tittle and Paternoster 2000, 326). Starting at age 10, the age-adjusted arrest rate rises precipitously. Somewhere between the ages of 15 to 19 the rate peaks at about 160 per 1,000. Then, it gradually slopes downward like an inverted *j*, until around age 55, after which the age-adjusted rate is practically zero.

Figure 3.1
Arrests Rates per 1,000 by Age

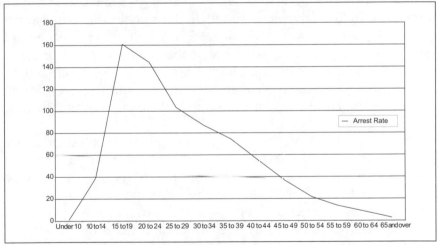

Data from U.S. Census estimates and the 1999 Uniform Crime Report.

The calculation of age-adjusted arrest rates clearly shows that arrests occur much more frequently during the late teenage years than at any other time in the life course. But these data must be interpreted carefully. They do not show the age of onset, that is, the age at which most people are *first* arrested. Instead, the data show that given their representation in the population, people aged 15 to 19 are arrested more often than people aged 40 to 44. However, this does not mean that most people are first arrested when they are 15, nor do the data show the prevalence rate for this age group. That is, we cannot assume, based on these data, that 160 out of every 1,000 15- to 19-year-olds are arrested, because some arrests undoubtedly involve repeat offenders—those who have been arrested more than once in a year.

To ascertain the age of onset of offending, a second technique must be used. This technique involves sampling individuals and either asking them to self-report on their first offense or else reviewing official records to see at what age each person first appears in the records. With this data, the hazard rate for first arrest (or first self-reported offense) can be calculated. The hazard rate is the rate at which persons in a sample experience some event, such as an arrest, determined from among those who have not yet experienced the event. For example, imagine that 100 males aged 20 are sampled and a check of official records reveals that at age 10 only one of them had been arrested. The hazard rate for first arrest at age 10 would be one in 100, or .01. Continuing to check the records, we find that at age 11 three more individuals were arrested. In this sample, then, the hazard rate for first arrest at age 11 would be 3 in 99, or .0303. This second rate is based on 99 individuals because the person who was arrested at age 10 is not eligible to have another first arrest. If we continued on in this fashion, we could calculate a hazard rate for first arrest for all ages up to the current age of our sample, which in this hypothetical example is age 20.

If we plot hazard rates against age, the result is a graph such as that shown in Figure 3.2. This figure, based on data from the National Youth Survey, shows the hazard rate for onset of serious offending by age and race (Elliott 1994). Because the graph plots the behavior of a relatively small number of people, it appears more jagged than plots of national arrest statistics by age, which are based on millions of arrests. Nevertheless, for both African Americans and whites the general shape of the hazard rate curve resembles that of the familiar inverted *j* of age-adjusted arrest rates. Up to age 11, the hazard rate is very low, less than 0.5 percent for the total sample. At age 12 a steep increase begins that peaks at age 16, when the hazard rate is 5.1 percent (Elliott 1994). The rate then declines to under 1.0 percent by age 27. After age 27, very few people initiate careers in serious violent offending. People who are going to commit such offenses at any time in the life course almost always begin doing so before age 30.

Figure 3.2
Hazard Rate for Onset of Serious Offending

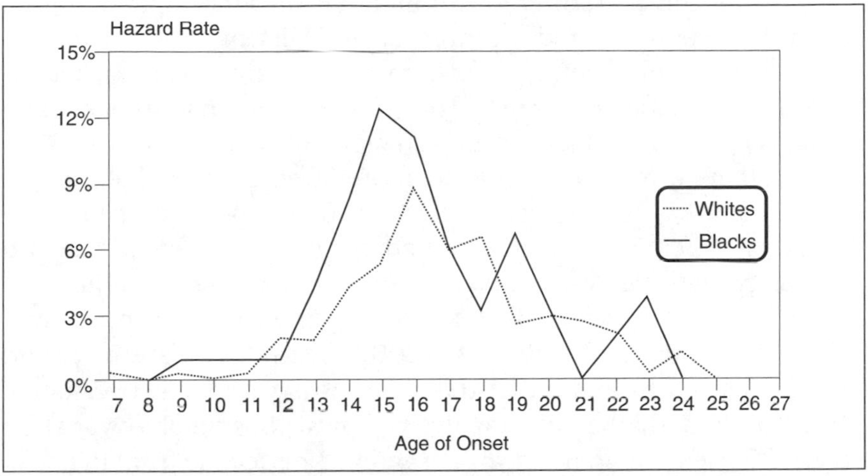

Reprinted with permission from Delbert S. Elliott (1994), *Criminology* 32(1):1–22.

A very similar pattern was observed in the Cambridge Youth Study (West and Farrington 1977, 6–8). When the subjects in that prospective study of 411 lower-class males were 20 years old, Donald West and David Farrington examined official court records. They found that by age 20 a total of 120 youths, which is about 30 percent of the sample, had compiled 360 official court convictions. Five boys were first convicted at age 10, and six others joined them at age 11. The percentage of youths first convicted increased sharply up to a peak at age 14, when 21 of the subjects were convicted for the first time. After age 14, declining numbers of youths initiated criminal activity in each succeeding year. The peak age for convictions occurred at 18, when 42 different youths were convicted. Thus, in this sample, the prevalence of delinquency was highest at age 18. From that point on, the prevalence rate declined and fewer and fewer of the subjects in the study were criminally active.

Data from a variety of different sources and studies paint a similar picture. The peak age for onset of offending occurs somewhere between 14 and 15. The highest prevalence rate occurs a year or two after that. After age 20, it becomes increasingly unlikely that a previously law-abiding person will initiate a criminal career. Almost everyone who is going to start has started by then. And, by age 20, most of those who started earlier have either desisted or begun to reduce their levels of criminal activity.

Whether this pattern holds for all types of offenses, at all times, and in all places is debated. Gottfredson and Hirschi (1990) claim that the relationship between age and crime is invariant, meaning that it is found in all societies at all times. They further claim that the age-crime relationship is not subject to explanation by sociological variables. The fact that young people commit more offenses than older people is simply a law of human nature. It is not something that is caused by the special experiences that youths undergo or by variation in standard sociological variables such as race or socioeconomic status. It just is.

Other scholars reject this extreme position (Steffensmeier and Allan 2000; Tittle and Paternoster 2000). Darrell Steffensmeier and Emilie Allan (106) argue that the claim of invariancy is overstated. They contend that careful analysis shows considerable variation across offense types in the peak age and rate of decline from the peak age. To illustrate their point, Steffensmeier and Allan calculated age-adjusted arrest rates for three different offenses: burglary, fraud, and gambling. The peak age for burglary arrests occurs at about 19, but for fraud offenses it is closer to age 25. Arrests rates for burglary decrease by over half just a few years after their peak at age 19. The decline in arrest rates for fraud is much more gradual over time. Arrest rates for gambling do not appear to follow the standard inverted *j* pattern at all. They peak at around age 20, decline slightly in the following few years, and then stabilize for about 30 years. Thus, for people in their early 20s, the age-adjusted arrest rate for gambling was just under 2 percent. For people in their early 50s, it was also just under 2 percent. Contrary to the invariance hypothesis, the shapes of these three age-crime curves do not correspond with one another. Thus, the relationship between age and crime varies from one type of crime to another.

There are other differences in the age-crime curve that belie the idea that it is invariant. One important difference involves racial and ethnic minorities. The invariance hypothesis predicts that the relationship between age and crime is the same for all types of people. Thus, we would expect that the proportion of arrests accounted for by youths would be the same for whites and nonwhites. For example, if white youths between the ages of 15 and 20 account for 60 percent of arrests of white people for burglary, then African-American youths of the same ages should make up a roughly similar percentage of burglary arrests for African Americans. But they do not. The adult percentage of arrests for African Americans is larger than the adult percentage of arrests for whites across all crime categories (Steffensmeier and Allan 1995). For African Americans, the dramatic drop-off in offending that is expected to occur at the end of the teenage years is not so dramatic. The slope of the right side of the age-crime curve is more gradual, less sharply pitched downward for African Americans than for whites. This means that there is a greater probability that African-American as opposed to white offenders will continue to be involved in crime in adulthood.

The reasons for the longer duration criminal careers of African Americans are complex, involving racial discrimination, economic inequality, and structural changes in the global economy. We will look into these matters later. But for now, we note that the relationship between age and crime appears to be different for African Americans than for whites.

One other aspect of the age-crime curve remains to be addressed, and that is whether the curve is invariant across cultures and historical periods. The evidence on this question is mixed. Gottfredson and Hirschi (1990, 124–126) examined data on age and crime from nineteenth-century England and Wales (1842–1844), England in 1908, and the United States in 1977. The general shapes of the curves they examined are quite similar, with involvement in crime peaking during the late teen years and then sloping down gradually. Since the data come from different countries and span over 130 years, they concluded that this was impressive evidence of cross-cultural and historical stability.

Other analyses, however, suggest that the shape of the age-crime curve does vary both cross-culturally and historically. Societal age-crime curves appear to be influenced by variation in the degree of age stratification in society. Age stratification refers to distinctions made between age groups in regard to the roles that members of different age groups are expected to occupy and in the relative social status of different age groups. Contemporary industrialized societies, such as the United States, Canada, and Western Europe, are highly age stratified. For the most part, youths have low status and are excluded from assuming responsible and productive economic roles until well after they reach physical maturity. In contrast, age stratification is less pronounced in small preindustrial societies. In these societies, the transition from youth to adult status occurs earlier, and youths are expected to assume adult roles close to the time that they reach physical maturity. In these types of societies, the age-crime curve is flatter and less skewed than it is in contemporary industrialized societies (Steffensmeier, Allan, and Streifel 1989).

Even within the United States, the relationship between age and crime has changed gradually over the course of the past century. Darrell Steffensmeier and his colleagues (1989) examined UCR arrest statistics from 1940 to 1980. Their analyses suggest that there has been a gradual shift toward greater concentration of offending among youth. As the end of the twentieth century approached, age curves became more peaked than they had been earlier. In addition, the peak of the age-crime curve appears to occur at younger ages. Other research also suggests that the nature of youth crime has changed recently. An examination of the criminality of the two Philadelphia birth cohorts, the first born in 1945 and the second in 1958, uncovered a dramatic increase in violent crime among the later cohort (Tracy, Wolfgang, and Figlio 1990).

Considered as a whole, the research on age and crime suggests a general, but not invariant, pattern. Involvement in many crimes, especially the garden-variety street crimes that constitute UCR Index offenses, is most widespread among teenagers and young adults. Involvement in these offenses declines rapidly among older age groups. The majority of those who commit index-type crimes have relatively short careers. This inverted *j* pattern has been found in many countries and over a broad span of time (Tittle and Paternoster 2000). The inverted *j* pattern describes population-wide age-crime curves when all crimes are lumped together. However, when crime categories are considered separately, it appears that the peak age for certain crimes occurs later and the decline in involvement for older age groups is more gradual. These divergent patterns are observed particularly for white-collar type crimes and other crime categories not included in the UCR Crime Index. Variations in the standard inverted *j* pattern are also found among different population groups, cultures, and historical periods (Steffensmeier and Allan 2000).

The finding that the relationship between age and crime varies among different population groups and over historical periods is particularly important for the life course perspective. Consistent with a central premise of the life course perspective, this finding suggests that trajectories in crime are influenced by social and historical conditions and changes (Magnusson and Cairns 1996). If the age-crime curve did not vary over time and place, and if it did not vary across population groups, it would mean that social and historical conditions have little impact on crime trajectories. It would mean that macrosociological conditions such as the degree of race-based inequalities in a society or the structure of a society's age stratification system have no bearing on involvement in crime. The criminal careers of African-American males in Harlem would be the same as those of white males in Hollywood. Trajectories in crime would be the same for Generation X as for teenagers in colonial America. If results such as these were true, it would call into question the life course principle of contextualism, that is, the idea that social and historical conditions shape trajectories in all domains of life.

However, the evidence reviewed on variations in the relationship between age and crime indicates it is unlikely that trajectories in crime are everywhere the same. Rather, they appear to be influenced by social and historical conditions. We elaborate on these influences in following chapters. To set the stage for that discussion, we turn now to a review of theoretical perspectives on adolescent trajectories in crime.

Adolescent Trajectories in Crime: Discovery of the Chronic Offender

Involvement in minor forms of crime and deviancy is so widespread among teenagers that it is statistically normal, especially for males (Moffitt 1990). Some time during their teenage years, the vast majority of individuals regardless of race, ethnicity, or class background begin to rebel against authority and to break the law. Many of the children who were trouble free when they were younger, who did not display antisocial tendencies, now become a source of headaches for their parents and teachers and a concern for law enforcement. For example, in the National Youth Survey, a significant proportion of respondents reported committing at least one delinquent act (Elliott and Huizinga 1983). Most teenage delinquencies—involving such offenses as truancy, petty theft, alcohol abuse, and recreational drug use—are not serious (Gold 1966; Short and Nye 1958). But serious violent crimes are not rare either. The University of Michigan Institute for Social Research conducts an annual cross-sectional survey of high-school seniors called *Monitoring the Future*. In the 1995 survey, which is representative of all U.S. high school seniors, nearly one out of five seniors (19 percent) reported committing a serious violent act in the past year (Institute for Social Research 1996). In light of the near universality of deviance among the young, it is only a slight exaggeration to say that in every generation society is invaded by a host of uncivilized barbarians who must be tamed (Wilson 1975).

Although minor forms of delinquency are very common among teenagers, not all teenagers restrict themselves to trivial offenses. There is significant variation among teenagers in both the rate and seriousness of their offending. Some teenagers commit very serious crimes, and for some teenagers involvement in crime and deviance is not a new thing. Rather, it is a continuation of troublemaking and antisocial behavior that began long before they reached age 13. These individuals are continuing on trajectories that they started to pursue much earlier. The flood of newcomers to crime may obscure the continuity displayed by those who were regarded as problem children in early childhood.

An important result of the life course and other developmental approaches has been the discovery that there are different trajectories in crime. The exact number of trajectories is not yet known, nor are all of the characteristics of these trajectories well understood. Nevertheless, it is clear that for some offenders onset occurs earlier and desistance later than normal. Furthermore, some offenders commit much more serious offenses and at much higher rates than normal.

One of the earliest and most influential investigations to identify different trajectories in crime was the first Philadelphia cohort study conducted by Marvin Wolfgang, Robert Figlio, and Thorsten Sellin (1972). In this study, data were gathered on a cohort of 9,945 boys born in Philadelphia in 1945 until they reached age 18 in 1963 (Wolfgang, Figlio, and Sellin 1972). Official police records were used to identify delinquents. An official contact meant that the police had filed a report on a delinquent event in which the individual was involved. The researchers tracked the number of official contacts of each boy and evaluated the seriousness of each contact. Thus, Wolfgang and his colleagues were able to identify nonoffenders, one-time offenders, and multiple offenders, those with two or more contacts (Wolfgang et al. 1972, 65).

Nearly 35 percent of the sample, a total of 3,475 boys, had at least one official contact, and taken together the delinquent boys were responsible for 10,214 offenses. A little less than half (46 percent) of the delinquents were one-time offenders. The remaining 54 percent (1,862) were repeat offenders. Not surprisingly, the repeat offenders accounted for the bulk of the total number of cohort offenses. They committed well over 8,000 offenses.

The fact that over one-third of the sample had an official police contact was surprising and indicated the widespread prevalence of delinquency. But even more surprising was the discovery of the *chronic offender.* Chronic offenders were defined as boys who had five or more contacts with the police. In this cohort, there were 627 chronic offenders. These offenders accounted for a hugely disproportionate share of the total number of offenses committed by the cohort. The 627 chronic offenders represent only 6.3 percent of the entire cohort, but they committed 5,305 offenses, which is over half of all the offenses committed by the cohort (Wolfgang et al. 1972, 88–89).

The chronic offenders stood out from the rest of the delinquents in the cohort in more ways than just their frequency of offending. They also committed much more serious offenses. The "chronic 6 percent," as they have become known, accounted for between 70 and 80 percent of the cohort's homicides, rapes, aggravated assaults, and robberies.

The discovery of the chronic 6 percent spurred a host of other cohort studies designed to replicate and extend the results of the Philadelphia cohort investigation. Wolfgang followed up his own research in another study of a cohort born in Philadelphia in 1958 (Tracy et al. 1990). The 1958 cohort was larger than the earlier one, including more than 27,000 subjects. Significantly, over 14,000 females were included in the second cohort.

As in the 1945 cohort, a small percentage of male youths (7.5 percent) were identified as chronic offenders. They accounted for 61 percent of all cohort offenses and an even larger share of the more serious offenses, such as homicide, rape, robbery, and aggravated assault. Chronic offending among females was rare. Of the females, only 1 percent were identified as chronic offenders (Tracy et al. 1990).

Since the pioneering studies in Philadelphia, other cohort studies have accumulated data that supports Wolfgang's findings. Lyle Shannon followed three cohorts of youths born in 1942, 1949, and 1955 in Racine, Wisconsin. A small percentage of youths in the cohorts appeared to be chronic offenders. Shannon estimates that in each cohort, about 5 percent of the subjects account for three-quarters of the felonies committed by the total cohort (Shannon 1988). In the Cambridge study, West and Farrington also observed that a small number of recidivists accounted for a large share of arrests (West and Farrington 1977).

Early analyses of longitudinal offending patterns identified three distinct groups: nonoffenders, one-time or short-term offenders, and long-term chronic offenders. However, as researchers have more closely examined offending trajectories using more sophisticated statistical techniques, the number of distinct patterns identified has increased. In a reexamination of the Cambridge data, Nagin and Land (1993) discovered evidence that the chronic group of offenders may comprise two subgroups: high-rate and low-rate chronics. The members of the low-rate chronic group were distinguished by the longevity of their criminal careers and by a flatter age-crime curve. During their teenage years, the low-rate chronics committed offenses at a rate that was actually lower than the short-term offenders. However, unlike the short-term offenders, the low-rate chronics continued to offend after age 20. By age 30, their offense rate was similar to that of the high-rate chronic offenders at the same age. Thus, the criminal careers of the low-rate chronic group did not appear to follow the typical age-crime curve. They had much flatter curves than normal (Nagin and Land 1993).

Explaining Offending Trajectories: Development or Propensity?

The fact that different offending trajectories exist is no longer seriously debated. As Nagin and Land (1993, 329) put it, the "observation that individuals have criminal careers in the sense that there are persistent differences across individuals in their rates of offending over time is unassailable." Longitudinal studies from the Gluecks onward have demonstrated that most individuals who become involved in crime and delinquency do so for only a relatively short period of time during their teenage years. But a small proportion of offenders commit offenses for a longer period of time. The active phase of their offending careers may stretch from age 10 or 11 into adulthood. At issue is how to explain the different offending trajectories.

There are two broad conflicting schools of thought on the problem of explaining offending trajectories. One school takes a life course or developmental approach, whereas the other school takes a propensity or general theory approach.

Those who take a life course or developmental perspective on antisocial behavior argue that the causes of antisocial behavior change over the life course (Bartusch et al. 1997). The factors that lead to early onset of offending are not the same as those that lead to onset at later ages. In effect, the life course perspective predicts that the different offending trajectories have unique causes, or at least that each trajectory has a few unique causes, although some causal mechanisms may overlap and operate across trajectories. This school of thought is sensitive to variation in experience as people age. It holds that what happens to people at each stage of the life course can have a causal impact on their behavior at that and subsequent stages. An important implication of this approach is that intervention strategies to prevent antisocial behavior must be sensitive to the age of the subject (Bartusch et al. 1997).

Propensity theorists place much less importance on age and on variation in experience over time. This school of thought holds that the causes of crime and other forms of antisocial behavior are the same at all stages of the life course. Criminal behavior results from an underlying behavioral propensity that remains stable across the life span (Gottfredson and Hirschi 1990). At an early point in the life course, each individual's propensity toward crime and deviance is established. From that point on, this innate propensity drives behavior independent of other factors and is largely resistant to change. Thus, according to this school of thought, the different offending trajectories that are observed in adolescence reflect only variation in an underlying propensity toward crime. They are not caused by differences in experiences.

The developmental and propensity approaches to offending are not necessarily mutually exclusive. Individuals may indeed vary in some stable propensity to commit offenses. Yet, how the propensity to offend is expressed may be shaped by external environmental contingencies. For example, individuals who share similar propensities but who experience different opportunities to offend can be expected to exhibit different levels of offending. Many life course theorists recognize that individuals vary in underlying propensities toward offending, but they argue that events and turning points in the life course nevertheless influence how propensities are expressed. They have proposed a variety of different theories to explain how underlying propensities are shaped by external conditions. Below, we review four of the best known and most influential of these theories.

Terrie Moffitt's Complementary Pair of Developmental Theories

One of the most important contemporary theories in the life course perspective is Terrie Moffitt's complementary pair of developmental theories. Moffitt (1993; 1997) argues that there are two qualitatively distinct types of offenders—*life-course-persistents* and *adolescence-limiteds.* According to Moffitt, these two types of offenders follow distinctly different trajectories in crime and antisocial behavior over the life course, and their differing trajectories are caused by fundamentally different factors.

Moffitt theorizes that the life-course-persistent trajectory is followed by a relatively small proportion of the population, somewhere between 4 and 9 percent of all males (Moffitt 1993). Offenders who follow this trajectory engage in a variety of antisocial behaviors throughout the life course (Moffitt 1997, 13). Their antisocial tendencies appear early in childhood and continue to be manifested through adolescence and into adulthood. As young children, these individuals stand out from other children as more aggressive and difficult to manage, in the opinion of their parents and teachers. They come to the attention of the police when they are still preteens, and during their teenage years they commit more serious offenses than other teenagers. Finally, as adults, these individuals continue to lead very troubled lives. While their peers settle down, get married, have children, and get jobs, the life-course-persistent offenders continue to follow patterns of antisocial behavior.

Moffitt's evidence for this type of offender comes from epidemiological studies of the prevalence of antisocial behavior at different stages in the life course and from longitudinal cohort studies of individual continuity in antisocial behavior. Epidemiological research on the prevalence of antisocial behavior consistently finds that between 4 and 9 percent of whatever age group is under investigation display high levels of antisocial behavior. Studies of preschool children, for example, find that about 5 percent are regarded by their parents as "very difficult to manage" (McGee et al. 1991). Costello (1989) found that in several countries roughly 4 to 9 percent of elementary school-aged boys were diagnosed with conduct disorder. As we noted above, in both the 1945 and 1958 Philadelphia cohort studies, 6 and 7.5 percent, respectively, of the males appeared to be chronic offenders (Wolfgang et al. 1972; Tracy et al. 1990). Finally, the prevalence of antisocial personality disorder among adult men is estimated to be around 5 percent (Robins 1985). Thus, at different points in the life course, researchers using different indicators of antisocial behavior consistently find that between 4 and 9 percent of males stand out from their age peers.

Because epidemiological research is based on cross-sectional samples, it cannot tell us whether the individuals designated as antisocial at early and late ages are the same or different people (Moffitt 1997, 13). Proof that the preschoolers who are regarded by their parents as difficult to manage grow up to be the same individuals that psychologists diagnose with antisocial personality disorder can come only from longitudinal studies that follow the same persons over time. After reviewing this research, Moffitt (1997, 15) concludes that a "substantial body of longitudinal research consistently points to a very small group of males who display high rates of antisocial behavior across time and in diverse situations."

Unlike the life-course-persistent trajectory, which is followed by only a small proportion of people, the adolescence-limited trajectory is ubiquitous (Moffitt 1997, 15). Individuals who follow the adolescence-limited trajectory commit offenses for only a relatively short period of time during their teenage years. They start offending around age 14 or 15, committing for the most part minor delinquencies. They continue to commit offenses for two to three years and then desist. Prior to entering their teenage years, these individuals "have no notable history of antisocial behavior and little future for such behavior in adulthood" (Moffitt 1997, 16).

The adolescence-limited trajectory mirrors the shape of the general age-crime curve. Indeed, according to Moffitt (1993; 1997), adolescence-limited offenders are responsible for the shape of the age-crime curve. The apparent peak in the age-crime curve that is observed in arrest statistics is caused by an increase in the prevalence of offenders, not a sudden increase in the individual rate of offending (Moffitt 1997, 15). The large number of adolescence-limited offenders who join the small number of life-course-persistent offenders makes it appear that offending peaks sharply in adolescence for everyone. In reality, though, the life-course-persistent and adolescence-limited offenders have distinctly different trajectories. Viewed over time, the trajectory of a life-course-persistent offender should be flatter because this person offends at a relatively constant rate from early childhood through at least early adulthood. In contrast, the trajectory of an adolescence-limited offender peaks sharply during the middle teenage years because this person starts and then stops offending as a teenager. Thus, adolescence-limited offenders display discontinuity in behavior.

Adolescence-limited offenders differ from life-course-persistent offenders in other ways as well. According to Moffitt, the antisocial behavior of adolescence-limited offenders is situation specific. That is, they behave well in some situations but not in others. For example, they may be good students in school during the week but drink and vandalize property on Friday and Saturday nights. Life-course-persistent offenders, on the other hand, tend to have trouble getting along with others in almost all situations. Their antisocial behavior is said to be generalized.

Evidence for the adolescence-limited trajectory comes from numerous studies showing that a very large majority of teenagers commit minor delinquencies but then stop before they reach age 20. Self-report studies of representative samples consistently find that large majorities of individuals engage in crime and delinquency during their teenage years (Elliott and Huizinga 1983; Hirschi 1969; Moffitt 1994). In the Dunedin, New Zealand, study researchers interviewed the male subjects when the subjects reached age 18. A whopping 93 percent admitted involvement in some sort of delinquent activity in the past year (Moffitt 1997, 16). Statistically speaking, complete conformity is abnormal.

If there really are two types of offenders as envisioned by Moffitt, then this strongly implies that we need two theories. Accordingly, Moffitt (1993; 1997) proposes two separate etiological theories for life-course-persistent and adolescence-limited antisocial behavior. Because Moffitt believes that antisocial behavior is stable in some individuals from very early childhood to adulthood, her theory of life course persistence focuses on factors present at the very earliest moments in the life course. Moffitt contends that the life-course-persistent pattern of antisocial behavior arises out of the combination of a "vulnerable and difficult infant with an adverse rearing context" (Moffitt 1997, 17). She envisions a child with a difficult temperament who is born to parents who are ill equipped to handle the child's problems. The child's difficult temperament flows from what Moffitt calls neuropsychological deficits. Deficits in neuropsychological conditions and processes may affect temperament in such areas as activity level and emotional reactivity; behavioral development in speech, motor coordination, and impulse control; and cognitive abilities in attention, language, and reasoning (Moffitt 1997, 18).

Children who suffer from neuropsychological deficits and who are born into disadvantaged or troubled families undergo negative encounters with their parents. The parents do not recognize or know how to properly respond to the child's problems. In interactions with the child, they do the wrong thing at the wrong time. Over time, this "chain of failed parent/child encounters" aggravates the behavioral problems or tendencies that flow from the child's neuropsychological deficits. Thus, a child with a neuropsychological deficit that promotes impulsivity grows up to be very impulsive because parents have not taken steps to help the child handle or ameliorate the behavioral effects of the condition. Thus, life-course-persistent antisocial behavior begins with interaction between problem children and problem parents. Moffitt's theory does not address how normal children—that is, those who do not have deficits—will be affected by inadequate parenting.

The early pattern of antisocial behavior persists into adolescence and later into adulthood. In part, this persistence is caused by the behavioral style that the individual developed as a child and carries over into later stages in the life course. The hyperactive child with poor self-control and limited cognitive abilities becomes an overactive adult who is self-indulgent and not very smart. When the person is a child, this constellation of traits leads to trouble, and it continues to do so as the person ages, producing continuous contemporary consequences. At each stage of the life course, this person's behavioral style gets him or her into trouble with others.

Persistence in antisocial behavior, and specifically criminal behavior, also results from the cumulating effects of problems and failure over time. Beginning early in life, individuals on a life-course-persistent trajectory behave in ways that limit their future opportunities. Because they are so difficult to be around, life-course-persistent individuals are often rejected and avoided by others. They have difficulty learning how to behave in a pro-social manner and so have few pro-social friends and little opportunity to practice conventional social skills. They do poorly in school and so never attain basic math and reading skills. Without these skills, their opportunities for legitimate employment are severely curtailed. Involvement in crime and delinquency leads to arrests and incarcerations, which further diminish opportunities for success in a conventional lifestyle. Cumulating consequences eventually ensnare the life-course-persistent individual in a deviant lifestyle from which escape becomes ever more difficult as time passes (Moffitt 1997, 21–23).

The theory of life course persistence is designed to explain continuity in behavior over a long period of time, especially criminal and deviant behavior. The theory of adolescence-limited antisocial behavior confronts a different empirical regularity—the lack of continuity that characterizes the offending trajectories of most individuals. What accounts for the pattern of widespread onset of delinquency in early adolescence that is followed shortly thereafter by the equally widespread pattern of desistance from delinquent behaviors? Why do children who have little or no history of behavior problems develop such problems in adolescence, and then why do they seem to spontaneously recover just a few years later?

As with her theory of life course persistence, Moffitt begins her theory of adolescence-limited offending by noting the age at which antisocial behavior first appears in this trajectory and arguing that the important causal factors must begin operating at that time. In the adolescence-limited trajectory, delinquent behavior first appears early in the teenage years. The causal factors that begin operating at this time include biological changes (puberty), the increasing importance of peer relationships, changes in age-graded societal expectations, and changes in teenagers' values, attitudes, and aspirations (Moffitt 1997, 25). Puberty brings with it an increased interest in sex and a rapid increase in physical strength (Steffensmeier and Allan 1995, 99). At about the same time that puberty occurs, teenagers begin to spend less time with their parents and more time with their peers. The importance of parents as a point of reference and center of attention begins to decline, while peers move front and center as objects of concern and interest. Children move away from their parents not only because they come to like their peers more but also because society expects it of them. Between the ages of roughly 12 and 17, they are expected to "grow up" and no longer behave like children. However, they are not yet given the opportunity to assume productive adult roles. They occupy an ambiguous and confusing middle ground between childhood and adulthood (Steffensmeier and Allan 1995). Finally, in the realm of cognitive development, they become acutely aware of what they perceive to be inequities in society's expectations. To teenagers it is exceedingly unfair that while they are expected to *behave* like adults, they are not given the opportunity to *be* adults or to have the autonomy and freedom of movement that goes with adult status. All of these changes leave young teenagers looking for something else, some way out of their ambiguous and stressful position in society.

Although it is easy to agree with the idea that life for teenagers is ambiguous and stressful, this does not explain why they respond to this predicament with delinquency. To explain the onset of delinquency in the adolescence-limited trajectory, Moffitt introduces the idea of *social mimicry*:

> Social mimicry occurs when two animal species share a single niche and one of the species has cornered the market on a resource that is needed to promote fitness. In such circumstances, the 'mimic' species adopts the social behavior of the more successful species in order to obtain access to the valuable resource. (Moffitt 1997, 25)

Moffitt argues that the idea of social mimicry can be applied to adolescence-limited and life-course-persistent delinquents. In the eyes of their peers, life-course-persistent delinquents appear to have a very valuable "resource" and that resource is mature status. They seem to behave like adults. They smoke, drink, have sex, skip school, and resist adult authority. Seeing that life-course-persistent delinquents get to act like adults and wanting to do the same themselves, adolescence-limited delinquents begin to copy or mimic the behavior of life-course-persistent delinquents, the "more successful species" in the ecology of teenagers. They begin committing minor delinquencies.

For youths following the adolescence-limited trajectory, delinquency is a way of cutting ties with childhood and staking a claim to adult status. It answers their needs for autonomy. By engaging in forbidden adult activities, teenagers clandestinely resist adult authority. These activities symbolize independence and, hence, are enormously rewarding to the adolescence-limited delinquent.

Despite all the fun, excitement, and thrills of misbehavior, adolescence-limited youths do not maintain their wrongdoing into adulthood. No doubt to the delight and relief of their parents, as adolescence-limited delinquents approach the end of their teenage years, they quit delinquent behaviors. Why? In Moffitt's view, the answer is that better routes to the valuable resource of mature status open up at the end of the teenage years. As teenagers near the end of their teenage years, as they graduate from high school, society's expectations for them change once again. By age 20, they are expected to get jobs and support themselves or to be in college, preparing for a career. They attain some of the privileges and autonomy that they have desired for so long. Because of these changes, the adolescence-limited delinquent begins to perceive delinquency and its consequences from a new perspective. Delinquency is no longer seen as the only way to establish autonomy from adult authority. Autonomy is now freely given by society; indeed, it is thrust upon older teens. Furthermore, the legal and social consequences of delinquency become more serious at age 18, and adolescence-limited delinquents soon realize that continued involvement in crime is likely to harm their future life chances. The rewards of crime decline while its costs increase (Moffitt 1997, 35). Desistance becomes the rational thing to do.

For adolescence-limited delinquents, desistance is not only rational; it is also relatively easy. They have good options for change. Unlike life-course-persistent delinquents, adolescence-limited delinquents are able to avoid the damaging effects of contemporary and cumulative continuity. Because adolescence-limited delinquents do not suffer from personality disorders or cognitive deficits and because they have learned how to behave in a pro-social manner, it is relatively easy for them to fit into the expected routines of employment or college. They know how to get along with others and how to follow rules. In addition, because their delinquent careers are shorter than the careers of life-course-persistent offenders, the process of cumulative continuity has less time to work. Adolescence-limited delinquents accumulate fewer of the negative consequences that accompany involvement in crime than life-course-persistent delinquents.

Thus, as they enter adulthood, the paths of adolescence-limited and life-course persistent delinquents diverge. The former begin to explore new pathways into conventional adult roles of employment, marriage, and family. The latter, however, discover that these options are closed to them. Life-course-persistent delinquents find themselves stuck in an antisocial lifestyle (Moffitt 1997, 37).

Sampson's and Laub's Age-Graded Theory of Informal Social Control

In a series of articles and in their seminal book *Crime in the Making,* Robert Sampson and John Laub have advanced an age-graded theory of informal social control to explain trajectories in crime and delinquency (Sampson and Laub 1993; 1997; Laub, Nagin, and Sampson 1998). As a control theory, their theory starts with the assumption that delinquency, crime, and deviance are natural. If people are not somehow controlled or prevented from following their natural inclinations, they will tend to behave in ways that society regards as antisocial or criminal. The theory of age-graded informal social control holds that the most important sources of control are informal bonds between people.

Sampson and Laub argue that at different stages in the life course individuals are potentially subject to different forms of informal social control. For children, informal family and school bonds are important. Children who are strongly bonded to their parents and children who care about school are less likely to be involved in delinquency than children who have difficult relations with their parents or who do not like school. As children move through the life course, the major sources of informal social control change. Parents and school are not as important for young adults as they are for children and teenagers. For young adults, employment and marriage are potential sources of informal control. Variation in the strength of informal controls influences the likelihood and degree of involvement in crime and deviance at all stages of the life course.

Sampson and Laub recognize that ontogenetic differences between individuals—that is, persistent underlying differences in temperament and criminal potential—may account for some of the variation in criminal behavior. But they do not develop an explicit theory of what these "child-effect" personality or behavioral factors might be. Rather, they focus much more heavily on factors that are external to the individual, which they call "structural variables" related to the family. These structural variables include family size, household overcrowding, family socioeconomic status, mother's and father's deviance, mother's employment, family disruption, residential mobility, and whether the parents are foreign born. They argue that these structural variables influence "family process variables," which refer to how family members relate to one another and specifically how the parents relate to and interact with their children. Important dimensions of family process include the use of harsh and erratic discipline by the parents, the mother's supervision of the child, parental rejection of the child, and the child's attachment to the parents. The structural variables are conceived to affect the process variables, which in turn are conceived as the direct cause of delinquency. Thus, the process variables mediate the effects of the structural variables (Sampson and Laub 1993).

Besides the family, the other important sources of informal social control in early childhood are schools and peers. Sampson and Laub argue that structural variables also influence the child's performance in and attachment to school as well as relationships with delinquent peers. Children born into families that have certain structural characteristics are less likely to perform well in school or to be strongly attached to school (Sampson and Laub 1993, 110–111). Children from large, poor families that move often and in which the mother is employed appear to be particularly disadvantaged in regard to school attachment. Children from these types of families are also more likely to have friends who are delinquent. Both school attachment and delinquent peers, in turn, are related to delinquency.

Based on rigorous and exhaustive statistical analyses of the Gluecks' data, Sampson and Laub conclude that the direct causes of juvenile delinquency comprise child effects, process effects, and, to a lesser extent, structural effects (Sampson and Laub 1993, 119). Child effects, in the form of early antisocial behavior, are related to later delinquency but not as strongly as bad parenting, attachment to school, and attachment to delinquent peers. The effect of family structure is largely mediated by the process variables. Thus, delinquency can be curtailed by strong informal social controls based in family, schools, and friends. Teenagers who lack such controls are at great risk of finding themselves on a trajectory toward serious adult crime.

As teenagers move into young adulthood, two factors begin operating that shape adult patterns in crime. First, as young adults, they potentially become subject to new forms of informal social control. These new forms of control include employment and marriage. Individuals who are lucky enough to find good jobs or enter good marriages or both become subjugated to new informal controls. According to Sampson and Laub (1993), exposure to these adult forms of social control can redirect the criminal trajectories of individuals who were seriously delinquent as youths.

But the chances that a seriously delinquent youth will find a good job or marry a supportive spouse are less than ideal because of the second factor that begins operating in adulthood. Youths who are seriously delinquent accumulate disadvantages as they age. These cumulative disadvantages "snowball," or pile up, over time, making it increasingly more difficult for the individual to exit from a life of crime. These disadvantages are generated most directly by official sanctions, such as arrest, conviction, and incarceration, which label and stigmatize individuals. Being officially labeled as a serious delinquent dramatically reduces future educational and employment opportunities (Sampson and Laub 1997, 147). The individual becomes trapped in a cycle in which crime leads to failure in conventional activities, which in turn motivates further involvement in crime. Thus, Sampson and Laub (1993; 1997) hypothesize that there is an interaction between early criminal propensities and societal reactions that influences the adult life chances of delinquent youths. Continuity in criminal behavior is not solely the result of underlying criminal propensities; it also is caused by societal reactions.

The distinguishing feature of Sampson and Laub's theoretical work is their claim that social processes can cause even seriously delinquent individuals to desist from crime. They argue that even for very committed offenders change is possible, and change can occur relatively late in life (1997). Adult social bonds to work and family can inhibit adult criminality and deviance (Sampson and Laub 1990; 1993; Laub et al. 1998). How do these bonds develop? Why do some individuals experience a change in fortune for the better while others literally have nowhere to go but prison? Sampson and Laub are appropriately cautious about drawing any definitive conclusions. They acknowledge that they cannot rule out the possibility that selection effects account for both desistance and entry into a good marriage or good job (Sampson and Laub 1993, 241–42). So, it is difficult to know for sure whether stable marriages lead to desistance, or whether high criminal propensity leads to marital instability and continuity in offending in adulthood. In the end, they suggest that "both social selection and social causation . . . seem to be at work in the unfolding of human lives over time" (242).

Terence Thornberry's Interactional Theory of Delinquency

Terence Thornberry argues that standard criminological theories ignore a basic feature of human behavior: it occurs in social interaction. The concept of interaction implies that human behavior has a give-and-take, back-and-forth aspect that plays out over time. During the process of interacting, all parties to the interaction are reciprocally affected. For example, a child's attachment to parents evolves over time as the parents and the child interact. What the child does at one point in time affects attachment at a later point, and in turn, what the parents do affects the child's feelings of attachment. Standard criminological theories, however, fail to take into account the back-and-forth character of human behavior. In standard models of delinquency, independent variables—such as attachment to parents—are assumed to effect dependent variables, such as delinquency. The causal effects are conceived as flowing only in one direction, from attachment to delinquency, and not from delinquency to attachment. This approach is mistaken because it ignores the interactional dimension of human development and behavior. It ignores the fact that a child's involvement in delinquency may affect attachment to parents, just as attachment to parents affects delinquency. Thornberry argues we should think of delinquency in interactional terms. We need to develop causal models of delinquency that take into account not only the effects of the independent variables on delinquency but also the effects of delinquency on the independent variables. In other words, we should develop reciprocal models of delinquency (Thornberry 1987).

The reciprocal model that Thornberry (1987, 873) proposes is similar to Sampson and Laub's age-graded theory of informal social controls. It is based on the premise that the "fundamental cause of delinquency is the attenuation of social controls over the person's conduct." His model incorporates three social control variables and three delinquency variables. Of the three social control variables, the most important one for explaining the onset of delinquency in early adolescence is attachment to parents. Attachment affects belief in conventional values and commitment to school, which are the two other social control variables. The three social control variables, in turn, affect associations with delinquent peers, delinquent behavior, and delinquent values. Following the standard logic of control-type theories, Thornberry argues that adolescents aged 11 to 13 who are strongly attached to their parents are likely to be committed to school and to believe in conventional values. Commitment and belief reduce the likelihood that the child will associate with delinquents, engage in delinquency, and hold delinquent values. Thus, children who are strongly attached to their parents are predicted to be at low risk for early onset of delinquency.

The interactional component in Thornberry's model lies in his stipulations that the social control variables are reciprocally related to each other and that the delinquency variables can act back upon the control variables. Regarding the reciprocal relationships between the social control variables, Thornberry assumes that over time attachment affects commitment and vice versa. Similarly, commitment to school affects belief in conventional values and the same is true in reverse. Children who are strongly attached to their parents are more likely to be committed to school, and over time commitment to school increases attachment to parents. This happy chain of socially conforming causality can be disrupted, however, if for some reason delinquent friends or activities enter the picture. Thornberry theorizes that if a child begins to associate with delinquent peers or engage in delinquent activities, these behaviors will have negative effects on the social control variables. Adolescents who begin hanging around with delinquents or engaging in delinquency are predicted to become less committed to school, to believe less in conventional values, and eventually to grow less attached to their parents.

As children develop over the life course, the causal importance of variables changes. For children in early adolescence, attachment to parents is conceived to be the most important variable. By middle adolescence (ages 15 to 16), as children begin to mature and become less dependent on their parents, delinquent peers and delinquent values become more important. What happens in the home becomes less important than what happens outside the home. Thornberry does not argue that parents are irrelevant to teenagers but that they are less important in middle adolescence than in early childhood as a "locus of control and interaction" (1987, 879). The power of the family to shape behavior declines in middle adolescence and is supplanted by interactions with peers. At this stage of the life course, the causal importance of delinquent values increases. Delinquent values are now conceived to determine associations with delinquent peers and involvement in delinquent activities. Holding delinquent values steers youths toward other delinquents and toward delinquent acts. Delinquent values are also assumed to reduce commitment to school and to be incompatible with belief in conventional values. Thus, the major change that occurs in midadolescence relates to the increased saliency of the delinquency variables relative to the family. The basic structure of Thornberry's theory, however, stays the same. The control variables and the delinquency variables are still seen as being locked in mutually reinforcing causal loops.

As individuals grow out of middle adolescence and into late adolescence (ages 18 to 20), new factors emerge to affect crime and delinquency and old ones recede in importance. According to Thornberry, two important new factors are commitment to conventional activities (employment, college, military service) and commitment to one's own family. These factors become potentially important sources of social control, while attachment to parents and commitment to high school become less important. During late adolescence, many individuals find work, begin to make plans to attend college, and begin to think seriously about marrying and raising their own families. In Thornberry's theoretical scheme, these developments are thought to lead naturally to reduced involvement in delinquent activities and less time spent with delinquent peers. The transition to the world of work helps one build a stake in conformity, and so does getting married. Individuals who make these transitions on time embark on trajectories that are increasingly removed from crime and delinquency. However, if these transitions do not happen, then the effects of the delinquency variables amplify and the individual's criminal trajectory is likely to continue.

Although Thornberry's theory is primarily a social psychological theory of delinquency, he does not ignore the external social realities that influence the interactional processes lying at the heart of his approach. In particular, he notes that social class is systematically related to the "initial values," or starting positions, of the interactional variables in his model (1987, 885). Children born into lower-class families are more likely to experience disrupted family processes and environments. Hence, the likelihood that they will develop strong attachments to their parents is less certain. Lower-class children are also likely to live in neighborhoods where delinquents are present and where delinquent values may coexist with conventional values. In contrast, middle-class youth are more likely to have stable families and to live in suburbs or city neighborhoods that provide greater insulation against exposure to delinquent values and role models. Social class provides an environmental framework within which the interactional processes identified by Thornberry develop.

John Hagan's Theory of Criminal Capital and Capital Disinvestment

One of the most important, provocative, and fertile ideas to arise in American sociology in the past 50 years is James S. Coleman's concept of *social capital*. Social capital is distinguished from human capital, which encompasses the skills, aptitudes, abilities, and credentials possessed by individuals that enable them to produce and succeed in life. It is also distinguished from physical capital, such as tools, machines, and factories. Social capital is not a property of individuals or of the physical implements of productions. Rather, it inheres in the structure of relations between people (Coleman 1988). It is something that groups of actors can possess in relative degrees and that individual actors can tap into to serve their ends. Social capital can take the form of obligations and expectations of trustworthiness between group members. It also encompasses how information is transmitted among group members. Finally, social capital is created when groups have strong norms accompanied by sanctions (Coleman 1988). Groups or social structures can vary along all of these dimensions of social capital.

From the perspective of the individual, social capital, like all forms of capital, is useful because access to it enhances the individual's ability to pursue ends and to satisfy needs. Consider an example adapted from Coleman that illustrates how high levels of trust in a group can enhance individual productivity or need satisfaction. Imagine a mother in a neighborhood in which everyone knows and trusts one another. The mother can allow her young child to play without her being present in a local park because she knows that some other parent will be watching to make sure that nothing bad happens. The mother can take a few minutes to run an errand or clean the house or perhaps just relax for a moment. The mother's freedom to pursue these ends is made possible by the social capital that exists in her neighborhood, the high level of trust between residents. Imagine another mother in a different neighborhood, one in which residents do not know or trust one another. This mother does not have the freedom to let her children play outside unsupervised. Hence, the mother's ability to accomplish other tasks is diminished because of the time and energy she must devote to her child.

Social capital typically carries positive connotations, but criminologists were quick to realize that it could also have negative aspects for society. For example, organized criminal groups may have high levels of trust between members, which permits them to organize and coordinate criminal enterprises, such as large-scale drug dealing. This sort of criminal enterprise can be carried out only by individuals working in concert who can depend on one another. In this case, the group's social capital is used to further the criminal ends of its members to the detriment of society.

John Hagan has taken the concept of social capital and used it to construct a developmental theory of street crime in America (Hagan 1991; Hagan 1997). His theory is distinguished from most others in the life course perspective by its explicit emphasis on historically based macrosocial and economic processes, most notably what he calls "capital disinvestment." Capital disinvestment is a process that has happened to minority communities and neighborhoods over the course of the latter half of the twentieth century. The original cause of capital disinvestment was the economic slowdown that occurred in the last quarter of the twentieth century. During this period, three distinct processes of capital disinvestment eroded the ability of minority communities to provide good jobs for their members: residential segregation, racial inequality, and the concentration of poverty. The absence of opportunities in the legitimate economy forced the members of these communities to adapt and develop alternative means of capitalization. These alternative means included reliance on deviance service centers and the drug economy to provide jobs. The processes of capital disinvestment overlap one another. But each also produces its own distinct effects and requires separate explication.

According to Hagan (1997), beginning in the 1970s the U.S. economy began to slow down after a long period of postwar expansion. During this slowdown, core manufacturing jobs in auto plants and steel mills began to disappear from American cities in the Northeast and Midwest. Jobs in manufacturing had provided a means of economic advancement for African Americans and other minorities. Although the economy eventually created new jobs, these jobs were located in areas in which African Americans were not welcome. Policies of residential segregation made it difficult for African Americans to leave inner-city neighborhoods and move to the suburbs, where the economy's new jobs were being created (Hagan 1997, 290). Young minority males and females were, in effect, trapped in communities in which few opportunities in the legitimate economy remained (see also Wilson 1987).

In addition to being located in areas from which African Americans were segregated, the economy's new jobs increasingly required advanced education and high-level technical skills. It was not easy for African Americans to fulfill these requirements. Opposition to affirmative action laws gained in strength during the last quarter of the century and restricted the access of African Americans to college and to programs that helped them secure good jobs in the legitimate economy. Racial differentials in earnings and educational achievement, which had been declining, began to grow again. Race-linked inequality, always a feature of American society, became worse after the mid-1970s. According to Hagan, the rise in racial inequality led to feelings of "resentment, frustration, hopelessness, and aggression" in America's minority youths (Hagan 1997, 291).

Finally, the third process of capital disinvestment is the concentration of poverty. Residential segregation and racial inequality combined to create hyper-ghettos. In hyper-ghettos, poverty is extreme and extensive. Community members lucky enough to have good jobs and a little money leave as quickly as they can. Only the most disadvantaged and discouraged are left behind. As a result, poverty is concentrated in hyper-ghettos, and the range in variation in economic resources becomes extremely narrow. Everyone is poor and everyone must struggle to survive.

The processes of capital disinvestment destroy conventional forms of social capital. In place of conventional forms of social capital, communities develop alternative forms of economic organization, which amount to what Hagan calls "forms of recapitalization" (Hagan 1997, 296). By recapitalization, Hagan means that communities attempt to organize whatever resources are available so that they can be used to help community members achieve their goals. Often, according to Hagan, the only economic resources that disadvantaged communities have at their disposal are illicit. People who live in disadvantaged communities have nothing to offer the outside world in the way of conventional economic resources. Their labor is not wanted, they cannot produce anything conventional of value, and they have nothing conventional to sell. But they can offer the outside world something that is not available via the conventional economy. They can offer access to illegal services and commodities, such as prostitution, gambling, and especially narcotic drugs. These communities become deviance service centers for conventional society, places where illicit services and commodities are provided for a price.

Young people who live in disadvantaged communities are drawn to the promise of the deviance service industry. In their eyes, becoming involved in the drug economy or prostitution is a way to get ahead. It's a way to get money, fine clothes, and fancy cars. Jobs in the legitimate economy are not available to them or to their parents. The prospects of going to college seem dim. The deviance service industry is the most promising employer around and so young people, lacking access to other sources of social capital, take advantage of what is available. They take positions in the drug economy.

Hagan notes that deviance service centers are not a new urban phenomenon. Indeed, they have a long history in America. Throughout the nineteenth and early part of the twentieth centuries, different ethnic groups used the deviance service industry as a means of social mobility. Participation in organized crime was a way to acquire the financial resources necessary to move out of the ghetto and into mainstream society. But times have changed, and the deviance service industry is no longer the mobility ladder it once promised to be. Rather than providing a route out of the ghetto and out of a life of crime, participation in deviance and vice is more likely to embed young people in a criminal lifestyle.

The process of criminal embeddedness links the historical community-level processes of capital disinvestments and recapitalization to the life course trajectories of individuals. Young people who become involved in the deviance service industry, and especially the drug economy, isolate themselves from conventional employment and educational trajectories. They spend time with other criminals like themselves. Their social contacts are with others in the deviance industry and not with people who might provide access to legitimate employment or who might help them succeed in school. Cutting ties with conventional others is one aspect of criminal embeddedness. The other aspect is the high probability, indeed near certainty, that the individual will eventually be arrested and be officially labeled as a criminal offender. Being labeled a criminal makes it exceedingly difficult, if not impossible, for young members of socially stigmatized minority groups to ever find a way out of crime and into the middle class. In ways that they probably cannot perceive or appreciate, their life course trajectories are set in a downward spiral of cumulating disadvantages from which there is little hope of escape.

Thus, Hagan's theory focuses on how broad changes and patterns in the economy and social structure are linked to the life course trajectories of individuals. Capital disinvestment has created neighborhoods and communities that have relatively little conventional social or cultural capital. The parents of children who grow up in these communities are not well equipped to help their children develop human capital. Because the parents do not have strong links to the conventional labor market, they also have few resources to help their children find decent jobs in the legitimate economy. Young people see the deviance service industry as the most promising source of employment. Individuals who succumb to the lures of the deviance industry risk becoming embedded in criminal lifestyles that isolate them from conventional educational and employment trajectories. Their trajectories in crime are characterized by continuity into adulthood. Hagan explains the severity and longevity of the criminal trajectories of urban underclass youth by emphasizing the powerful shaping force of personal and neighborhood social disadvantages. Individual-level differences in personal constitutions do not figure prominently in his theory.

The powerful impact that capital disinvestment has had on inner-city life is undeniable. Yet, even though inner-city ghettos undoubtedly make healthy development a more risky prospect, we must avoid falling into the trap of environmental determinism. Even in the most disadvantaged communities, there are always variations in outcomes. The deviance service centers described by Hagan may indeed draw many young people into a life of crime, but not everyone succumbs to their charms. Despite obstacles and disadvantages, many inner-city families try hard and successfully to protect their children from the lures of street life (Jarrett 1997; Anderson 1990). Good opportunities may be few and far between, but many young people do get jobs in the legitimate economy and try to rise above their circumstances via the traditional routes of work and education (Newman 1999). Genetic endowments do not by themselves determine developmental outcomes, and neither do environments. Developmental outcomes are always a matter of probabilities and interactions.

Ethnographies of Street Crime

Support for Hagan's theory of capital disinvestment and criminal embeddedness comes from a number of ethnographic studies of inner-city life. These ethnographies capture the complex and hard realities of living in poverty in urban America. In a long-term study in Milwaukee, John Hagedorn interviewed gang members in 1987 and again in 1992. His interviews reveal the anger and alienation of those who are disenfranchised. The young men and women in his study had conventional aspirations and surprisingly conventional ethical beliefs about the immorality of drug dealing. Yet, they felt trapped and frustrated by the lack of legitimate opportunities, and they expressed a clear-eyed view of how the world works for those who come from disadvantaged backgrounds. One young man involved in the drug economy expressed his views on himself and his situation in this way:

> I'm a mad young man. I'm a poor young man. I'm a good person to my kids and stuff, and given the opportunity to have something nice and stop working for this petty-ass money I would try to change a lot of things . . . I feel I'm the type of person that given the opportunity to try to have something legit, I will take it, but I'm not going to go by the slow way, taking no four, five years working at no chicken job and trying to get up to a manager just to start making six, seven dollars. And then get fired when I come in high or drunk or something. Or miss a day or something because I got high smoking weed, drinking beer, and the next day come in and get fired; then I'm back in where I started from. So, I'm just a cool person, and if I'm given the opportunity and I can get a job making nine, ten dollars an hour, I'd let everything go; I'd just sit back and work my job and go home. That kind of money I can live with. But I'm not going to settle for no three, four dollars an hour, you know what I'm saying? (Hagedorn, 1994, 208–209)

While making "nine, ten dollars an hour" is a rather modest financial objective, it is, in the eyes of this young man, not one he is likely to reach. The interview continued with a short exchange in which the young man expressed in equal parts both wild optimism and sober resignation about his future:

Interviewer: Five years from now, what would you want to be doing?

Young Man: Owning my own business. And rich. A billionaire.

Interviewer: What do you realistically expect you'll be doing in five years?

Young Man: Probably working at McDonald's. That's the truth. (Hagedorn 1994, 209).

But the drug market offers other opportunities to make money. It provides, if not a way out of the ghetto, at least a chance to have a more comfortable life in it. The young men in Hagedorn's study recognized that selling drugs involves trade-offs. They recognized that selling dope is morally wrong, but they felt compelled to do it as a matter of survival. One long exchange with a drug dealer illustrates the moral compromises some men make in the ghetto:

Interviewer: Do you consider it wrong or immoral to sell dope?

Dealer: Um-hum, very wrong.

Interviewer: Why?

Dealer: Why, because it's killing people.

Interviewer: Well, how come you do it?

Dealer: It's also a money-maker.

Interviewer: Well how do you balance things out? I mean, here you're doing something that you think is wrong, making money. How does that make you feel when you're doing it, or don't you think about it when you're doing it?

Dealer: Once you get a (dollar) bill, once you look at, I say this a lot, once you look at those dead white men [*presidents' pictures on currency*], you care about nothing else, you don't care about nothing else. Once you see those famous dead white men. That's it.

Interviewer: Do you ever feel bad about selling drugs, doing something that was wrong?

Dealer: How do I feel? Well, a lady will come in and sell all the food stamps, all of them. When they're sold, what are the kids gonna eat? They can't eat dope 'cause she's gonna go smoke that up, or do whatever with it. And then you feel like 'wrong.' But then, in the back of your mind, man, you just got a hundred dollars worth of food stamps for 30 dollars worth of dope, and you can sell them at the store for seven dollars on 10, so you got 70 coming. So you get 70 dollars for 30 dollars. It is not wrong to do this. It is not wrong to do this! (Hagedorn 1994, 210–11)

Other men in Hagedorn's study had an even harder take on life. They were not troubled by any moral qualms in their drug dealing. As far as they were concerned, both the buying and selling of drugs were a matter of personal choice. Consider this exchange:

Interviewer: Do you consider it wrong or immoral to sell dope?

Dealer: I think it's right because can't no motherfucker live your life but you.

Interviewer: Why?

Dealer: Why? I'll put it this way . . . I love selling dope. I know there's other niggers out here love the money just like I do. And ain't no motherfucker gonna stop a nigger from selling dope . . . I'd sell to my own mother if she had the money. (Hagedorn 1994, 214)

Tied in as they are to the income made possible by selling drugs, it is hard to imagine that either of these dealers is ever going to look for, let alone find, a way out of a life of crime. In a Philadelphia ghetto community studied by Anderson (1990), the drug economy served as an employment agency for many young men. Anderson noted that

> Young men who 'grew up' in the gang, but now are without clear opportunities, easily become involved; they fit themselves into its structure, manning its drug houses and selling drugs on street corners. (Anderson 1990, 244)

Growing up in a disadvantaged, drug-ridden neighborhood promotes criminal embeddedness in other ways as well. It exposes youths to delinquent values that do not promote behavior likely to be regarded favorably by mainstream society. This value system emphasizes the importance of being "bad" and being tough. In an extraordinarily perceptive ethnography of youths in Clarendon Heights, a low-income housing project in a northeastern city, Jay MacLeod (1987) depicts this worldview. For the "hallway hangers" (as MacLeod calls them), a group of teenage white males who live in the project, being bad is the top priority. Slick, a member of the group, explained its meaning and importance this way:

> You hafta make a name for yourself, to be bad, tough, whatever. You hafta be, y'know, be with the 'in' crowd. Know what I mean? You hafta. It's just all part of growing up around here. You hafta do certain things. Some of the things you hafta do is, y'know, once in while you hafta, if you haven't gotten into a fight, if you have a fight up the high school, you're considered bad. Y'know what I mean? If you beat someone up up there, especially if he's black, around this way . . . if you're to be bad, you hafta be arrested. You hafta at least know what bein' in a cell is like. (MacLeod 1987, 26)

In contrast, pursuing culturally promoted goals, such as doing well in school, leads to ridicule and social ostracism, as this exchange between MacLeod, Slick, and two other hallway hangers illustrates.

> *MacLeod:* So how is it that to be what's good down here, to be respected. . . .
>
> *Slick:* You gotta be bad.
>
> *Frankie:* Yeah, if you're a straight-A student, you get razzed.
>
> *Slick:* Then you're a fucking weirdo, and you shouldn't be living here in the first place.
>
> *Shorty:* No, you got people down here who don't drink and don't smoke.
>
> *Slick:* Who? Name one.

Shorty: Stern. John Stern.

Frankie: Yeah, but like he's saying, whadda we think of John Stern?

Shorty: Fucking shithead (*all laugh*). (Macleod, 1987, 26)

Commitment to the group and to its value system inhibits youths in Clarendon Heights from pursuing conventional trajectories in education and occupation. There are always exceptions, of course. The John Sterns of the neighborhood will probably achieve some measure of conventional success. But for the hallway hangers, breaking away from the group to pursue an education or an occupational career is less likely to happen because of their embeddedness in the gang. For any of them to strive as individuals for upward mobility would betray their friends, as is illustrated by this exchange:

MacLeod: Do you have anything else to add about kids' attitudes down here?

Jinks (a hallway hanger): I'd say everyone more or less has the same attitudes toward school, fuck it. Except the bookworms—people who just don't hang around outside and drink, get high, who sit at home—they're the ones who get an education.

MacLeod: And they just decided for themselves.

Jinks: Yup.

MacLeod: So why don't more people decide that way?

Jinks: Y'know what it is Jay? We all don't break away because we're too tight. Our friends are important to us. Fuck it. If we can't make it together, fuck it. Fuck it all. (MacLeod, 1987, 119–120)

Youths who decide to stick with the group become embedded in a lifestyle from which it becomes increasingly difficult to escape. Disadvantages begin to accumulate. Because of their criminal activities, they eventually compile extensive official criminal records and bad reputations in the community. As they spend more time and energy in the world of drugs and crime, they accordingly have less time to spend in legitimate pursuits, such as school and the entry-level jobs that provide social contacts and employment experiences. Schooling, contacts, and a good work history are crucial prerequisites for making the transition to adult employment. Youths who become criminally embedded are likely to lack all of these prerequisites. Hence, they have little chance of ever finding much success in legitimate occupations. The trajectories they established in adolescence are likely to extend into adulthood.

Summary

For criminologists, the teenage years are where the action is. As we have learned in this chapter, the early teenage years witness an explosion of deviant and lawbreaking behavior among a substantial proportion of every teenage cohort. The small percentage of youths who started engaging in crime before becoming teenagers build criminal momentum during the second decade of life. As they grow stronger, more autonomous, and more daring, they become a serious menace to society. But they are not alone. Some time between the ages of 13 and 17, almost everyone gets into the act, as virtually all adolescents briefly engage in crime or delinquency. Thus, teenagers rightly command the attention of life course criminologists.

In this chapter, we have reviewed the evidence on age and crime. That age and crime are strongly related is not debated seriously by criminologists, but there is considerable dispute over the details of this relationship. The most thorough analyses indicate that at the aggregate level the shape of the age-crime curve varies over historical periods, societies, and demographic groups. Careful analysis also indicates that the relationship between age and crime is not the same for all individuals. The delinquent trajectories followed by many individuals mirror aggregate-level patterns in that they resemble an inverted *j*. Onset occurs in midadolescence, between the ages of 14 and 16. It is followed by a brief period of involvement in delinquency that then dwindles and finally ceases in late adolescence, around age 19 or 20. But some individuals follow trajectories that are flatter or less peaked than normal over time. These individuals tend to start earlier in life, to offend at higher rates than normal, and to continue to offend at the ages when most of their age peers are desisting.

Life course theorists have devoted considerable attention to explaining these different trajectories, and we have reviewed the major theories that they have proposed so far. A number of distinctions can be drawn between life course theories. Different theorists emphasize different causal factors. Terrie Moffitt, for example, places great importance on innate temperamental differences to explain variation in criminal trajectories. John Hagan, on the other hand, stresses the importance of macrohistorical and economic changes and their impact on the life chances of disadvantaged minorities. Robert Sampson, John Laub, and Terence Thornberry focus on shifts in the nature and balance of informal social controls over the life course.

Despite these differences in emphasis, if we permit ourselves some theoretical license, we can begin to outline a general theory of crime and the life course.

Such a theory would begin with the family. Children who come from troubled families are more likely to embark on delinquent trajectories than children whose parents are calm, loving, and supportive. But it is a mistake to assume that parents alone are to blame if their children turn out wrong. The extent to which parents can provide calm, loving support to their children is influenced by two important factors. One factor is innate temperamental differences among children. Some children appear to be born with difficult temperaments, making it hard for parents to respond to them in a calm and loving fashion. The second factor that affects how parents relate to their children is the neighborhood environment. Parents whose economic circumstances force them to live in economically disadvantaged neighborhoods have a more difficult time raising their children than parents who have the financial means to live elsewhere. Disadvantaged neighborhoods may affect how families raise their children in a number of ways, such as by providing greater opportunities for delinquency and more exposure to delinquent role models.

As most children enter their teenage years, the salience of parents as the locus of control, support, and interaction begins to decline. At this point in the life course, peers move front and center as the primary object of teenagers' attention and concern. Teenage peers model and reinforce behavior for one another. Thus, peers are a major influence on trajectories in crime and delinquency during the teenage years.

Important changes also take place in the realms of biology and psychology during the teenage years. Biologically, these years bring sexual maturity and rapid increases in physical strength, and they bring explosive developmental changes in the teenage brain associated with emotions, perceptions, and reasoning ability. Psychologically, they bring a desire for greater autonomy and independence from parents. The desire to be treated like an adult becomes paramount. These biological and psychological developments have much to do with the onset of delinquency among teenagers. They make certain types of offenses more feasible, such as those that require physical strength. They also serve as a source of motivation for other offenses and forms of deviancy in which teenagers attempt through rebellious behavior to stake a claim to adult status. In a highly age-stratified society such as the United States, there is a large gap between the timing of these biological and psychological transitions and the socially appropriate time for making the transition to adult status. The former transitions occur early in the teenage years, whereas the later transition is delayed until the late teenage years or even the early 20s.

One consequence of the teenage drive for autonomy and independence is that teenagers venture out into the community without the protective supervision of their parents more often and for longer periods of time than do young adolescents. But the communities and neighborhoods into which they go are not all the same. Communities vary in a number of important ways that may strongly influence individual trajectories in crime and delinquency. They vary in the number and types of criminal and legitimate opportunities they offer, in the availability of deviant and legitimate role models, in the degree of police presence, and in the style of policing that is used. For teenagers in economically disadvantaged and racially segregated inner-city neighborhoods, all of these variables tend to converge in the wrong direction. These neighborhoods present a surfeit of criminal opportunities and few legitimate ones. Gangs are a strong presence, whereas fully employed adults are few and far between. The police do not hesitate to arrest, nor are the courts chary to convict and incarcerate adolescent troublemakers. Hence, compared to their middle-class suburban counterparts, youth in these neighborhoods are at much greater risk of becoming involved in serious crime and of becoming embedded early on in a criminal lifestyle.

Policy Implications

Nowadays, it is politically fashionable to ridicule government programs aimed at helping people, especially programs aimed at reforming and rehabilitating troubled youth. It is not uncommon to hear cynics argue that by the time children become teenagers, there is little we can do to change them. According to this perspective, if crime prevention is going to work at all, it has to be implemented when children are as young as age 2 or 3. The argument is based on the well-known finding that children who display conduct disorders early are more likely to become serious delinquents and adult criminals later. However, as Elliott Currie (1998, 101) notes, "[I]t's a long leap from this common finding to the pessimistic insistence that a child's future is set in stone at age 3." That early disorders are empirically related to later delinquency may tell us only what happens if we do not do anything to deal with the problems of troubled youths. It does not tell us what would happen if we really did try to deal with them. In addition, recent advances in our understanding of how the teenage brain develops clearly indicate that for teenagers there is still time to change direction and to establish new behavior patterns.

Programs that invest in vulnerable at-risk youth can make a difference. One program that has shown evidence of success is the federal Job Corps, a carryover from the 1960s. The Job Corps, which combines intensive skill training with support services for its participants, significantly reduces violent crime among its graduates (Currie 1998, 102). Another program for at-risk youth that showed promising results was the Quantum Opportunity Program. Like the Job Corps, this program provided support services as well as training for minority youths from welfare homes. Students were randomly selected for the program, and they stayed in it throughout their high school years. Two years after the program ended, follow-up evaluations found the students in the program averaged half as many arrests as a control group. Program participants were also less likely to be on welfare and more likely to be in college (Currie 1998, 102–103). Thus, children from disadvantaged backgrounds can be helped to find better, more productive paths through life, but we have to be willing to try.

Most teenagers don't become embedded in a criminal lifestyle. But even those who do are not necessarily fated to become career criminals. It's true that the best thing to do is to prevent children from embarking on serious criminal trajectories in the first place, but we should not just abandon those who have already begun serious delinquent careers. Although it may be difficult, it is not impossible to halt the downward slide of youths who already are in trouble.

One approach that has shown promise is called multisystemic therapy (MST). MST is based on a view of the individual that resonates well with the multifactor, multicausal approach of life course theory. Individuals are seen as "nested within a complex of interconnected systems" that include family, peers, school, and the community (Currie 1998, 105). Problems may crop up in any of these systems, and treating youths requires responding comprehensively to issues in all of them. It makes little sense to teach youths job-related skills and expect them to become law-abiding taxpayers if there are no jobs in the community. Thus, the MST approach recognizes that we must do more than just help troubled youths overcome their individual deficiencies; we must also take steps to ensure that the necessary supports and opportunities are in place in the community.

The MST approach has been carefully evaluated at sites in South Carolina and Missouri. The clients in both programs were a tough group and had certainly earned the label "troubled youth." Most had multiple arrests, often for serious violent offenses. Many did not live with their biological parents. Despite all the strikes against them, youths who completed the MST program had significantly fewer arrests and time spent incarcerated than youths who received more traditional individualized treatment (Currie 1998, 105–107). What makes the difference in the MST approach compared to other forms of treatment is the recognition that individuals must be viewed in the context of their larger environments. Treating only the individual and ignoring the environment is almost guaranteed to fail. ✦

Chapter 4

Adulthood

Desistance and Cumulating Disadvantages

Age is a high price to pay for maturity.

—Tom Stoppard

Overview

A s they begin the third decade of life most people have left or are in the process of leaving their involvement in street crime. The decline in offending that started toward the end of the teenage years continues into the early twenties and then more or less stops because the bottom has been reached. The vandalism, shoplifting, petty thefts, fistfights, illegal drug use, and drunkenness so common among teenagers as to be statistically normal become decidedly abnormal for a substantial majority of people after the age of 25. By the early twenties the number of active offenders decreases by over 50 percent from its peak at around age 17. For example, the age-specific arrest rate for burglary peaks at age 17, but by age 21, it is only half as high (Blumstein and Cohen 1987). By the late 20s, only about 15 percent of offenders are still active (Moffitt 1997). Desistance sometime between the ages of 20 and 30 is the normal pattern.

Of course, it is not really correct to say that all offending stops completely. Adults drive over the speed limit, roll through stop signs, and on occasion have more than a few drinks before getting behind the wheel to head home from work or a party. According to national surveys, a nontrivial proportion of the American adult population uses illegal drugs. For example, the 1999 *Household Survey on Drug Abuse,* conducted by the U.S. Department of Health and Human Services, found that between 10 and 15 percent of adults aged 21 to 45 reported using an illicit drug in the past month. Adults in their thirties and forties may assault their spouses, abuse their children, cheat on their taxes, and engage in a breathtakingly wide and innovative variety of white-collar crimes related to their occupations (Gabor 1994; Evans et al. 1997). As we will see in the next chapter, white-collar offenders are often much older than street offenders when they first enter the justice system. As measured by arrests, the average age of onset for white-collar offenders is 10 or more years later than it is for street offenders (Weisburd, Waring, and Chayet 2001; Benson and Kerley 2000). Nevertheless, for a substantial majority of people, offending declines substantially in frequency and seriousness as they enter adulthood.

Yet, not all delinquents and street offenders quit. Some persist in their involvement in crime beyond the teenage years. Thus, the important question for life course researchers now becomes what differentiates those who desist from those who persist. A related question concerns the effects of involvement in crime on other domains in life. How does involvement in crime and delinquency as a teenager affect adult trajectories in employment and family? As we will see, in adulthood the damaging consequences of criminal embeddedness begin to materialize, greatly diminishing chances for normal developmental patterns.

Hard quantitative data on older criminals are hard to come by. As they enter their forties and fifties, we lose sight of the men and women who led lives characterized by serious offenses in young adulthood. They become lost in the vast archipelago of American state prisons, mental hospitals, skid rows, or in many cases, cemeteries. Thus, to learn more about the life course of older criminals, we must often rely on qualitative research.

Cumulative Disadvantages: Desistance and the Adult Consequences of Juvenile Crime

Although most people age out of crime, the transition to adulthood is not always smooth. For some offenders, early and extensive involvement in crime and delinquency has detrimental effects on trajectories in other domains of adult life. To have been arrested, convicted, and incarcerated are accomplishments that tend to diminish rather than enhance one's attractiveness to employers, potential spouses, and college admissions officers. The idea that involvement in crime may causally affect other domains of life has received relatively little attention from researchers (Thornberry and Christenson 1984). But it is an important part of the life course perspective on crime and illustrates the fundamental principle that trajectories are interconnected. Events in one trajectory may influence the course of other trajectories.

A growing body of research indicates that teenage delinquency and crime have significant negative effects on a number of adult outcomes. Adult outcomes refer to activities and accomplishments that are commonly associated with adult status in modern societies. These outcomes include getting a job, marrying and starting a family, and obtaining educational credentials. All of them play important roles in the desistance process. In adulthood, there is a reciprocal, back-and-forth relationship between trajectories in crime and trajectories in other domains of life. For example, involvement in crime affects the likelihood of entering into a stable marriage, and marital stability in turn affects the likelihood of desistance from crime.

Crime, Employment, and Desistance

The idea that economic conditions, especially employment opportunities, are linked to crime is popular with politicians and the public. For a variety of reasons, it makes sense to assume that economic conditions somehow drive crime rates. The most simple and straightforward reason is that people mired in poverty may commit crimes simply as a means of survival. Another more complicated potential explanation focuses on economic inequality and relative deprivation. According to this view, it is not absolute poverty that drives crime but rather the gap in wealth and income between the rich and the poor (LaFree 1998). When this gap is large or growing, the poor supposedly become frustrated by their relative lack of financial resources compared to the rich. They turn to crime out of frustration or because they believe their time is better spent on income-producing criminal activities than in legitimate employment. Other potential explanations for why economic conditions may be causally related to crime focus on the lifestyles of unemployed persons or the social control that employment can exert over people who might be inclined toward crime (Piehl 1998).

Although there are a number of theoretically plausible reasons for assuming that economic conditions drive crime, empirical research on the relationship has proved surprisingly inconclusive (Piehl 1998; Freeman 1995). Researchers have used several different strategies to investigate the link between crime and the economy, including time-series analyses, cross-sectional area studies, and individual comparisons. Time-series studies, which attempt to compare indicators of economic conditions and crime rates over time, appear to be sensitive to the variables included in the analysis and the time period covered (Freeman 1995). Contradictory results are common. Cross-sectional studies compare areas, such as states, cities, or neighborhoods, on their economic conditions and their crime rates. These studies tend to find that crime rates are higher wherever economic conditions are bad. In particular, indicators of economic inequality seem to be consistently associated with crime rates (Chiricos 1987; Freeman 1995). However, as with time series studies, the statistical models used in cross-sectional studies are not perfect and the results to date suggest that the effect of economic conditions on crime is modest (Freeman 1992).

Both time series studies and cross-sectional studies rely on aggregate data. These studies can tell us a good deal about general patterns in the economy and in crime, but they are one step removed from the individuals who make decisions either to commit a crime or to get a job or to do both. Studies that investigate the economic circumstances and criminal behavior of individuals over time, or that compare the circumstances of those who commit crimes with those who do not, offer perhaps the best way to evaluate how the job market affects crime (Freeman 1995). From the perspective of the life course approach, individual studies are important because they have the potential to tell us something about how trajectories in crime may be shaped or influenced by trajectories in other domains of life, such as occupational trajectories. However, at this level of analysis, the question of causal order is complicated. Research suggests that individual economic incentives such as, for example, being poor or unemployed influence individual involvement in crime and delinquency, but the reverse also seems to be true. That is, involvement in crime and delinquency appears to influence occupational and employment trajectories (Hagan 1993; Freeman 1995; 1992).

There is no debate about the fact that the people who populate American prisons and jails come disproportionately from groups with low incomes and poor employment records. Analyses of the employment records of persons in the criminal justice system routinely find little evidence of stable employment (Weisburd, Wheeler, Waring, and Bode 1991). Studies of juvenile delinquents also show that those who end up in jail or under arrest are more likely to have low incomes or be unemployed than their peers who avoid contact with the criminal justice system (Wolfgang, Figlio, and Sellin 1972; Thornberry and Christenson 1984; Allan and Steffensmeier 1989). For example, a study of inner-city African-American youth found that "30 percent of those who committed a crime held a job at the same time of the survey compared with 46 percent of those who had not committed a crime" (Freeman 1987).

In the United States, evidence indicates that the population of criminals overlaps considerably with the population of people at the lower end of the income distribution, but this does not necessarily mean that poverty or unemployment causes crime. There are other explanations for the correlation between crime and unemployment. One alternative explanation points to ontogenetic factors. Criminals may simply be people with "personal characteristics" that make it difficult for them to succeed in society (Freeman 1995). Impulsivity or low intelligence, for example, may cause individuals to be both poor employment prospects and criminally active. Another explanation is that the causal order is reversed. Instead of joblessness causing crime, it is crime that causes joblessness. This would happen if criminals reject jobs because they find working at crime more attractive and rewarding than working at a legitimate job, or if their involvement in crime makes them unattractive to potential employers. In either case, it is involvement in crime that precedes reduced achievement, if not complete failure, in occupational trajectories.

A solid body of research indicates that the latter explanation applies in many cases, with crime causing unemployment and low occupational attainment, rather than vice versa. An analysis of the Cambridge data found that teen delinquency and crime at ages 16 to 17 predicted adult unemployment at ages 18 to 19 and 21 to 22 (Hagan 1993). Similarly, Robert Sampson and John Laub (1993) found that the subjects in the Gluecks' sample who were officially defined as delinquents and who had high levels of delinquency were significantly more likely to have low job stability than the nondelinquents or the less-active delinquents.

Other studies find similar results (Tanner, Davies, and O'Grady 1999; Thornberry and Christenson 1984). The effects that involvement in crime can have on occupational trajectories in some cases appear to be enduring and widespread across social groups. Tanner et al. (1999) analyzed data from the National Longitudinal Survey of Youth (NLSY), which contains information on a nationally representative sample of over 6,000 youths followed from 1979 to 1992. In this study, the researchers selected a subsample of individuals who were between ages 14 and 17 and enrolled in school in 1979. In 1979, the youths were asked to self-report on five measures of crime and delinquency, including skipping school, drug use, property damage, violence, and contact with the justice system. In 1992, these same respondents, now between the ages of 27 and 30, were asked about their educational attainment and occupational status. The results of regression analyses clearly revealed the powerful negative effects of teenage delinquency on adult status attainment. All of the delinquency indicators had consistently significant and negative effects on educational attainment for both males and females. For males, greater involvement in drugs and property crime in 1979 was associated with lower occupational status in 1992, 13 years later. Because both educational attainment and occupational status are known to be strongly correlated with race, ethnicity, socioeconomic status, and cognitive abilities, the researchers included measures of these variables in their statistical models. The significant negative effects of delinquency on education and occupation remained even after the controls were included in the models. Teenage delinquents appear to pay for their youthful indiscretions later in life.

Although Tanner and his colleagues found that delinquency affects adult outcomes independently of socioeconomic status, other research suggests that being delinquent has much more harmful delayed consequences for persons from disadvantaged class or race backgrounds. Beginning in 1976, John Hagan followed a sample of Toronto youths from high school into their mid-20s. Thirteen years later, in 1989, having been delinquent as a teenager had significant negative effects on adult occupational attainment for working-class youths who identified with a "subculture of delinquency." However, for nonworking class youths, involvement in delinquent acts did not limit their occupational achievements as adults (Hagan 1991). Hagan's research suggests that the impact of crime on occupational trajectories depends on social class as much as it does on overt behavior. Involvement in delinquency is much more costly over the long run for working-class youths than it is for middle- and upper-class youth.

This theme that crime has differential effects on occupational trajectories depending on your social background is elaborated in Mercer Sullivan's important ethnographic study of lower-class youth (1989). Sullivan studied youths in three ethnically distinct New York City neighborhoods, one white, one Hispanic, and one African American. In all three neighborhoods, kids often became involved in "crimes for money before they had much access to employment" (Sullivan 1989, 216). Although their initial trajectories in crime were similar, delinquent youths from the white neighborhood soon diverged from their counterparts in the African-American and Hispanic neighborhoods. The white youths tended to desist from crime and move into legitimate employment as they neared the end of their teenage years. African-American and Hispanic youths, however, tended to persist in their criminal behavior and over time became embedded in a criminal lifestyle (Hagan 1993).

The reasons why the white and minority youths followed different trajectories are complex and involve patterns in residential segregation, the structure of the labor market, and racial preferences in the justice system. According to Sullivan, the white youths lived in a neighborhood in which many of the adults were employed in desirable blue-collar jobs. The adults were in positions that enabled them to link neighborhood young people to good jobs through personalized referral networks. In contrast, in the minority communities, "many . . . parents had no jobs . . . and those parents who were employed tended to work in government jobs that recruited by bureaucratic means rather than through personal networks" (p. 80). As the minority youths grew up, they could not count on their parents or other neighborhood adults to help them find jobs. Those minority youths who were interested in going to work had to rely on more impersonal methods to find employment. In addition, because of race-based residential segregation, the neighborhoods in which the minority youths lived were physically isolated from the main centers of employment in the metropolitan area. Taken together, the "social ties between residents and local employers reinforced physical proximity to produce a much greater supply of youth jobs" for the white youths than for the minority youths (Sullivan 1989, 104).

Besides better access to jobs, the white youths enjoyed other advantages that helped reduce the negative consequences of involvement in crime and delinquency. In all three neighborhoods, youths involved in crime eventually came to the attention of the criminal justice system. But their experiences in the justice system were markedly different. By using money and personal connections, the parents of the white youths were better able to influence the criminal justice system than were the parents of the minority youths. As a result, the encounters that white youths had with the criminal justice system resulted in less severe formal sanctions than those received by minority youths. For minority youths, arrests were more likely to lead to formal court appearances and to confinement. The more severe formal sanctions that the minority youths received stigmatized them and further isolated them from legitimate occupations (Sullivan 1989, 241).

Sullivan's work illustrates how trajectories in crime and employment can become intertwined and how they are influenced by the surrounding social context. For the white youths in his study, teenage delinquencies did not have severe detrimental consequences for their occupational trajectories because their parents were able to protect them from the stigma of criminal justice processing. Because they lived in neighborhoods that provided them with access to good jobs, the white youths eventually took up legitimate occupations. Thus, for the white youths, crime and employment were not tightly connected. They received a free pass. For the minority youths, however, crime was not free and not without consequences. Because their parents were unable to protect them from the criminal justice system, they were more likely to be confined and stigmatized. Their entanglements with the justice system kept them out of school, further isolating them from legitimate employment. Rather than gradually becoming embedded in the world of legitimate employment like the white youths, the minority youths gradually became embedded in crime networks (Hagan 1993, 473). Their trajectories in crime were intimately and negatively intertwined with their occupational trajectories.

Sullivan's study is unique in that it compares youths from different racial and ethnic backgrounds. Studies by other researchers, however, suggest that the experiences Sullivan found are common among disadvantaged minority youths. In disadvantaged communities characterized by concentrated poverty and extremely limited opportunities for legitimate employment, crime becomes a way of life for many young people long before we would expect them to start their occupational careers. In these communities, young people, especially young minority males, seem to come to the conclusion early on that good jobs are not and never will be available. A well-paying legitimate occupation does not seem to be in the cards for them. Their response often is to turn to other ways to make money, primarily through gangs and drugs. For example, in a Philadelphia ghetto community studied by Anderson (1990), the drug economy served as an employment agency for many young men. Anderson noted that "Young men who 'grew up' in the gang, but now are without clear opportunities, easily become involved; they fit themselves into its structure, manning its drug houses and selling drugs on street corners" (Anderson 1990, 244). In an ethnography of the Diamonds, a Puerto Rican gang in Chicago, Padilla (1992) observed a similar process. From the young Puerto Ricans that he interviewed, Padilla learned that their involvement in the gang and in the drug economy began while they were still only young teenagers aged 13 to15. Membership in the Diamonds was attractive to these youngsters in part because it promised a way to make more money than they thought they could get by working at the low-paying jobs available in their neighborhood (Padilla 1992).

But the income that the Diamonds earned through the gang and the drug economy came at a price. Their affiliation with the gang led to problems at school and to encounters with the police. They were expelled from school and arrested often (Padilla 1992, 166). Over time, the youths found themselves without educational credentials and with reputations as troublemakers and criminal records that made it difficult for them to progress to adult employment or to college, transitions that most young people easily make when they near the end of their teenage years.

The ethnographies by Sullivan, Anderson, and Padilla suggest a process is at work in disadvantaged minority communities in which some youths become embedded in crime (Hagan 1993). Youths who become criminally embedded begin their involvement in crime early. They develop criminal skills and make friends and contacts with other similarly inclined individuals. Over time, because of their criminal activities, they eventually compile extensive official criminal records and bad reputations in the community. As they spend more time and energy in the world of drugs and crime, they accordingly have less time to spend in legitimate pursuits, such as school and the entry-level jobs that provide social contacts and employment experiences. Schooling, contacts, and a good work history are crucial prerequisites for making the transition to adult employment. Youths who become criminally embedded are likely to lack all of these prerequisites. Hence, they have little chance of ever finding much success in legitimate occupations.

Ethnographic work is powerful because it brings us close to lived reality. From Sullivan, Anderson, and Padilla, as well as others (Moore 1991; Hagedorn 1988), we learn what it feels like to grow up in a poverty-stricken ghetto community. But the objection can be raised that these studies necessarily focus on relatively small and nonrandom samples of individuals. It is possible that there is something unique about the communities and individuals included in these studies that differentiate them from the general population. Representative samples secured through random-sampling techniques might tell another story.

An important study by Richard B. Freeman suggests otherwise. Freeman analyzed data from three different large random sample surveys of poor and minority youths: the 1979–1988 National Longitudinal Surveys of Youth (NLSY), the 1989 National Bureau of Economic Research's (NBER) Boston Youth Survey (BYS), and the 1979–1989 NBER Survey of Inner City Youth (ICY) in Boston, Chicago, and Philadelphia (Freeman 1992). The results replicate the findings from ethnographies in showing that involvement in crime often precedes unemployment. Importantly, Freeman's careful analyses suggest that the process identified in ethnographies applies generally among disadvantaged youths. What appears to be the most damaging consequence of teenage crime is the risk of contact with the criminal justice system, which leads to being officially labeled. For example, the analyses of the NLSY surveys show "that the most serious involvement with the criminal justice system—jail or probation—*had massive long-term effects on employment* while lesser involvements had small and often negligible effects" (Freeman 1992, 217, emphasis in original). Similar results were found in the Boston Youth Survey and in the Survey of Inner City Youth. In Boston, youths who had been in jail had "exceptionally low chances of employment" compared to youths who had committed crimes but not been caught (221). Analysis of the ICY survey showed that "having been in jail is the single most important deterrent to employment" (222). Thus, having a criminal record greatly increases the likelihood of unemployment (Freeman 1992, 226).

In addition to showing how crime reduces employment, Freeman's analyses show that crime also is strongly associated with reduced educational attainment and that, for disadvantaged youths, being a criminal initially may be considerably more lucrative than working at a legitimate job. From the survey evidence, it appears that "crime offers relatively high hourly pay to disadvantaged youth" (233).

This research on the effects of crime on employment illustrates two important principles of the life course approach. First, events that occur in one trajectory can have implications for trajectories in other domains of life. The type of trajectory that a person follows in crime and delinquency seems to have particularly profound potential consequences for his or her educational and occupational trajectories. Involvement in crime and delinquency as a youth often precedes and leads to restricted employment opportunities as a young adult. Contact with the criminal justice system that results in formal sanctions, such as conviction and confinement, appears to have particularly detrimental consequences. Thus, for some people, trajectories in crime and occupation may be strongly linked. However, the degree to which trajectories in crime and occupation are linked depends on larger structural conditions in society. And that is the second life course principle illustrated by this research. Social conditions shape trajectories and the impact of events on trajectories. Early involvement in crime appears to be more harmful to the occupational and educational careers of disadvantaged minority youths than it is to white middle-class youths. Minority and lower-class youths are more likely to become embedded in criminal lifestyles from which it is difficult to escape. Middle-class white youths, on the other hand, stand a much better chance of avoiding the harmful occupational consequences that delinquency entails for minority youths. In effect, for white middle-class youths, the connection between delinquency and unemployment is not as strong as it is for youths who come from disadvantaged backgrounds.

Although it is increasingly clear that early involvement in crime affects later occupational trajectories, we should not forget that the relationship between crime and employment is reciprocal. Just as crime affects employment, so does employment affect crime. Indeed, obtaining stable employment appears to be an important turning point in criminal careers. In *Crime in the Making,* Sampson and Laub carefully investigated the effect of job stability on desistance. They found that it is one of the strongest predictors of desistance from crime in adulthood (Laub and Sampson 1993; Sampson and Laub 1993). Recognizing that selection effects might account for the correlation between job stability and reduced involvement in adult crime, Sampson and Laub took great pains to control for prior differences in criminal potential and for sample selection bias. The effects of job stability on general deviance, excessive alcohol use, and arrest remained consistently negative. The delinquents who somehow managed to find stable jobs in their late teens and early twenties were much less likely to continue their involvement in crime in their thirties than their counterparts who did not find jobs. The effects of job stability on deviance were also observed in the control sample. Recall that the Gluecks' study involved both a delinquent sample and a control sample of nondelinquents. Sampson and Laub found that even in the control sample, job stability was the strongest predictor of the frequency of adult arrest. Finding stable employment, then, is an important way out of crime.

Marriage, Children, Family, and Desistance

Another important turning point in the life course is marriage. Marriage entails new responsibilities and a strong emotional commitment to another person. From the perspective of life course theory and standard criminological theories, there are a number of reasons to think that marriage and family life can have a potentially profound influence on trajectories in crime. For example, social-bond theory would predict that a good marriage could be an important source of informal social control (Laub, Nagin, and Sampson 1998). To the extent that a young man is emotionally attached to his wife and his children, he is likely to curb his criminal inclinations out of respect for his wife's wishes and a desire not to jeopardize his family life.

Another interpretation of the relationship between marriage and desistance comes from differential association theory. Mark Warr (1998) argues that time spent with a spouse or children at home is time that cannot be spent with criminal peers on the street. Time spent working to provide a living for one's spouse and children is also time taken away from the risky attractions of street life. Getting married reduces one's contact with friends in general and delinquent friends in particular. Reduced exposure to delinquent friends leads to reduced involvement in crime and deviance (Warr 1998).

Qualitative and quantitative evidence suggests that, for some men, becoming involved with a woman and getting married can be a route out of crime. However, the relationship between marriage and crime is complex. It is not simply the case that criminals who get married stop committing offenses whereas those who do not get married continue to offend. As with employment and crime, understanding how marriage and family life intersect with crime requires close attention to temporal order and causal sequencing. There are times when crime affects marriage and family life, and there are times when the reverse appears to be true. That is, marriage and family life can reduce involvement in crime and other forms of deviance (Sampson and Laub 1993).

Consider first how involvement in crime and delinquency early in life affects marital stability later in life. In their reanalysis of the Gluecks' data, Sampson and Laub (1993) found that childhood behavior problems were negatively correlated with marital stability in adulthood. The boys who were most seriously delinquent as teenagers were least likely to be in strong stable marriages in their 20s and 30s. Their marital histories were characterized by conflict, separation, and divorce. Just as early involvement in crime reduces educational attainment and employment stability, it can reduce marital stability.

However, although extensive involvement in crime appears to be incompatible with marital stability, this does not mean that young criminals have no family life. To the contrary, evidence from two longitudinal studies of inner-city youth, the Rochester Youth Development Study (RYDS) and the Pittsburgh Youth Study (PYS), suggests that early involvement in delinquency is strongly associated with becoming a parent as a teenager. Recall that the RYDS and PYS are longitudinal studies that have tracked samples of inner-city youths in Rochester, New York, and Pittsburgh, Pennsylvania, since 1988. Youths were between 12 and 13 when they were first interviewed for the study and they have been reinterviewed every six to twelve months thereafter. In a recent analysis of the RYDS data that was available up to 1996, researchers found that males who got involved in delinquency early and who frequently used drugs were much more likely to father children as teenagers than their less-delinquent peers (Thornberry et al. 2000). According to the researchers, just over one-quarter of the males in the sample (28 percent) became teenage fathers. However, while

> Seventy percent of high-frequency drug users became teen fathers, only 24 percent of the nonusers or low users did. Similarly, while nearly half (47 percent) of the high-rate delinquents later became teen fathers, only 23 percent of the nondelinquents or low-rate delinquents did. (Thornberry et al. 2000, 3)

For reasons that are not yet understood, a smaller percentage of the males in the Pittsburgh study became fathers before their 19th birthday than in the Rochester sample (12 percent to 28 percent, respectively). Nevertheless, delinquency still appeared to have the same positive effect on the risk of becoming a teen father. In the PYS, 19 percent of the high-rate delinquents fathered children, compared to 9 percent of nondelinquents or low-rate delinquents (Thornberry et al. 2000, 4).

Delinquency alone, of course, is not the only cause of teenage parenthood. It is just one of a constellation of factors that seem to be associated with having children early in life. Race, neighborhood characteristics, parents' level of education, intelligence, and, not surprisingly, early sexual activity are also significantly correlated with teen fatherhood. But even when researchers control for these other factors, chronic delinquency and drug use still significantly increase the likelihood that a boy will become a teen father (Thornberry et al. 2000, 3).

Having children is a normal and expected part of the life course. Eagerly anticipated by most married couples, it is truly a profound, life-altering transition that can have dramatic effects on all dimensions of the life course. Like many other transitions in the life course, however, society has age-graded expectations for this transition. When a transition is made off time, that is, at an inappropriate time in the life course, it can have detrimental consequences for the individuals making the transition and for those with whom their lives are entangled. This general principle of the life course approach is especially true in the case of the transition to parenthood. Teenagers who have children are making what has been called a *precocious transition*, that is, a transition that occurs much earlier than is normative or expected in society (Smith et al. 2000). Teenagers who make this precocious transition by having children suffer many negative educational, financial, social, and health consequences (Furstenberg, Brooks-Gunn, and Morgan 1987; Lerman 1993). They are less likely to complete school and achieve financial security and more likely to be socially isolated and have poor health than teenagers who avoid having children. Equally important, the children of these teenage parents are at risk for suffering the same negative developmental consequences as the parents.

The negative consequences for children of having teenage parents are compounded when a parent is caught up in the criminal justice system. Children whose parents are incarcerated are more likely to grow up in poverty, and they are less likely to form a strong attachment to the imprisoned parent (Sandifer and Kurth 2000; Johnston and Carlin 1996). They also appear to be at greater risk to engage in deviant and criminal behavior themselves, compared to children who grow up in similar socioeconomic circumstances but whose parents are not incarcerated (Hagan and Dinovitzer 1999).

Thus, trajectories in crime influence trajectories in family life as much as the other way around. Often the influence of crime on family life is not beneficial. However, there are exceptions to this pattern. In some cases, trajectories in crime and drugs can be changed for the better by events that occur in the domain of family life. What matters most is the development of high-quality marital bonds (Sampson and Laub 1993). In *Crime in the Making,* Robert Sampson and John Laub found that delinquents who had the good fortune to establish strong attachments to their spouses were more likely to reduce offending or desist altogether than delinquents who were not married or who were in poor quality marriages. The effect of strong marital attachment on offending remained even after controls for individual differences among delinquents were added to the statistical analysis. Good marriages can facilitate the desistance process.

The effect of a good marriage on criminal offending does not occur all at once. It is a gradual process that cumulates over time. Careful statistical analyses of the Gluecks' data show that the longer time an offender invests in a good marriage, the more likely that marriage is to have a preventive effect on his criminal trajectory (Laub et al. 1998, 237). Offenders who enter into good marriages gradually become committed to their spouses. This commitment appears to function as a source of informal social control that grows slowly over time and leads toward desistance.

Thus, getting married or meeting a "good woman" can be an important turning point in the life course of male offenders. It begins a process in which the offender starts building ties to conventional others and engaging in conventional activities (Shover 1996). Establishing a mutually satisfying relationship with a woman changes the way formerly criminal men view themselves and their lives. Neal Shover's (1996, 126) interviews with men who had extensive criminal careers illustrate the power of these new social bonds to shape both behavior and attitude:

> When I reached the age of 35 it just seemed like my life wanted to change. I needed a change in life, and I was tired of going to jail. I wanted to change my life and stay out here. And by meeting the woman that I met it just turned my life completely around. . . . When I met her it just seemed like something in my life had been fulfilled.

Another of Shover's (126) informants, a man who had served many years in prison, described how his wife helped him avoid going back to a life in crime even when he was unemployed and under stress:

> I loved my wife—I love her still—and she talked to me a lot. . . . And if it wouldn't been for her, no tellin' where I'd be at, 'cause I'd most likely had a gun in my hand and robbed a bank or something. Or took something from somebody to get some food you know. . . . She helped me along.

Good marriages and other types of supportive social relationships can change the lives of criminals in other ways, too. They bring the former offender into contact with a different crowd of people, conventional people whose daily routines do not include stealing or getting arrested. For some offenders, these new relationships provide a secure and rewarding social niche within which the offender can develop new interests and new activity patterns:

> Through [his girlfriend] I met a whole lot of straight people, you know, that I enjoyed bein' around, you know. Like her people, her parents, her sisters and brother, you know, her mother. I enjoyed bein' around them. And they was straight, you know, never been incarcerated, never been affiliated with the law and shit like that. I enjoyed bein' around them, because they did some things—like, we played cards, played little games, you know. I like sports, you know; we'd sit down and talk about sports, and do things of that nature. (Shover 1996, 127)

For those who have spent many years following a criminal lifestyle, changing this trajectory and finding a route out of crime is difficult. It is highly unlikely that these individuals will ever catch up to their age peers in regard to occupational attainment and financial security. Nevertheless, even for career criminals desistance is not impossible. The creation of strong bonds with conventional others and involvement in legitimate activities are the most important contingencies through which some men redirect their trajectories in crime (Shover 1996; Sampson and Laub 1993). At all ages, offenders who are unable to establish these bonds are unlikely to stay away from crime for long.

Cognitive Changes and Desistance

Along with the objective contingencies of bonds to conventional others and involvement in legitimate lines of action come psychological or cognitive changes in career offenders who desist (Shover 1996). These changes seem to arise out of a combination of advancing age and the hard experiences that accompany a life of crime. In one of the few studies of older criminals, Neal Shover (1996, 131) concluded that advancing age had several effects on the attitudes of career criminals. Age brought greater interest in employment and secure bonds to others. Like most people, as criminals age they also become better at calculating the likely outcomes of different courses of action. Past experience has taught them that not all crimes are successful and that eventually they will be arrested and confined. In short, "aging, with its accumulating stock of experiences, makes men less audacious and more capable of acting rationally." Underlying the maturity that comes with age are two more profound changes in the cognitive orientations of those career criminals who turn away from crime. They develop a new perspective on themselves, and they become increasingly aware of time (Shover 1996, 131).

In his interviews with aging criminals and his exhaustive review of the literature in this area, Shover discerns a developmental pattern of changed identity among these men. They develop a new, more critical and evaluative perspective on themselves and their former activities. From this perspective, they look back on what they did and who they are and come to see themselves in terms that are not flattering. One man interviewed by Shover (1996) describes his former self in this way:

> I saw myself for what I really was. I saw what I was. I saw it. With my own eyes I saw myself. I could see it just as plain as I'm looking at you now. And I know that what I looked at was a sorry picture of a human being. . . . I was a self-made bastard, really. (131)

From this new perspective, activities that had previously seemed exciting, thrilling, and cool are now viewed as simpleminded or just plain dumb:

> Hey man, everybody got the nature to want to live good, you know, a desire to live good. And I thought that was the best way to do it, you know, by stealing, you know. I could get things that I ordinarily couldn't get by working. But, man, now I don't look at it that way. I think I was stupid. (1996, 132)

The aging criminal comes to see his youthful perspective on life and self as misguided and leading only to defeat rather than the good life he had envisioned.

The cognitive changes that accompany long-term involvement in crime are not limited to men. Although few studies have examined the criminal careers of women, those that have suggest that male and female offenders follow similar psychological trajectories. Female criminals come to realize that life on the streets is a grinding and dangerous existence. After years of being embedded in crime, they gradually come to appreciate that it offers no chance of success. They recognize that they have lost or are in danger of losing everything, and they become overwhelmed with a sense of personal despair. Ira Sommers and Deborah Baskin interviewed women with long histories of involvement in drugs and street crime (Sommers, Baskin, and Fagan 1994). The life stories of these women often mirror those of men. A woman named Stephanie was 27 and had been using and selling crack for half a decade when she was interviewed. She described how she came to recognize the futility of her life on the streets:

> I knew that, uh, I was gonna get killed out here. I wasn't havin' no respect for myself. No one else was respecting me. Every relationship I got into, as long as I did drugs, it was gonna be constant disrespect involved, and it come . . . to the point of me getting killed. (90)

Another subject interviewed by Sommers and Baskin was Gazella, a 38-year-old Hispanic woman who had been involved in drugs and crime for over two decades. Like Stephanie, Gazella came to see that drugs and crime were taking her nowhere except to isolation and despair:

> I'm 38 years old. I ain't no young woman no more, man. Drugs have changed, life styles have changed. Kids are killing you now for turf. Yeah, turf, and I was destroyin' myself. I was miserable. I was . . . I

was getting high all the time to stay up to keep the business going, and it was really nobody I could trust. (90)

I didn't have a place to live. My kids had been taken from me. You know, constantly being harassed like three days out of the week by the Tactical Narcotics Team [police]. I didn't want to be bothered with people. I was getting tired of lyin', schemin', you know, stayin' in abandoned buildings. (91)

As offenders age, they encounter ever more negative and stressful situations on the street. They become ever more marginalized from the traditional life structures that support most of us—family, friends, children, and work. Daily life on the street is tough and wearing even on the hardiest of souls. A 27-year-old Hispanic woman interviewed by Sommers and Baskin described it this way:

You get tired of bein' tired, you know. I got tired of hustlin', you know. I got tired of livin' the way I was livin', you know. Due to your body, your body, mentally, emotionally, you know. Everybody's tryin' to get over. Everybody will stab you in your back. Nobody gives a fuck about the next person. (92)

For some long-term offenders, the steady accumulation of hard knocks eventually wears them down and leads to a psychological crossroads. They start to reevaluate the rewards and costs of crime. The rewards come to be seen as less and less pleasing and the costs as more and more certain and intolerable. This change in calculus appears to be an important step in the desistance process (Sommers et al. 1994; Shover and Thompson 1992).

Exactly why some career criminals experience this psychological turning point is not well understood. One factor that seems to be involved is that as offenders get older they find that doing time in prison is increasingly grueling, and the thought of incurring a long prison sentence evokes fear. The deprivations of imprisonment grow increasingly burdensome. When asked what had finally convinced her to quit drugs and crime, a woman named April responded to Sommers and Baskin this way:

Jail, being in jail. The environment, having my freedom taken away. I saw myself keep repeating the same pattern, and I didn't want to do that. Uh, I had missed my daughter. See, being in jail that long period of time, I was able to detox. And when I detoxed, I kind of like had a clear sense of thinking, and that's when I came to the realization that, uh, this is not working for me. (91)

April's concerns were echoed by Denise, who also experienced a realization that she no longer was willing to risk being imprisoned:

> I saw the person that I was dealing with—my partner—I saw her go upstate to Bedford for two to four years. I didn't want to deal with it. I didn't want to go. Bedford is a prison, women's prison. And I couldn't see myself giving up two years of my life for something that I knew I could change in another way. (91)

Confinement has other effects besides the fear that it provokes in offenders. It also provides them with time for doing nothing but thinking about themselves and their lives, and through a process of introspection their views change. The words of one of Shover's informants illustrate this process:

> I had a lot of time to think. Every time you go to jail . . . think about them nights, man. I'd be in them cells, I got to be by myself, and I can't go to sleep. I got to think, and if you sit down and think enough, something is going to come to you. . . . First thing, you going to start to figure things out. (132)

As offenders start to figure things out, some of them come to see that time is like a nonrenewable liquid asset, something that can be spent, but that once spent cannot be replenished (Shover 1985). A man whom Shover (1985) interviewed in prison described how the future had come to seem increasingly valuable to him.

> I'm older (now) and I don't have much time. I guess you start looking at how much time you have left, and what to do with that time. . . . I'm 42 now. I got 20 years left and I'm sitting here doing this dead time. You know, nothing out of my life but dead time. . . . Every year that goes by, it seems like it's quicker, you know. Life, before you're 21 it seems like it's forever, before you turn 21. And after you do, time seems like it's flying by. (84)

Older criminals are not unique in their growing awareness that time is not a limitless resource and that one's time will eventually run out. These types of changes also are common among nonoffenders. Studies of ordinary people find that as males age, their orientation toward time changes from "time-since-birth" to "time-left-to-live" (Shover 1985, 85). Most people become increasingly introspective as they age (Levinson 1978). We think more about the future and the inevitability of death. Although the apparent similarities in experience between offenders and nonoffenders are striking, they must be interpreted cautiously. There have been no controlled studies that purposely compare the time orientations of offenders with nonoffenders through the life course, and there is some evidence that offenders come to differ psychologically as they age into midlife (Hagan 1997).

In a panel analysis of Canadian youth that covered almost twenty years, Hagan (1997, 133) demonstrated that individuals who were involved in the subculture of delinquency as youths were more likely to be depressed in midlife than youths who were not involved in delinquency. Intriguingly, psychological differences between delinquents and nondelinquents were not observed at the start of the panel analysis. That is, when they were young, delinquents were no more likely to be depressed than nondelinquents. The differences in what Hagan calls "despair in the life course" only appeared at midlife. Hagan (1997, 133) attributes this delay to a "sleeper effect," an effect that is not apparent immediately but that becomes apparent with the passage of time.

Summary

Hagan's research brings together many of the themes that we have tried to develop in this chapter. These themes include the principle of interconnectedness in the life course and the structural consequences of cumulating disadvantages. Youths who become involved in subcultural delinquency tend to leave school prematurely. Their failure to obtain educational credentials eventually leads to unemployment or to poor episodic employment. However, their poor experiences in the labor market are caused only in part by their lack of schooling. Recent changes in the global economy also contribute. As a result of globalization and technological developments, manual-labor jobs are less needed in developed economies than they were in the past. Increasingly, in developed countries such as Canada and the United States, manual laboring jobs have disappeared. Transnational corporations have moved them to developing countries in South America or East Asia or Mexico, where labor costs are cheaper. In the past, these jobs absorbed lower-class youth who were not inclined to pursue upward mobility through education, providing them with some measure of financial security and a reasonable standard of living. This option is no longer available. Education is now required for a man or a woman to have any sort of chance at a decent livelihood. To compete successfully in the labor market of a developed country demands education and technical skills. The connection between educational and occupational trajectories, always close, has grown even tighter.

Thus, trajectories in crime intersect with trajectories in education, occupation, marriage, family, and psychological perspectives. Heavy involvement in delinquency as an adolescent is connected to reduced educational attainment, which is in turn connected to occupational failure and finally to increased depression and despair later in life. Lower-class youth, and especially lower-class youth from racial or ethnic minorities, are particularly susceptible to being caught up in this chain of cumulating disadvantages. Structural changes brought on by globalization in labor markets have reduced the number of alternative pathways for them to find financial security as adults. Structural changes have increased the likelihood that delinquent youths and lower-class minority youth in general will be trapped on the pathway of cumulative disadvantage.

Policy Implications

The disadvantages that accompany long-term commitment to a criminal lifestyle render it difficult for career criminals to assume a conventional life. Career criminals who have finally had enough and who want to go straight face daunting obstacles. They typically lack educational credentials and marketable skills. They have poor employment histories and extensive criminal records. They may have health problems associated with alcohol and drug abuse and the hard life on the streets. Finally, unless they have been extraordinarily lucky, they usually don't have a network of supportive family and friends to help them. The cards are stacked against them. Yet, change is possible. The work of Sampson and Laub shows that even individuals with extensive and long-term involvement in crime can reach turning points and embark on new trajectories.

Adult offenders have one thing going for them that may facilitate prosocial change in their lives. Because of their years of experience on the streets, in jail, and in prison, they suffer from no illusions about what the criminal life is like. As the life stories presented in this chapter show, adult offenders clearly understand the futility and dangerousness of a life in crime. They no longer need to be warned that they are heading for a fall. They've already fallen. For them, the warnings of impending disaster that they heard from parents and teachers when they were teenagers have become harsh realities. Adult offenders, thus, are perhaps more likely to be psychologically ready to change than young delinquents and more willing to take advantage of opportunities for a fresh start.

Some research supports the idea that older offenders are more amenable to change than younger ones. In a study of the effects of employment on recidivism, Christopher Uggen found that employment significantly reduced criminal activity among offenders over 27, but it had little effect on teenage offenders or those in their early twenties (Uggen 2000). This result suggests that we must pay attention to the timing of interventions. What works at one stage of the life course may be ineffective at another.

Providing opportunities for good stable employment, then, may be one way to assist older offenders. They are more likely to be psychologically ready to change their lives than younger offenders who are still excited by the thrills of the street. The work of Sampson and Laub supports the deterrent effects of employment on crime and indicates that change is possible even for individuals with extensive criminal records.

But we need to be realistic about the chances for prosocial change in adult offenders. Although some offenders do experience cognitive changes as they grow older, not everyone has an epiphany while sitting in prison. Some offenders do their time, get out, and go back to their old ways. We also need to recognize that older offenders face a multitude of problems. Just providing jobs is not likely to be enough in most cases. Older offenders are often afflicted with drug and alcohol problems that must be attended to. They are unlikely to have marketable skills. They may also be socially isolated, lacking supportive family and friendship networks. Thus, successful programs to help older offenders will require multifaceted approaches, approaches that combine education, job training, and drug treatment and that strive to create support networks (Currie 1993). ✦

Chapter 5

White-Collar Crime and the Life Course

. . . the generalization that criminality is closely associated with poverty obviously does not apply to white-collar criminals. With a small number of exceptions, they are not in poverty, were not reared in slums or badly deteriorated families, and are not feeble-minded or psychopathic. They were seldom problem children in their earlier years and did not appear in juvenile courts or child-guidance clinics.

—Edwin H. Sutherland

Overview

In 1940, when Sutherland penned the words quoted above, there was no life course perspective on crime. Yet, the ideas that criminals grow up in troubled families, that they start out as problem children, and that they suffer mental or psychological deficits were mainstays of American criminology. Today, over half a century later, these same ideas undoubtedly would strike a responsive chord among life course researchers. However, just as Sutherland's contemporaries developed the criminological theories of his day based on samples that excluded white-collar criminals, so have life course researchers focused on similarly restricted samples. Sutherland's contemporaries ignored white-collar criminals, and so have today's life course researchers and theorists.

The proponents of the life course perspective are not unique in their neglect of white-collar criminals. With a few exceptions (Paternoster and Simpson 1993; Passas 1990; Braithwaite 1989a; 1989b; Lasley 1988; Hirschi and Gottfredson 1987), criminologists generally have not sought to apply standard criminological theories to white-collar crime.

Nevertheless, for both practical and theoretical reasons, white-collar crime is an important form of criminal behavior that neither criminologists nor society can afford to ignore. On the practical side, the economic costs of white-collar crime are generally assumed to dwarf those of ordinary street crime (Benson and Cullen 1998; Shover, Fox, and Mills 1994; Coleman 1989; Levi 1987). In addition, some forms of white-collar crime, such as manufacturing unsafe products, maintaining unsafe work environments, and polluting the environment, can have substantial harmful physical effects (Benson and Cullen 1998). Although it is difficult to put a precise figure on the extent of physical harm, it is not an exaggeration to say that thousands, perhaps hundreds of thousands, of consumers, workers, and members of the general public suffer annually from these offenses (Coleman 1994; Cullen, Maakestad, and Cavendar 1987; Brodeur 1985; Frank 1985; Reasons, Ross, and Paterson 1981). Finally, like street crime, white-collar crime has social costs. Social costs include the detrimental effects that crime may have on the mentality, emotions, and behavior of people generally. For example, a social cost of street crime is the fear of victimization that it may create in people who are not themselves directly victimized. White-collar crimes are thought to create a sense of distrust, to undermine public confidence in government and business, and perhaps to provide street criminals with rationalizations for their own crimes (Shover et al. 1994; Kramer 1984; Clinard and Yeager 1980; Conklin 1977; Edelhertz 1970). These are potentially important social costs of white-collar crime. Taken together, the economic, physical, and social costs of white-collar crime make it a public problem of the first magnitude.

White-collar crime also raises troubling theoretical issues for the life course perspective. These issues involve the relationship between age and crime, continuity in behavior, the importance of antisocial personality traits, and the influence of social context on behavior. Little is known about the age distribution of "respectable" offenders who commit business-related crimes. Yet, the data that are available indicate that most of the people who are convicted of white-collar crimes are substantially older than those convicted of typical street crimes (Weisburd, Waring, and Chayet 2001; Benson and Moore 1992; Weisburd, Chayet, and Waring 1990). An analysis of newspaper reports on persons convicted of lucrative business crimes in the late 1980s found that the modal age of the offender was between 40 and 50 (Steffensmeier and Allan 1993). White-collar offenders often commit their first officially recorded offense at an age when most street criminals have long since desisted from crime. They don't fit the pattern presumed by most theories in the life course perspective.

There are other discrepancies between white-collar crime and the life course perspective. With respect to juvenile delinquents and common street criminals, a major finding of the life course approach has been that there is often substantial continuity in their antisocial behavior over time. But a history of antisocial behavior does not appear to describe the behavioral trajectories of white-collar offenders. Street criminals are thought to have troublesome or confrontational personalities that make it difficult for them to fit in with society. Whether white-collar offenders have distinctive personalities is unknown. In addition, unlike so many street criminals, white-collar criminals do not appear to come from disadvantaged circumstances. The social context of their offending does not resemble that of street offenders. Thus, these important elements of the life course perspective must be considered anew in light of white-collar crime.

A final reason for considering white-collar crime is that these types of offenses may be on the rise (Weisburd, Wheeler, Waring, and Bode 1991). Over the past 50 years, changes in the American economy have greatly increased the number of white-collar jobs. As the American populace moved off the farm and into cities, the nature of work changed. Manual labor that took place outdoors or in factories was gradually replaced by office work. As men and women started working in white-collar occupations, they discovered abundant opportunities for white collar crime. A broader cross-section of the American population than ever before now has access to the tools of white-collar crime—pens, computers, and, most important, legitimate access to somebody else's money (Weisburd et al. 1991). The growth of modern state bureaucracies has placed enormous sums of money in the hands of ordinary middle-class people who would never have had access to it in the past (Weisburd et al. 2001). As state and federal government programs have increased in size and number, they have become targets for the commission of fraud both by those who administer the programs and by those who benefit from them.

Other broader changes in the functioning of American society have also contributed to the expansion of opportunities for white-collar crime. Increasingly, we must rely upon people with specialized knowledge and skills in all areas of daily life. Specialists fix our household appliances and our cars. They invest our money and handle our legal affairs. We have no choice but to trust these individuals. Who could master all of the complexities of modern electronic appliances, cars that run on computer chips, as well as the ups and downs of the stock market, and still have a life? Like it or not, trust is unavoidable in modern society. But with trust always comes the possibility of violations of trust. Experts may take advantage of us. Some argue that the most distinctive characteristic of white-collar crime is that it is a violation of trust (Shapiro 1990).

In this chapter, we explore these and other issues related to white-collar crime and the life course perspective. We begin with a discussion of some of the definitional complexities raised by the concept of white-collar crime and then pull together what little is known about the life histories and criminal trajectories of white-collar offenders. The empirical foundations of this chapter are much less well established than those of preceding chapters. Because we do not have at our disposal a host of carefully designed longitudinal studies of white-collar offending, we rely on original data analysis in some places.

The Concept of White-Collar Crime

Edwin Sutherland first coined the phrase "white-collar crime" (Sutherland 1940), and he is revered for his brilliantly original exposition of this form of crime. The distinguished British criminologist Herman Mannheim once suggested that if there were a Nobel prize in criminology, Sutherland would have won it for his work on white-collar crime (Mannheim 1965, 470). But despite the novelty of his choice of words, Sutherland was not the first to notice the form of criminality that has come to be known as white-collar crime. In 1908, E. A. Ross published a blistering attack on "criminaloids," the upper-class businessmen and robber barons of his day who stole with a pen rather than a gun (Ross 1977). A deeper look into the historical record reveals that from biblical times onward, what we today would call white-collar crime has been officially disapproved of and subject to legal sanctions in many societies (Geis 1988). Nevertheless, it is undeniably true that white-collar crime has never been a top priority issue for criminologists or political leaders. In all types of societies from monarchies to democracies, those in power have always used the law primarily to control and repress threats posed by the lower social classes. Before Sutherland, predatory business practices were not conceived of as criminological problems. So, his tireless efforts to reshape the way that criminologists thought about crime deserve high praise.

Sutherland used several different definitions of white-collar crime, but they all combined the characteristics of the individuals who committed the crimes with the nature of their criminal behavior. His most frequently cited formulation defines white-collar crime "approximately as crime committed by a person of respectability and high social status in the course of his occupation" (Sutherland 1949). From the start, Sutherland's definition provoked controversy, which has continued to the present day (Shapiro 1990; Hirschi and Gottfredson 1987; Tappan 1947).

The debate over the definition of white-collar crime has several interrelated dimensions. The first involves the nature of the actor. Should a distinction be made between offenses committed by individuals versus those committed by groups of individuals acting in concert for some type of organization? The second issue concerns whether we should include the social status of the offender as part of the definition of white-collar crime or rely solely on the nature of the behavior involved in the offense. Finally, there is the question of what should count as crime. Many white-collar offenses are treated as violations of regulations rather than criminal laws. Should we count regulatory violations as part of white-collar crime or reserve the term strictly for offenses prosecuted under criminal law?

Regarding the nature of the actor, the question is, should criminologists make a distinction between crimes committed by corporate entities versus those committed by individuals? Illegal acts committed through or for the benefit of a business entity or any formal complex organization are typically called "corporate" or "organizational" crimes (Clinard and Yeager 1980; Clinard and Quinney 1973). Antitrust violations, such as bid rigging and price-fixing, are classic examples of corporate crime (Simpson 1987). Corporate or organizational crime is often distinguished from "occupational" crime, which refers to illegal acts committed by an individual or group of individuals for personal gain. Embezzlement is the classic example. Organizational crime differs from occupational crime in that the offense of the former is committed with the support of and for the benefit of an organization rather than for the benefit of an individual.

Although criminologists often draw a sharp line between corporate and occupational crime, it makes more sense to think of the distinction in terms of a continuum based on the degree of overlap between individual and organizational interests (Coleman 1994; Wheeler and Rothman 1980). At one end of the continuum are offenses such as embezzlement, which are committed strictly for personal gain and without any support from the organization. At the other end are offenses committed solely to advance the interests of the organization, such as the illegal disposal of toxic waste. In between are offenses in which both personal and organizational motives are served. For example, in the case of consumer fraud by a small-business owner, the interests of the organization (the business) and the individual (the business owner) coincide closely. Even in very large organizations where it is often correct to think of offenses as primarily benefiting the organization, individuals may nonetheless reap personal benefits in the form of promotions or bonuses for their willingness to violate the law to further corporate interests (Wheeler and Rothman 1980).

Some criminologists have questioned whether it makes sense to think of corporations as actors in the same way that we think of individuals as actors (Cressey 1989). The distinguished criminologist Donald Cressey (1989) argues against treating corporations as criminal actors for the purposes of criminological theory. In his view, criminological theory should focus on real people, on individuals who think, decide, and act in organizations. Corporations do not act, but people do. Treating a corporation as though it were a person is misplaced anthropomorphism, and trying to explain corporate as opposed to individual behavior leads to conceptual confusion rather than clarity. According to Cressey, the distinction between corporate and occupational crime is unnecessary.

Other scholars disagree (Yeager and Reed 1998; Braithwaite and Fisse 1990). They contend that corporations do indeed act and that corporate actions are more than simply the sum of the acts of individual organizational members. John Braithwaite and Brent Fisse (1990) provide a persuasive illustration. They note that in a corporation, each member of a board of directors can vote to declare a dividend, but only the board as a collectivity has the power to declare a dividend. The collective action of the board is qualitatively different from the actions of the individuals that make up the board. The board's collective decision may result from processes such as "groupthink" or the group risky-shift phenomenon, which do not apply when individuals make decisions in isolation from one another (Janis 1972; Wallach, Kogan, and Bem 1964). Hence, it makes sense conceptually to treat corporations and other organizational entities as distinct objects of explanation.

With its focus on individuals, Cressey's position is more amenable to the life course perspective than is the position that corporate crime should be treated separately from the individuals who make up the corporation. Of course, this compatibility does not make Cressey's position correct (Geis 1995). Regardless of whether it makes ontological sense to think of corporations as actors, it is still the case that individuals within organizations commit criminal acts. Indeed, the organization must be recognized as an important causal element in shaping the behavior of the individuals who hold positions in it (Simpson, Paternoster, and Piquero 1998). Just as a neighborhood subculture may shape the criminal behavior of street offenders, organizational subcultures can shape the criminal behavior of organizational members (Braithwaite 1989b). Thus, it is appropriate to consider whether the life course perspective can help us understand criminal behavior in organizational settings and, vice versa, whether an examination of offending in organizations may illuminate life course theory.

A second issue in the debate over the definition of white-collar crime concerns the social characteristics of the actor. Should the characteristics of the actor be included in the definition, or is it better to define white-collar crime solely in terms of behavior? By including the social status of the perpetrator as part of his definition of white-collar crime, Sutherland is said to have confused explanation with definition (Shapiro 1990; Edelhertz 1970). If only people of high social status can commit white-collar crimes, then variation in social status cannot be used to explain white-collar crime. As far as Sutherland was concerned, this result was acceptable because he questioned whether variables such as social status or poverty were causes of crime (Sutherland 1940). His differential association theory focused on how actors come to define law-violating behavior as acceptable or unacceptable, as opposed to how their position in the social structure may drive them to crime.

Other white-collar crime scholars have rejected Sutherland's approach to defining white-collar crime. In its place, they have proposed definitions that focus on the nature of the behavior involved in white-collar crime (Shapiro 1990; Edelhertz 1970). Edelhertz (1970, 3), for example, proposes that white-collar crime be defined as "an illegal act or series of illegal acts committed by non-physical means and by concealment or guile, to obtain money or property, or to obtain business or personal advantage." Shapiro (1990) urges scholars to abandon white-collar crime altogether and to focus in its place on violations of trust. What is distinctive about these "offense-based" definitions of white-collar crime is that they make no mention of the social characteristics of offenders. Persons from all walks of life may violate trust or commit illegal acts of deception, such as fraud. Hence, social status and other offender characteristics can be treated as causal variables just as they are in investigations of those who commit street-crime offenses.

For researchers interested in applying life course theory to white-collar crime, offense-based definitions have several attractive features. As noted above, if offender characteristics are not included in the definition of white-collar crime, then these characteristics are free to vary. Researchers can investigate whether and how the social status of individuals, for example, influences the characteristics of the white-collar offenses they commit. Further, researchers can investigate how the social status of offenders influences official societal reactions to their crimes (Benson and Walker 1988; Wheeler, Weisburd, and Bode 1982; Hagan, Nagel-Bernstein, and Albonetti 1980). Freedom to explore connections between status and reactions to white-collar crime is particularly desirable for life course researchers. They can explore the collateral consequences that involvement in white-collar offending has on trajectories in other domains of life and investigate whether these consequences vary depending on the social status of the actor (Benson and Kerley 2000; Benson 1984).

Offense-based definitions also have methodological advantages over offender-based definitions. Offense-based definitions make it more feasible to gather data on large samples of offenders. This is difficult to do with offender-based definitions. Researchers can simply draw samples of persons arrested or convicted of particular types of offenses that are presumptively white-collar offenses. This strategy has been used in a number of important quantitative studies of white-collar offenders in the federal justice system (Weisburd et al. 1991; Benson and Walker 1988; Hagan et al. 1980).

Offense-based definitions are not without their drawbacks, however. Sampling offenses rather than offenders raises the likelihood that researchers will miss the most powerful white-collar offenders. These individuals are the ones most likely to avoid being arrested, tried, or convicted (Shapiro 1985; Mann 1985). They rarely appear in sampling frames based on official records. Further, offense-based definitions may lead researchers to include offenders and offenses that are clearly not white-collar in nature. For example, according to Edelhertz's definition of white-collar crime as a nonviolent property offense committed by means of concealment or guile, a wino who cons another wino out of his bottle could claim to be a white-collar criminal.

The final definitional issue to be addressed concerns what types of illegalities to include in studies of white-collar crime. Should the definition of white-collar crime be restricted only to acts punishable under criminal law, or should it include acts punishable under civil and administrative law (Cullen et al. 1987)? This issue arises mainly in regard to corporate or organizational crime, but it may also apply to acts by individual professionals such as doctors, lawyers, or stockbrokers. These and other professional occupations are subject to administrative sanctions by regulatory authorities. John Braithwaite has clearly articulated the arguments in favor of the broader definition:

> To exclude civil violations from consideration of corporate crime is an arbitrary obfuscation because of the frequent provision in the law for both civil and criminal prosecution of the same corporate conduct. In considerable measure, the power of corporations is manifested in the fact that their wrongs are so frequently punished only civilly. (Braithwaite 1982, 1466)

Braithwaite's point is not well taken by lawyers and businessmen. As they see it, including civil and administrative violations broadens the subject matter of white-collar crime beyond concern with strictly criminal behavior. This expansion strikes those who take a strictly legalistic view of crime as a conceptual mistake. Crime carries with it a degree of social stigma and moral condemnation that mere regulatory violations do not. Hence, legal scholars argue that it is a mistake to lump together convicted criminals with those who have been merely sanctioned administratively. Not surprisingly, businesspersons agree with legal scholars on this point. They think that offenses that are not prosecuted criminally cannot be placed in the same category as those that are (Orland 1980; Tappan 1947).

The idea of conceiving the subject matter of criminology so as to include behavior that may not be legally defined as criminal is not unique to white-collar crime scholars. Researchers working within the life course perspective occasionally define their subject matter as "antisocial behavior," rather than criminal acts, under the assumption that crime is only one manifestation of a general behavioral style that includes deviant, aggressive, or otherwise untoward behavior. Sometimes this approach is taken because the research subjects are very young children who are not legally capable of committing criminal offenses. But it may also be used in the study of teenagers and adults. Similarly, though they are generally antithetical to many aspects of the life course approach, Gottfredson and Hirschi (1990, 10) argue that crime, deviant behavior, sin, and even accidents share "common elements" to such a degree that it is a mistake to think of them as distinct phenomena. They suggest that crime should be defined generically "as acts of force or fraud undertaken in pursuit of self-interest" (1990, 15). Note that their definition makes no mention of criminal law, nor does it require that the acts in question be potentially subject to criminal law. Thus, white-collar crime scholars are not alone among criminologists in including within their domain of study acts and behaviors that may not be legally defined as crimes.

Applying the Life Course Approach to White-Collar Offenders

Applying the life course perspective to white-collar crime is difficult because of the paucity of longitudinal data on white-collar offenders. There are no prospective longitudinal studies that include information on white-collar type offenses. Until recently, most of what was known about the social characteristics and social backgrounds of the people who commit white-collar offenses came from case studies of individuals or corporations that were selected primarily because of their high social status or because they had committed particularly egregious offenses. Following Sutherland's original definition of white-collar crime, many researchers have investigated cases involving high-status individuals, such as corporate executives, professionals, and high-ranking public officials (Ermann and Lundman 1992; Hills 1987; Cullen et al. 1987; Hochstedler 1984). These individuals, of course, look nothing like traditional street criminals. They occupy positions of power and influence. They have families and are financially stable. Some are active in civic affairs and known as "pillars of the community." Indeed, part of the reason the offenses appear so shocking and interesting is that the perpetrators do not come from disadvantaged backgrounds and do not have histories of run-ins with the law. At first glance, their offenses seem completely out of character and not part of a pattern of deviant behavior. This image of white-collar offenders is widespread among the general public and law-enforcement officials (Wheeler, Mann, and Sarat 1988; Benson 1985b). It suggests that the life course trajectories of white-collar criminals differ from those of common criminals along almost all relevant dimensions, such as occupation, education, family background, and, of course, criminality.

That there are such high-status offenders cannot be denied. There is no shortage of case studies that document their existence. Nevertheless, it is important to keep in mind that these cases were selected for study precisely because they were unusual and precisely because they fit preexisting conceptions about the high social status of white-collar offenders. Do they present a misleading picture of the average white-collar offender? Evidence that not all those who commit business-related offenses occupy positions of high social status has been around for some time (Spencer 1965; Cressey 1953). For example, some of the subjects in Cressey's (1953) classic study of embezzlement were low-level clerks or cash register attendants and not corporate executives. More recent evidence suggests that contemporary white-collar criminals are often not economic elites.

Beginning in the 1980s, several studies called into question the classic stereotype of the white-collar offender (Weisburd et al. 1991; Croall 1989; Daly 1989). These studies were based on relatively large samples of individuals convicted in U.S. federal courts of presumptively white-collar offenses (Benson and Kerley 2000; Benson and Moore 1992; Weisburd et al. 1991). A very important study, *Crimes of the Middle Classes*, by David Weisburd, Stanton Wheeler, Elin Waring, and Nancy Bode, was based on a sample of 1,094 persons convicted between 1976 and 1978 in U.S. federal courts of eight selected offenses: bank embezzlement, tax fraud, credit fraud, mail fraud, securities fraud, false claims, bribery, and antitrust activity (Weisburd et al. 1991). These offenses were called the criterion offenses. For comparative purposes, the researchers also collected data on a sample 204 persons convicted of non-white-collar criterion offenses.

This data set is one of very few that include a large random sample of offenders and that contain information on the social-class backgrounds of offenders as well as information on their criminal histories. David Weisburd and Elin Waring have recently extended the original study by gathering data on the original sample's criminal activities for over ten years following their convictions in federal court (Weisburd et al. 2001).

At about the same time, Brian Forst and William Rhodes put together another data set similar to the one collected by Wheeler et al. (1988). The Forst and Rhodes study sampled persons convicted of ten offenses tried in U.S. federal courts between 1973 and 1978. Of the 10 criterion offenses, six were white-collar crimes: bank embezzlement, bribery, false claims and statements, income-tax violations, mail fraud, and postal embezzlement. The four remaining offenses, which represent common crimes, include bank robbery, homicide, narcotics offenses, and postal forgery. The sample included 2,643 individuals sentenced for the six white-collar crimes and 2,512 individuals sentenced for the four common crimes.

Both Wheeler and colleagues and Forst and Rhodes gathered data primarily from the Pre-sentence Investigation Report (PSI). PSIs are prepared by federal probation officers for judges. They describe the offense of conviction and provide detailed information on the defendant's educational, medical, employment, family, and criminal history (Weisburd et al. 1991, 14). In a sense, the PSI is like a retrospective life history, with the probation officer serving as the interviewer. In preparing PSIs, probation officers attempt to give judges a sense of who offenders are, where they came from, and what brought them before the court. Because judges regard evidence of prior criminal activity as an extremely important factor in sentencing, information on the nature and timing of prior arrests and convictions is usually quite detailed in the PSI. Although PSIs contain a wealth of social information, they are administrative documents produced to satisfy administrative needs. As Weisburd and colleagues (1991, 15) note, PSIs are "filtered through the eyes of probation officers and may be subject to whatever biases they may bring to their work."

The Wheeler et al. and Forst and Rhodes data sets are the only two data sets I am aware of that contain personal and social information on large samples of white-collar offenders. Although they can be used to address issues relevant to the life course perspective, they have a number of shortcomings that make them less than ideal for such an endeavor. Neither data set was assembled with the life course perspective in mind. The researchers were primarily interested in the treatment of white-collar offenders in the criminal justice system. Information was gathered on the social backgrounds of offenders primarily so that the researchers could investigate whether and how the social and class characteristics of offenders influence their treatment in the justice system (Weisburd et al. 1991, 13). Both data sets contain very detailed information on how the cases were processed in the courts and on the seriousness and mechanics of the offenses. Personal information on the offenders' occupations and families at the time they committed the offenses—that is, as adults—is also relatively comprehensive. Information on the early childhood and adolescent histories of the offenders, however, is much skimpier.

In addition to the shortcoming of relying primarily on the PSI as a data source, both studies have other weaknesses. The sampling frames draw from populations of convicted offenders. Thus, the studies can tell us only about white-collar offenders unfortunate or inept enough to get arrested and convicted. We can learn nothing about offenders who were clever, lucky, or powerful enough to avoid detection in the first place (Weisburd et al. 1991, 19). Because of their sampling designs, only persons who committed particular white-collar crimes are included in the sample. Other federal white-collar crimes could have been included, and doing so might have provided a different picture of offenders (Weisburd et al. 1991, 18). Finally, data on individuals who violated civil or administrative law are lacking.

Despite these shortcomings, both data sets provide a unique opportunity to further our understanding of white-collar offenders and their criminal careers. They paint a picture of the white-collar offender that does not correspond with the image presented in most case studies. Rather than being high-powered corporate executives, professionals, or politicians, the vast majority of those who violate white-collar statutes are middle-class individuals. Their offenses tend not to be ingeniously complex but rather straightforward and simple. Surprisingly, as we will see, many of the persons convicted in U.S. federal courts of violating white-collar crime statutes have prior criminal records (Weisburd et al. 2001; Benson and Moore 1992; Weisburd et al. 1990; Benson and Walker 1988).

In the following sections, we analyze the Wheeler et al. and Forst and Rhodes data sets to learn more about the social locations, criminal careers, and backgrounds of white-collar offenders. We begin by examining the social location of the white-collar and common offenders at the time of their convictions in federal court. By social location, we mean where the offenders stand in the social structure of American society. The indicators of standing include demographic characteristics and the standard markers of social status: employment and educational attainment. In addition, we explore marital status, homeownership, financial assets, and community involvement. Our goal in this section is to get a sense of who the white-collar criminal is (Croall 1989) and to see how white-collar criminals differ from common criminals.

After we have learned a little about who the white-collar offenders are, the next step is to look back into their lives to see if we can discern traces of the trajectories that brought them into U.S. federal court. As noted above, PSIs have their limits as retrospective life histories. Nevertheless, we can examine the offenders' criminal careers. Some data are also available on family background and performance in high school. By comparing the white-collar and common offenders, we hope to get a sense of how their life courses may have differed.

The Social Locations of White-Collar and Common Offenders

Table 5.1 presents information on the demographic characteristics, employment history, and educational attainment of the individuals in the Wheeler et al. and Forst and Rhodes data sets. For comparative purposes, information is also included on sample members who were convicted of common crimes.

Beginning with demographic characteristics, in both data sets the white-collar offenders are overwhelmingly males. They constitute 85.5 percent of the Wheeler et al. white-collar sample and 77.6 percent of the Forst and Rhodes sample. The common offenders are also disproportionately male. In both samples, dramatic differences are observed between white-collar and common offenders in race and age. Over 80 percent of Wheeler et al. white-collar offenders are white, compared to only 34.3 percent of common offenders. In the Forst and Rhodes sample, the comparable figures are 73.9 and 49 percent white for the white-collar and common criminals, respectively. The age differentials between white-collar and common criminals are nearly identical in both samples. On average, the white-collar criminals are ten years older than the common criminals. If you invited the more than 3,500 white-collar criminals represented in both studies to a party, the middle-aged white males would be the least likely to feel out of place.

Table 5.1
Demographic, Employment, and Education Characteristics of White-Collar and Common Criminals

	Wheeler et al.[1]		Forst and Rhodes	
	Common Criminals	White-Collar Criminals	Common Criminals	White-Collar Criminals
Demographic Characteristics				
Sex (Male)	68.6%	85.5%	84.2%	77.6%
Race (White)	34.3%	81.7%	49.0%	73.9%
Age (Mean Age)	30	40	30	41
Education				
High-School Graduates	45.5%	79.3%	45.7%	71.2%
College Graduates	3.9%	27.1%	3.3%	17.0%
Employment				
Unemployed	56.7%	5.7%	59.1%	30.2%
Steadily Employed[2]	12.7%	58.4%	24.1%	65.8%

[1]Adapted with permission from Tables III and IV from Wheeler, Stanton, David Weisburd, Elin Waring, and Nancy Bode, 1988, "White Collar Crime and Criminals," *American Criminal Law Review*, 25:331–57.

[2]In the Wheeler et al. study the reference period for steady employment is five years. In the Forst and Rhodes study, the reference period is two years.

The standard image of the white-collar offender pictures him as a "him" and as a person of power and accomplishment, a member of the upper social classes. The data on education presented in Table 5.1 suggest that this image is misleading. Just over one-quarter of the Wheeler et al. white-collar sample and less than one-fifth of the Forst and Rhodes sample are college graduates. Thus, in these two samples a sizable majority of the white-collar criminals were not college graduates. Although they are much better educated than common criminals, most of the white-collar criminal samples lack one of the standard markers of high social status that Sutherland and other white-collar scholars often refer to as distinguishing white-collar criminals (Wheeler, Weisburd, Waring, and Bode 1988, 360).

Not surprisingly, the white-collar offenders were much more likely to be employed at the time that they committed the criterion offense than the common offenders. Yet, the data on employment also suggest that many white-collar offenders are not entrenched in the occupational mainstream. At the time of the criterion offense, over 90 percent of the Wheeler et al. white-collar criminals were employed. In the Forst and Rhodes sample, about 70 percent were employed. The high rate of employment results in part from having to hold an occupational position in order to commit certain types of white-collar crimes. In stark contrast, a majority of common criminals in both data sets were unemployed at the time of their offense, and most had not been steadily employed prior to conviction. These results clearly indicate differences in employment between common and white-collar offenders. However, these dramatic differences should not blind us to the fact that steady employment does not characterize the employment history of a substantial proportion of white-collar offenders. In the Wheeler et al. data set, over 40 percent of the white-collar offenders did not have uninterrupted employment during the five years preceding their conviction. In the Forst and Rhodes study, a two-year reference period was used, but the results are very similar. Nearly 35 percent of the white-collar offenders were not steadily employed for two years prior to their conviction. These results suggest that a notable proportion of the white-collar offender population "cannot depend on steady and stable employment at the time of their crimes" (Wheeler et al. 1988, 340).

Besides education and employment, there are other markers indicating where an individual stands in the structure of American society. For adults, marital status, homeownership, and the accumulation of financial assets can be thought of as indicators of whether an adult is conforming to society's age-graded expectations. Adults are supposed to settle down, get married, buy homes, and begin to accumulate a nest egg of financial savings. White-collar criminals are much more likely to conform to these expectations than common criminals (see Table 5-2). In the Forst and Rhodes data set, over 60 percent of the white-collar criminals were married at the time of their conviction, versus less than 30 percent of the common offenders. A similar rate of marriage is observed in the Wheeler et al. white-collar sample

(58 percent). About half (50.3 percent) of the Forst and Rhodes white-collar criminals owned homes, and so did 45.3 percent of the Wheeler et al. sample, but only 11.8 and 6.6 percent of the common criminals in the two samples owned homes. Finally, at the time of conviction, just over one-third of the Forst and Rhodes white-collar criminals had financial assets in excess of $10,000. Less than 5 percent of the common offenders were similarly well-off financially (Benson and Kerley 2000). The Wheeler et al. white-collar criminals were also much better off financially than the common criminals. The median for financial assets for white-collar criminals is $11,000 versus $180 for common criminals.

Table 5.2
Adult Integration Into Society for Common and White-Collar Criminals

	Wheeler et al.[1]		Forst and Rhodes	
	Common Criminals	White-Collar Criminals	Common Criminals	White-Collar Criminals
Married	——	58%	28.2%	61.9%
Own Home	6.6%	45.3%	11.8%	50.3%
Financial Assets Greater Than $10,000	——	——	4.5%	35.3%
Median Assets	$180	$11,000	——	——

[1]Adapted with permission from Table 3.3 in Weisburd, David, Stanton Wheeler, Elin Waring, and Nancy Bode, 1991, *Crimes of the Middle Classes: White-Collar Offenders in the Federal Courts*, p. 63. New Haven, CT: Yale University Press.

When a white-collar criminal appears at sentencing, it is not unusual for his or her lawyer to ask for a reduced sentence because the client is supposedly an upstanding citizen who has made a substantial contribution to the community (Mann, Wheeler, and Sarat 1980). A defense attorney, of course, has a professional obligation to put his or her client in the best possible light. But is it really true that the average white-collar criminal is a pillar of the community? The data presented in Table 5.3 suggest that defense attorneys may be stretching the truth in many cases. In the Forst and Rhodes white-collar sample, the PSIs indicated that under 20 percent of the white-collar criminals were involved in social or other community groups and barely over 10 percent were involved in church or other religious activities. White-collar criminals are twice as likely to attend church regularly as common criminals, 31.3 to 15.8 percent respectively. Yet, nearly seven out of 10 white-collar criminals apparently have other things to do on Sunday mornings. At least they are not hanging out with other criminals. Only 8.4 percent of the white-collar criminals were judged to have criminal friends, compared to 36.2 percent of the common criminals.

Table 5.3

Community Activities and Criminal Friends for Common and White-Collar Criminals

	Common Criminals	White-Collar Criminals
Involved in Community Groups	4.7%	18.7%
Involved in Church	3.3%	11.8%
Attend Church Regularly	15.8%	31.3%
Criminal Friends	36.2%	8.4%

Note: Data are from the Forst and Rhodes sample.

Although white-collar offenders lead more conventional lives than common offenders, it is misleading to describe them as highly integrated into community life. Over 80 percent of white-collar offenders are *not* involved in community groups. Nearly 90 percent are *not* involved in church-related activities, and about 70 percent do not attend church regularly. Nor can it be safely assumed that all white-collar criminals have high social status. Most are not college educated, and well over a third lack steady employment. Taken together, these results indicate that many of the people who violate what are often thought of as white-collar statutes are not pillars of the community. Rather, they appear to be quite ordinary people leading middle-class lives.

Although the evidence reviewed above modifies our image of the typical white-collar offender, it certainly does not indicate that white-collar and common criminals are the same. White-collar offenders may not always come from the privileged sectors of society, but neither do they share social space with common criminals. White-collar offenders occupy distinctly different places in the American social structure than common offenders. Based on their analyses, Weisburd et al. concluded that

> . . . [W]hatever else may be true of the distinction between white-collar and common criminals, the two are definitely drawn from distinctively different sectors of the American population. While there is substantial diversity in the types of people that are found in white-

collar crime, even the lowest end of our offender hierarchy is easily distinguished from offenders in common-crime categories. . . (White-collar offenders) appear to represent the very broad middle of society. (1991, 73)

The life course perspective prompts us to ask how they arrived at these different locations. What social and criminal trajectories did they follow? We turn to these questions now, beginning with trajectories in crime.

White-Collar Criminal Careers

The term "white-collar criminal career" seems like an oxymoron. The white-collar criminal is generally thought to be a "one-shot" offender, whose first encounter with the criminal justice system is his or her last (Weisburd et al. 1990). To make a career out of crime involves a commitment to deviance and nonconformity that is assumed to be the antithesis of the white-collar criminal's lifestyle.

Contrary to the popular image of the white-collar criminal as a person who has never done anything wrong, a substantial proportion of the white-collar criminals in the Wheeler et al. and Forst and Rhodes data sets have prior criminal records. As Table 5.4 shows, in both samples approximately four out of ten offenders have a prior arrest. One-third of the sample members have prior convictions. Nevertheless, as a group the white-collar offenders appear to be much less involved in crime than common criminals. Over 80 percent of the common criminals in both samples have prior arrests.

Table 5.4
Prior Arrests and Convictions for Common and White-Collar Criminals

	Wheeler et al.[1]		Forst and Rhodes	
	Common Criminals	White-Collar Criminals	Common Criminals	White-Collar Criminals
Prior Arrests	89.5%	43.4%	81.8%	39.3%
Four or More Prior Arrests	—	12.0%	51.0%	15.4%
Prior Convictions	81.4%	35.4%	73.9%	31.3%

[1]Adapted with permission from Table 3.3 in Weisburd, David, Stanton Wheeler, Elin Waring, and Nancy Bode, 1991, *Crimes of the Middle Classes: White-Collar Offenders in the Federal Courts*, New Haven, CT: Yale University Press; adapted from Table 2 in Weisburd, David, Ellen F. Chayet,and Elin Waring, *Crime and Delinquency*, 36(3):342–55. Copyright © 1990 by Sage Publications. Reprinted by permission of Sage Publications.

Deciding what it takes to qualify as a "career criminal" is a matter of judgment. Different cutoff points can be used. The passage of "three strikes and you're out" laws suggests that for society in general the threshold number is three. Lawmakers apparently assume that individuals with three convictions have demonstrated that they are not just fooling around when it comes to crime, but rather are seriously committed to troublemaking. Several studies on persistence in criminal careers indicate that a reasonable cutoff point to use to identify serious offenders is four arrests or convictions. Analyses of the Philadelphia cohort data, West and Farrington's Cambridge data, and Shannon's Racine cohort data indicate that the probability that a first offender will be rearrested or reconvicted ranges from 0.5 to 0.6. This probability increases after each subsequent event. Up to a point, the more arrests or convictions a person has, the more likely he or she is to persist in crime and to be rearrested or reconvicted again. This "persistence probability" reaches a plateau of between 0.7 and 0.9 following the fourth event (Blumstein, Cohen, Roth, and Visher 1986, 89). So, the chances that someone who has been arrested four times will be rearrested for a fifth time is high. If we use four arrests as the cutoff point, 12 percent of the white-collar criminals in the Wheeler et al. sample and 15.4 percent in the Forst and Rhodes sample qualify as career criminals.

As we learned earlier, many white-collar offenders are not persons of high social status. This finding raises an important question about the repeat offenders in our white-collar crime samples, and it illustrates how definitions may change results. Would our results on prior criminal activity have been different if we had defined white-collar crimes in Sutherland's terms as crimes committed by persons of high social status? Perhaps recidivism occurs only among low status white-collar criminals.

David Weisburd and his colleagues (1990) explored this question in the Wheeler et al. data. They analyzed the criminal histories of a "selected group of offenders who held elite positions or owned significant assets, and who committed their crimes in the course of a legitimate occupation" (Weisburd, Chayet, and Waring 1990, 347). (Unfortunately, the Forst and Rhodes data set does not contain information that would permit similar analyses.) Using this definition, they were left with only about one-third of their original sample. With this more restrictive definition of white-collar crime, a smaller proportion of offenders had prior criminal records. It would not be correct, however, to say that all of these high-status offenders had led saintly lives.

Over one-quarter of the high-status offenders had criminal records. Ten percent of the restricted sample of offenders had prior felony convictions. Thus, even elite white-collar offenders may have criminal careers.

Having established that many white-collar criminals are repeat offenders, it becomes important to determine how their criminal careers resemble or differ from those of common criminals. The important dimensions of career offending are age of onset, desistance, and specialization (Blumstein et al. 1986). Recall that in earlier chapters we learned that most offenders are arrested for the first time in their mid-teenage years and have desisted by the mid-twenties, and most offenders do not specialize in any one type of crime. Are these patterns evident among white-collar offenders?

With respect to age of onset of offending, white-collar offenders do not follow the standard pattern. In the Wheeler et al. data, the mean age of onset for the entire sample of white-collar criminals is 35 (see Table 5.5). In the Forst and Rhodes data set, the mean age for the white-collar sample is 41, and it is 30 for the common criminals. If we consider only criminals with prior arrests, the mean age of onset declines to 27 for the Forst and Rhodes white-collar criminals and to 24 for the Wheeler et al. white-collar criminals. The common criminals with prior records in the Forst and Rhodes sample have a mean age of first arrest of 20. For the 60 percent of white-collar criminals whose first offense was the criterion offense, the average age was 41. As measured by arrests, most white-collar offenders truly are "late starters."

Table 5.5

Age of Onset for Common and White-Collar Criminals

	Wheeler et al.[1]		Forst and Rhodes	
	Common Criminals	White-Collar Criminals	Common Criminals	White-Collar Criminals
Onset Age First-Time Offenders	—	35	30	41
Onset Age Repeat Offenders	—	24[2]	20	27

[1]Adapted from Table 4 in Weisburd, David, Ellen F. Chayet, and Elin Waring, *Crime and Delinquency*, 36(3):350. Copyright © 1990 by Sage Publications. Reprinted by permission of Sage Publications.

[2]Based on offenders with three or more arrests.

If white-collar offenders are often late starters, are they also late stoppers? When and how does desistance take place in white-collar criminal careers? What little is known about desistance in white-collar crime comes from a recent study by Weisburd, Waring, and Chayet (2001). They took the original Wheeler et al. data set and supplemented it by adding data from the "rap sheets" that the FBI keeps on all offenders. Weisburd and Waring recorded information about all arrests for ten years after the date of the offenders' original criterion offense.

We must use caution in drawing conclusions about white-collar criminals and desistance from the Weisburd and Waring study. As they note, questions about desistance are always difficult to answer with certainty. We can never be sure, except in the case of death, that the last crime we have observed is the last one an offender will ever commit. This is the problem of censoring. After the data-collection period ends, our view of offenders and their activities is censored. However, compared to recidivism studies, in general, the ten-year follow-up period in this study is relatively long. It seems safe to assume that offenders who have not been rearrested for 10 years really have desisted.

What we learn from Weisburd and Waring about desistance is that white-collar offenders do not follow the patterns typical among street criminals. Street criminals usually "age out" of offending by the time they reach their thirties. In the Weisburd and Waring sample, however, the average age of desistance for white-collar offenders who had any arrests after the criterion offense is 43. Close to half (47 percent) of the white-collar offenders who reached the age of 50 by the end of the study had been arrested after age 50. With a longer follow-up period, the percentage of new arrests would go up (Weisburd and Waring 2001, 37). Ten percent of the offenders who made it to age 70 had arrests in their eighth decade of life. Overall, compared to common crime samples, a larger proportion of white-collar offenders appear to continue offending late in the life course (Weisburd and Waring 2001, 38).

The causes of desistance from white-collar crime probably are not the same as those for desistance from street crime. Street offenders may quit some types of crimes simply because as they get older they do not have the energy and agility to carry out certain offenses, such as robbery and burglary, anymore. In a sense, their opportunities to offend decline with age. This explanation does not seem to fit in the case of white-collar crime because the offenses are not physically demanding and because opportunities for white-collar crime may actually increase with age. As offenders grow older, they may move into more trusted occupational positions and hence have more opportunities to take advantage of their employers or others.

Another explanation often given for desistance from crime involves changes in informal social control. Street offenders appear to be most likely to desist when they establish strong informal social bonds to family or work. But white-collar offenders are much more likely to already have these bonds when they commit their offenses. So, it seems unlikely that an increase in informal social control contributes to desistance from white-collar crime.

Weisburd and Waring (2001, 41) speculate that the most likely cause of desistance from white-collar crime may be the cognitive changes associated with aging. As they reach and pass middle age, white-collar offenders, like other offenders, may come to the realization that time is passing them by and that they don't want to risk wasting any more of their remaining time in trouble with the law. The hard-driving executives who are willing to do anything for company and career may have a change of heart as they enter their fifties. Even the relatively small risk of incarceration that goes with white-collar crime may strike older offenders as an unacceptably high risk to take.

Criminal career researchers have devoted considerable attention to the matter of specialization in offending. Specialization exists when offenders commit the same type of crime repeatedly, whereas versatility means that offenders commit a wide variety of different types of offenses. Most research on specialization finds little evidence for it (Farrington, Snyder, and Finnegan 1988; Kempf 1987; Wolfgang, Figlio, and Sellin 1972). Most offenders appear to exhibit considerable versatility in their offenses (Gottfredson and Hirschi 1990). Indeed, Gottfredson and Hirschi (1990, 91) consider the evidence against specialization to be overwhelming.

Although the evidence against specialization in the careers of ordinary street offenders is strong, white-collar offenders may be different. Unlike many common crimes, white-collar crimes often require that one have special skills or hold a particular occupational position in order to commit the offense. It takes effort and persistence to learn how to commit some white-collar crimes or to secure the occupational niche necessary for the offense. White-collar offenders may have to invest more time and effort in their offenses than do common criminals. Hence, they have more motivation to capitalize on this investment by specializing in particular offenses than common offenders.

In support of this line of reasoning, in one of the few studies to compare white-collar and common offenders, Benson and Moore (1992) found evidence for greater specialization among white-collar offenders. In the Wheeler et al. data, over one-third of the white-collar criminals with prior arrests had at least one other arrest for a white-collar crime (Weisburd et al. 1990). As indicated in Table 5.6, in the Forst and Rhodes sample of white-collar criminals, 28 percent of the repeat offenders had at least one prior arrest for a white-collar crime

With the Forst and Rhodes data, it is possible to track offending patterns relatively closely. Using prior arrests, we can identify three types of criminal career patterns: "one-time offenders," "generalists," and "white-collar specialists." One-time offenders are those who have no other arrests besides the one for the criterion offense that brought them into federal court. They make up 61 percent of the sample. Generalists make up 32.3 percent of the sample. These are individuals who have prior arrests that are primarily for non-white-collar offenses (see Table 5.6).

Deciding where to draw the line between generalists and white-collar specialists is an arbitrary undertaking. Clearly, someone whose arrest record contains a smorgasbord of offenses ranging from check kiting to illegal drugs to spousal abuse is a generalist. Equally clearly, someone who has been repeatedly arrested for stock fraud can be considered a specialist. But what about someone whose arrest record consists mainly but not exclusively of white-collar offenses? For example, should a person who has three arrests for securities fraud and one for drunk driving be considered a specialist in white-collar crime or a generalist? There is no consensus on this point.

If we say that at least half of a person's arrests must be for white-collar offenses before we can call him or her a specialist, then relatively few offenders specialize in white-collar crime. In Table 5.6, the persons categorized as specialists are those who have prior arrests in addition to the criterion offense, with at least half of their total number of arrests being for white-collar offenses. Prior arrests for embezzlement, fraud, corporate crime, and "other white-collar offenses" were classified as white-collar offenses. By these criteria, white-collar crime specialists constitute only 7 percent of the sample. Weisburd, Waring, and Chayet (2001) also found some evidence of specialization in their reanalysis of the Wheeler et al. data, but not a lot. Their analyses suggest that the likelihood of specialization depends on the type of white-collar offense. Persons whose criterion offense was securities fraud appeared to be most likely of all the white-collar offenders to specialize exclusively in white-collar crime (Weisburd and Waring 2001, 47). Overall, both the Wheeler et al. and the Forst and Rhodes data indicate that it is not unusual for white-collar criminals to have prior experience with white-collar type crimes, but it is also not unusual for them to have prior experience with other types of crime, too.

Table 5.6
Specialization Among White-Collar Criminals

	Percent
Wheeler et al. Data	
Chronic Offenders With Prior Arrests for White-Collar Crime[1]	34.0
Forst and Rhodes Data	
White-Collar Criminals With Prior Arrests for White-Collar Crime	28.0
Types of Offenders	
One-Time Offenders	61.0
White-Collar Specialists	7.0
Generalists	32.3

[1]Adapted from Table 5 in Weisburd, David, Ellen F. Chayet, and Elin Waring, *Crime and Delinquency*, 36(3):342–55. Copyright © 1990 by Sage Publications. Reprinted by permission of Sage Publications.

The results on the prior criminal records of white-collar offenders mirror what we learned about their social characteristics. They both coincide with and diverge from the popular image of the white-collar offender. They agree with the popular image in that as a group the white-collar offenders clearly are much less criminal than the common street crime offenders. Yet, they diverge from the popular image of the white-collar offender as a one-shot offender, someone who has only made one mistake in life. Once again, white-collar offenders appear to be not exactly what we expected.

Family Background and Educational Trajectories

Thus far, we have learned that in adulthood white-collar criminals occupy distinctly different social locations in American society than street criminals, and they have distinctly different criminal trajectories. To what extent do these social and criminal differences stem from earlier experiences in the life course? In other words, do white-collar and common criminals end up in different places as adults because they started out in different places as children?

Life course researchers have devoted considerable attention to the effects of family background and early childhood socialization on later criminality. Early childhood socialization experiences are considered crucial either for preventing or for failing to prevent later deviance and criminality. However, there has been "no significant effort to link white-collar crime to family background or abnormalities in early socialization" (Coleman 1987).

The Forst and Rhodes data set has four measures of family background that provide a glimpse of the early years of white-collar criminals. These measures tell us if the defendant "was raised in a family environment," "had family members with a criminal record," "was an abused, neglected or abandoned child," and if the "parents or guardians had difficulty providing the necessities of life." Because we have the same data on the sample of common criminals, we can explore whether the individuals in the two samples began life in the same or different kinds of family environments.

Table 5.7
Family Background and School Performance for White-Collar and Common Criminals

	Common Criminals	White-Collar Criminals
Family Background		
Raised in a Family Environment	96.0%	95.9%
Abused or Neglected as a Child	17.9%	6.3%
Raised in Poverty	24.6%	15.3%
Criminal Family Members	18.6%	6.2%
School Performance		
Poor Academic Performance	52.4%	25.0%
Poor Social Adjustment	44.8%	20.9%

Note: Data are from the Forst and Rhodes sample.

As Table 5.7 shows, the vast majority of white-collar and common criminals begin life in some type of family environment, but this environment is much more likely to be a troubled one for common criminals. Just under one-quarter of the common criminals (24.6 percent) come from poverty-stricken families in which the parents had diffi-culty providing the necessities of life. In contrast, only 15.3 percent of white-collar criminals come from deprived backgrounds. Common criminals are almost three times as likely to have been abused or neglected as children than white-collar criminals (17.9 to 6.3 percent, respectively). They are also three times as likely to come from families with criminal members. White-collar and common criminals are likely to begin life in different places.

The statistical gap between white-collar and common offenders widens in school. Indeed, by the time they are in school, the two groups can be clearly distinguished. Two measures in the data set rate the defendant's "overall academic performance in school" and "over-all social adjustment in school." Table 5.7 shows that about half of all common offenders had below-average or poor academic perfor-mance and social adjustment in school, while only a quarter of white-collar offenders had the same problems. By the time they are in school, half of the common criminals already appear to be following trajectories slanting toward trouble and difficulty. In contrast, the per-centage of white-collar offenders with below-average academic per-formance or social adjustment in school is much smaller.

Conviction as an Event in the Life Course of White-Collar Offenders

In earlier chapters, we learned that involvement in crime and delinquency often has collateral consequences, particularly when offenders become entangled with the criminal justice system. John Hagan and Alberto Palloni (1988) have argued that we should think of crime as an event in the life course that has ripple effects through-out offenders' lives. For common criminals, the most detrimental col-lateral consequences involve educational failures that reduce occupational opportunities.

Because white-collar offenders start their criminal careers at much later ages than common offenders, the collateral consequences of crime are different for them. For juvenile delinquents, involvement in crime and the criminal justice system may prevent or delay them from making certain age-graded transitions in education and employment on time. Failure to make these transitions on time has detrimental consequences in the form of cumulating disadvantages. It "knifes off" future occupational opportunities and leads to a reduced standard of living (Moffitt 1993; Sampson and Laub 1990). White-collar offenders, however, tend to be much older when they first become entangled with the criminal justice system. By the time they are first arrested and convicted, most have already finished school and have well-established occupational trajectories. For white-collar criminals, involvement in the justice system does not knife off future opportunities as severely as it seems to do for street criminals. Unlike juvenile delinquents, white-collar criminals already have acquired human capital and a comfortable standard of living before they become ensnared in the justice system.

There are few studies that investigate the collateral consequences of involvement in white-collar crime. Those that are available suggest that the severity of the consequences of exposure as a white-collar criminal depend on the class status and occupational position of the offender. For example, Benson (1984) investigated loss of socioeconomic status (SES) among a small sample of individuals convicted of white-collar crimes in a U.S. federal court. He compared the offenders' SES at the time of the offense, at the time of conviction, and at times after conviction. The results indicated that loss of SES is not spread evenly among the white-collar criminal population. Professionals, such as doctors and lawyers, and individuals employed in the public sector or in licensed occupations are much more likely to lose SES than private businessmen or those employed by private businesses (Benson 1984). As the time from the point of conviction lengthened, however, nearly all of the white-collar criminals eventually regained their former level of SES.

Although one might assume that the more serious the crime you commit, the more likely you are to suffer negative labeling and collateral consequences, this does not appear to be the case for white-collar criminals. Indeed, the more serious the white-collar crime, the less likely the offender is to lose his or her job after being caught (Benson 1989). For some white-collar criminals, their class positions seem to protect them from collateral consequences, such as job loss. Individuals who hold managerial or employer positions are less likely to lose their jobs than are workers (Benson 1989). For example, analyses of the Wheeler et al. data revealed that among the offenders in the sample, those who committed antitrust and securities fraud offenses were most likely to be owners or officers of companies. These offenders also committed the most serious offenses with respect to the number of persons victimized and the amount of money lost during the offense. The typical bank embezzler, on the other hand, is an employee who commits a less serious offense. Yet, antitrust and securities fraud offenders were much less likely to lose their jobs after their offenses were discovered than bank embezzlers (Weisburd et al. 1991). Less than 5 percent of the antitrust offenders and less than 15 percent of the securities fraud offenders were fired or left their jobs after the offense was discovered. Far fewer bank embezzlers escaped so unscathed; over three-quarters (76.8 percent) of the bank embezzlers lost their jobs after their offenses came to light.

Considered in light of the evidence reviewed in earlier chapters, these investigations of white-collar criminality suggest that position in the class structure influences the collateral consequences of crime throughout the life course. Among juvenile delinquents and young adult criminals, collateral consequences are more serious and persistent for ethnic minorities from the lower classes than they are for white middle-class delinquents. Among white-collar criminals, the collateral consequences of crime are more serious for employees and workers than they are for owners and managers.

White-Collar Crime and the Life Course Reconsidered

The analyses presented in this chapter indicate that the individuals who are convicted for violating federal white-collar crime statutes come more from the middle than the upper social classes. This result must be viewed with caution, however. Because our analyses are based on samples of convicted offenders, they can tell us nothing about those who avoid conviction in the first place. It may be that upper-class offenders are simply better at avoiding conviction than middle-class offenders. After all, upper-class offenders have more money to use to hire top-notch legal defense teams, and good white-collar crime lawyers make sure that their clients keep away from courtrooms (Mann 1985). But the relationship between class status and legal sanctioning is complex, and the ability of upper-class individuals to avoid criminal prosecution is not simply a matter of money (Shapiro 1984; 1985). To explore this issue fully is beyond the scope of this book. So, we will have to be satisfied with noting that what we have learned thus far about white-collar offenders and the life course represents only a small part of the story that will eventually be told.

Although they do not fit the classic stereotype of the white-collar offender, the theoretical significance of middle-class offenders should not be ignored. They are not powerful business executives, but neither are they marginalized lower-class outsiders. Their trajectories in crime do not fit either the life-course persistent or adolescence-limited patterns identified by Moffitt (1997). On the other hand, neither do they resemble the powerful corporate executives popularized by Sutherland (1949) and others. So, where do they fit in criminological theory, and how may life course theory be applied to them?

White-collar offenders do not appear to follow the conventional trajectories in crime identified by life course theory. Their official offending careers start relatively late in life, when they are more or less securely ensconced in the middle class. It is possible, of course, that they start breaking the law much earlier than their official records indicate. However, because white-collar crimes tend to involve an occupational position, it is unlikely that they were committing white-collar crimes as teenagers. In the various social domains of adult life, most white-collar offenders appear to follow conventional trajectories. Early precursors of antisocial behavior or early hints of trouble in the life histories of typical white-collar offenders are hard to find. For most of these individuals, their offenses appear to come out of nowhere. Their crimes do not appear to be part of longstanding patterns of antisocial conduct, nor do they appear to be deeply rooted in a troubled family background. With respect to the life course approach, these patterns do not coincide with the typical image of trajectories in crime. They also suggest that theories that rely on latent personality traits (Moffitt 1993; Gottfredson and Hirschi 1990) are not appropriate for explaining white-collar crime. White-collar crime appears to be a function of adult life experience rather than the outcome of an antisocial personality or a troubled family background.

Regarding crime during adulthood, life course researchers have focused on identifying factors that distinguish those who stop offending from those who persist. Persistence in offending is thought to be caused either by an underlying propensity toward crime or by the narrowing of legitimate opportunities that results from the stigma associated with involvement in crime, or both. To explain desistance, Sampson and Laub (1993) proposed an age-graded theory of informal social controls. Transitions that increase informal social controls in adulthood, such as getting married or finding a good job, are hypothesized to lead to desistance from crime. Because onset into offending in adulthood is assumed to be very rare, life course researchers have ignored this pattern. However, as the data presented in this chapter demonstrate, most white-collar offenders do not begin to offend until they are well into adulthood. From the perspective of life course theory, how can this pattern of late starting be understood?

Part of the explanation lies in the occupational nature of white-collar crimes. Because opportunities for many white-collar crimes arise out of occupational positions, only individuals in certain occupations can commit certain types of white-collar offenses. Access to these positions is usually limited to individuals who have completed schooling and are accordingly in their twenties or thirties. Access to these jobs also tends to be limited to individuals who do not have prior criminal records. Hence, the first time white-collar offender will tend to be older simply because only older individuals can get the jobs that provide opportunities for white-collar crime. This explanation accounts for the age distribution of white-collar offenders, but it does not explain why particular individuals choose to commit white-collar offenses. Many other individuals have similar opportunities but do not offend.

Travis Hirschi and Michael Gottfredson (1987) argue that those who take advantage of white-collar crime opportunities are those with low self-control. Criminal propensity theorists take essentially the same tack. But there is something unsatisfying with these sorts of explanations. How could someone have enough self-control to get a good job but not enough self-control to resist taking advantage of the criminal opportunities the job presented? Why do some people hold occupational positions for long periods of time before committing their first white-collar offense? If criminal propensity is a stable personality trait, then why don't white-collar criminals take advantage of the opportunities presented by their occupational positions immediately? That they don't take immediate advantage is suggested by the late age at which most first time white-collar offenders are arrested. The average age of onset is around 40, an age at which it is safe to assume that most people have been in an occupational position for some time. If low self-control or high criminal propensity does not explain white collar crime, then we have to look elsewhere.

The life course perspective directs our attention to trajectories in other domains of adult life that may trigger involvement in white-collar crime, such as family life and occupation. Interviews with white-collar offenders indicate that some see themselves as responding to emergencies in family economic circumstances when they decide to become involved in white-collar crime (Benson 1985a; Rothman and Gandossy

1982; Daly 1989). Women appear more likely to become involved in white-collar crimes for family reasons than men (Daly 1989; Rothman and Gandossy 1982).

For other individuals, changes in motivational stressors that arise out of one's occupation are implicated (Weisburd et al. 2001). For example, a sudden downturn in business revenues may force a small businessperson to resort to unlawful means to keep the business afloat (Benson 1985a). A building contractor that I once interviewed thought he was going to lose his business because of a cash-flow problem. He conspired with his accountant to set up a check-kiting scheme and explained his involvement this way:

> I was faced with the choice of all of a sudden, and I mean now, closing the doors or doing something else to keep that business open. . . . I'm not going to tell you that this wouldn't have happened if I'd had time to think it over, because I think it probably would have. You're sitting there with a dying patient. You are going to try to keep him alive. (Benson 1985, 598)

Individuals who work in large corporations are subject to a complex combination of microfactors related to their occupational careers and macrofactors related to the structure and culture of the organizations within which they work. At times, these factors may exert pressure on individuals and make corporate offending a rational response (Simpson et al. 1998). For example, persons convicted of antitrust violations sometimes claim that in their industries technical violations of antitrust laws are just part of doing business. Consider these explanations of bid rigging from a public building contractor:

> It was a way of doing business before we even got into the business. So it was like why do you brush your teeth in the morning or something. . . . It was part of the everyday . . . It was a matter of survival. (Benson 1985a, 591)

> All you want to do is show a bid, so that in some cases it was for as small a reason as getting your deposit back on the plans and specs. So you just simply have no interest in getting the job and just call to see if you can find someone to give you a price to use, so that you didn't have to go through the expense of an entire bid preparation. Now that is looked on very unfavorably, and it is a technical violation. (Benson 1985a, 592)

These white-collar offenders appear to be responding to perceived problems in their lives or businesses (Weisburd et al. 2001). From the perspective of life course theory, the key point is that some white-collar crimes do not reflect continuity in behavior but rather discontinuity. They are not part of a pattern of antisocial conduct. Their causes are rooted not in the unfolding of innate developmental tendencies, but rather in contemporaneous circumstances of offenders' lives. ✦

Chapter 6

Historical and Structural Contexts

African-American men born in the U.S. and fortunate enough to live past the age of 18 are conditioned to accept the inevitability of prison. For most of us, it simply is the next phase in a sequence of humiliations.

—from *Soledad Brother,* by George Jackson

Overview: Four Million Babies in History

A central premise of the life course perspective is that the structure of the life course is shaped by historical conditions and can be reshaped by social change (Elder 1995). So far, we have only touched upon this premise as we have followed developmental trajectories from birth to adulthood. We have taken little note of the historical and macrosociological contexts in which the 4 million babies born each year play out their lives. But historical and macrosociological conditions matter. They play an important role in how individuals sort themselves out and are sorted into different trajectories and positions over the course of their lifetimes.

Thus, this chapter explores the effects of social and historical change on the life course and crime. We also consider the role of the state in shaping the life course. Very little attention has been paid to the ways in which the modern state shapes the life course in regard to crime. Like other life course theorists, criminologists have portrayed the individual lives of their subjects as "if they were occurring in a stateless society" (Mayer and Muller 1986).

How can the state influence crime and the life course? The most obvious answer is by what the state chooses to criminalize, by how effectively and fairly it enforces the criminal law, and by the penalties it imposes on those who are convicted. Arrest, conviction, and punishment are events in the life course that can dramatically affect opportunities for and the timing of other important trajectories in life (Hagan and Palloni 1988). They can easily disrupt family, educational, and occupational trajectories. They may also have effects on psychological trajectories.

Besides the obvious ways in which the state's machinery of criminal justice can affect individual life courses, other actions by the state may have less obvious but nonetheless profound consequences for trajectories in crime. Governmental decisions and policies in areas such as public housing and transportation can determine where people live and can have highly detrimental effects on the structural conditions of their neighborhoods. Neighborhood conditions, in turn, shape the life course in many ways. The rise of the welfare state and the welfare society has had deep and multitudinous effects on the structure of the life course in the United States and other western democracies. Indeed, in many ways the welfare state has created the modern life course, or at least certain stages within it (Mayer and Muller 1986).

Governments can choose to spend tax dollars on welfare, or education, or employment, or prisons, or in other ways. Their decisions about different institutional structures influence whether individuals have opportunities to participate (willingly or unwillingly) in institutions (Sutton 2001). If a government chooses to build prisons rather than, say, counseling centers, then teenagers who are disreputable or troublesome are likely to be sent to prison rather than given treatment. The detrimental effects of imprisonment on development follow in due course. In this sense, individual life courses are shaped by governmental decisions about the institutions that manage individual movement through the life course. These managerial institutions include families, schools, hospitals, the military, churches, labor markets, and others (Sutton 2001, 354–55).

Societies and governments vary in how they respond to troublesome people. Consider how differently drug addicts are treated in the United States, which views hard drug use as a criminal violation that should be handled by courts and prisons, compared to Britain, which classifies drug use as a medical problem to be treated by the National Health Service (Sutton 2001, 355). These different approaches to the problem of drugs represent different historically contingent ways of managing the life course.

In this chapter, we step back from our focus on individuals and consider how social change in American society and state actions have influenced the structure of the life course. We also briefly consider the relationship between social change and crime in other societies. The relationship between social change and the state is terribly complex, and it is often hard to tell which comes first. Government action may promote social change through legislation and regulation. Yet, at times legislation and regulation only follow or codify changes in behavior patterns that have occurred prior to and independent of state actions (Freidman and Ladinsky 1967). In hopes of keeping our discussion reasonably simple, we ignore the issue of causal order and treat social change and state actions separately. Our goal is to identify some of the major social changes that have occurred in the United States and to speculate on how they may have influenced crime and the life course.

The Maturity Gap

The maturity gap is thought to play a significant role in adolescent involvement in crime (Felson 1998; Steffensmeier and Allan 1995; Moffitt 1993). Recall that the maturity gap refers to the disjunction of physical and social age for adolescents in modern industrialized societies. Young people today reach physical and sexual maturity at earlier ages than ever before, but they reach social maturity at later ages than ever before. By social maturity, we mean the ability to assume a productive adult role in the economy. Of course, teenagers can always get minimum-wage jobs. These are not the jobs, however, that teenagers want to have when they are adults, and neither are these the jobs that society expects them to be holding as adults. Access to the type of job that will enable a person to build a career and support a family is increasingly restricted to those with advanced training and education. It takes time to accumulate these forms of human capital. Hence, there is a gap, a maturity gap, between physical and social maturity.

The maturity gap arose out of a long historical transformation in the nature of work that began with the industrial revolution. This transformation altered the balance between the physical and intellectual requirements of work, and it dramatically changed the social organization of work. Prior to industrialization, traditional tasks on the farm and around the home placed great demands on physical strength and endurance. Work was conducted close to home and organized around the productive roles of family members. For the family to survive and prosper, everyone had to contribute. Children assumed productive roles early in life, and they learned how to work from their parents and other adults (Felson 1998).

The world prior to industrialization was well suited to adolescents. They have physical strength and stamina in abundance, and what they needed to know they could learn by watching others. There was plenty of demanding and important work for them to do. Hence, they had an important economic function to play.

Because teenagers in the nineteenth century could undertake important economic roles, they were less likely to develop the feelings of rebellion and isolation so common among teenagers of today (Steffensmeier and Allan 1995, 106). Teenagers' economic function also made it appropriate for them to expect to assume a legitimate reproductive function much earlier in life than today. For both males and females, marriage and children typically occurred during the later teenage years. Thus, at age 16 a male could look forward to marrying and starting a family within just a few years, when he was 18 or 19. His schooling would be done and he would know most of what he needed to support himself and a family (Felson 1998).

In preindustrial societies, the transition from youth to adult occurs smoothly and naturally (Steffensmeier and Allan 1995). The timing of important life transitions is closely linked. Youngsters complete whatever training or schooling they need at about the same time they reach physical and sexual maturity. They are ready to marry and work, and society is ready for them to do so. By age 18 or 19, many youths are already tied down by raising their own children and not available for crime and delinquency. As soon as they are married, they have legitimate access to sex. Thus, sex as delinquent behavior is not a problem (Felson 1994, 79).

The situation of teenagers in the modern world could hardly be more different. They live in a world in which almost all of the available work requires at least a high school diploma. Anyone who really wants to get ahead must obtain a college degree. Few jobs require much in the way of muscular strength or endurance. Rather than working with things and with one's hands, modern jobs require working with people or data. Specialization is the order of the day, even for traditional manual labor jobs. For example, Marcus Felson (1994, 81) notes that the humble occupation of "butcher" is now subdivided into a number of specialized tasks, including, "animal stunner, shackler, sticker, head trimmer, carcass splitter, offal separator, shrouder, hide trimmer, boner, grader, smoked meat preparer, and hide handler." These changes in work add up to one big problem for teenagers in society today. They deny teenagers the possibility of assuming any important economic functions (Steffensmeier and Allan 1995; Felson 1994).

Because today's teenagers are in no position to assume productive roles in the economy, it follows that neither should they assume reproductive roles. As long as sex is conceived primarily as a reproductive activity, the sexual urges of teenagers have no legitimate outlet. Sexual activity, thus, becomes a form of deviance, something that must be hidden from the adult world.

Another aspect of the changed situation that confronts modern teenagers is the role of school as a status system in their lives. Because work has become so much more technical and demanding, prolonged education has become the norm rather than the exception. In the 1920s, less than 20 percent of young people graduated from high school, but by midcentury the figure was well over 50 percent (Greenberg 1977). The social importance of education is reflected in the passage of compulsory education laws and in programs designed to keep young people in school. These laws have forced teenagers to spend more time in school and in the company of their peers. The school has become an arena within which teenagers compete for status with one another and within which they assert their need for autonomy from school authorities.

For many, perhaps most, students, high school is a frustrating experience that can have criminogenic effects. In school, they are denied autonomy and told what to do by teachers and school administrators. For students who do not enjoy school, who see no long-term value in it, and who resent being treated in a degrading manner, delinquency is a form of rebellion and a way to assert autonomy from school authorities (Messerschmidt 1993). For some teenagers, delinquency may be a form of what Alvin Gouldner calls the "conflictual validation of the self" (Gouldner 1970, 220–21). It's a way to find out who you are. The criminogenic power of the school is illustrated in the Cambridge data, in which the peak age for delinquency is the year preceding high school graduation, and when the age of mandatory schooling was raised by a year in England, the peak age for delinquency also rose by a year (Greenberg 1977). Paradoxically, the modern high school may be a source of juvenile delinquency.

The rise of the maturity gap is a major development in human history and in the history of the life course. It exemplifies the inextricable nature of the connections between social and historical change and the structure of the life course. Its impact on trajectories in crime have been profound and are not yet fully understood.

Changing Families and Households

Since the end of World War II, the forms that families and households take in the United States have changed dramatically (LaFree 1998). The two-parent household in which the father works while the mother stays home is no longer the norm. Because families can play such an important part in preventing or provoking youth involvement in crime, it makes sense to think that changes in the American family have something to do with changes in crime. In this section, we look at two important developments in families and households: the increase in nonfamily households and the rise in divorce rates.

Following the end of World War II, the number of nonfamily households in the United States increased dramatically. Nonfamily households are those in which none of the individuals residing in the household are related by birth, marriage, or adoption. The percentage of nonfamily households in the United States nearly tripled between 1950 and 1995, from 11 percent to 30 percent. During this period, the total number of family households increased by 13 percent, but the total number of nonfamily households increased by 73 percent (LaFree 1998, 142). Most of the increase in nonfamily households was caused by the growing number of young adults who were choosing not to get married and to move out of their parents' home. Between 1950 and 1980, the percentage of single men between the ages of 18 and 24 living in nonfamily households leaped from 1 percent to 13 percent. Young women, as well, were choosing to avoid marriage and family life. The proportion of unmarried women in their 20s jumped from 28 to 58 percent between 1960 and 1985. Although most young people do eventually get married, their marriages are much less stable than in the past.

Starting in 1958, divorce rates in the United States, which had been relatively stable for most of the first half of the century, began to rise. Between 1958 and 1979, the national divorce rate more than doubled. After that, it stabilized at a high rate. Presently, about two out of every three first marriages end in divorce or separation (LaFree 1998, 143).

These changes in the form of households and families have criminological consequences. The increase in nonfamily households means that young people are subject to less informal social control than if they were living with their parents. As soon as young people are out on their own, they have greater privacy and autonomy to do what they want, including engaging in deviant and criminal acts. Routine activity theory warns us that more households also mean that there is simply more stuff available to be stolen (Felson 1998). Each new apartment set up by a single person is likely to be stocked with a TV, stereo components, and other valuable and stealable items. Furthermore, because the single person probably works or goes to school, the apartment is left unprotected much of the time. Multiply this situation by several million households and you have created a land of opportunity for burglars. Nonfamily households create opportunities for both offending and victimization. Accordingly, they make trajectories in crime easier to pursue.

Divorce has similar criminological consequences for offending and victimization. Families control offending in several ways. They regulate the behavior of family members, especially by supervising children. The bonds of love and respect that develop between family members moderate behavior in prosocial ways. A consistent research finding is that children who care about their parents are less likely to engage in deviant behavior that might embarrass their parents. Surely the same is true in reverse for parents. Families also protect their members from victimization, thus making it harder for others to offend (LaFree 1998, 136–37).

When people divorce, many of the benefits of marriage are lost. Divorced people set up separate households and stock them with goods. Divorced people are free from the subtle constraints on behavior that being married imposes. Perhaps most important in regard to crime and the life course, divorce affects how and where children are raised. At a minimum, divorced parents have a more difficult time supervising their children than parents in intact marriages, and the effects of divorce on children may extend well beyond the problem of supervision. Depending on the terms of the divorce settlement, divorce may lead to a pronounced decline in the standard of living of women and children. As a result of no-fault divorce laws, mothers who receive custody of their children often do not receive the financial support from their husbands that divorced mothers did in the past. Cut off from the income they had when they were married, they become unable to maintain their former standard of living. Divorced women with children are often forced by economic realities to move to less desirable neighborhoods, where their children are exposed to more criminogenic influences.

Coupled with the rise in divorce has been an increase in out-of-wedlock births. Taken together, these two trends mean that in the 1990s more children than ever before in the history of the United States are likely not to spend their childhood with both of their biological parents. According to Sandra Hofferth, 84 percent of children born in the early 1950s were living with both their biological parents when they reached age 14. Children born in the 1980s were not likely to be as lucky. Only one-third of children born in that decade were still living with both biological parents by age 14 (Hofferth 1985). As the twentieth century drew to a close, about half of all two-parent families included a stepparent. More than four out of 10 children born in the 1990s will be raised in single-parent families at least some time during their formative years (LaFree 1998, 144).

Like other crime-related risks, changes in the form of families and households were more prevalent among African Americans than whites. The proportion of female-headed households among African Americans has historically always been higher than among whites. Although the percentage of households headed by females grew for both African Americans and whites between 1960 and 1995, the rate of increase was much higher for African Americans. In 1960, the proportion of African-American households headed by a female was a little over 20 percent. By 1995, female-headed households accounted for almost 50 percent of all African-American households. In contrast, during the same period the percentage of white households headed by a female grew from about 9 percent to about 14 percent (LaFree 1998, 148). Gary LaFree notes the following:

> Regardless of the specific measure used, African Americans have been less likely than whites to adhere to the traditional form of the postwar family. Compared to whites, blacks have higher divorce rates, higher rates of children born to unmarried mothers, and lower marriage rates. (1998, 147)

Some of the notable differences between African Americans and whites in prevalence of involvement in criminal careers undoubtedly can be traced to these differences in family experiences.

Like the rise in the maturity gap, the breakdown in the family and the increase in nonfamily households represent a sea change in society. How children are raised is linked to whether parents stay together. How adults spend their time and who they associate with are linked to the nature (family or nonfamily) of the households they reside in. As marriages become less stable and as young people increasingly spend their time in nonfamily households, new patterns of interaction and behavior arise, with far-reaching criminological implications.

The Prison Experiment and the War on Drugs

The most direct way that governments affect trajectories in crime is through the criminal justice system. The criminal justice system includes police, courts, and prisons, as well as the legislative bodies that establish the laws governing the operation of these institutions. How these institutions operate determines who is brought into the criminal justice system, how long they stay, and what happens to them while they are there. As we have seen in previous chapters, for some individuals contact with the justice system has very negative effects on the life course. It cuts off individuals' access to legitimate opportunities and deepens and extends their involvement in criminal lifestyles.

In the latter half of the twentieth century, two major interrelated developments in criminal justice policy have greatly increased the number of people who become ensnared in the criminal justice system: the war on drugs and what has been called the "prison experiment" (Currie 1998). Both of these developments have had particularly dramatic and largely negative impacts on minorities and the communities in which they live.

The "prison experiment" began in the early 1970s, when incarceration rates in the United States started to rise with unprecedented speed. Between 1925 and 1970 the incarceration rate in American prisons remained relatively steady, averaging about 110 per 100,000 (Mauer 1999). But then things began to change. In 1972, the total incarceration rate, which includes inmates in jails as well as federal and state prisons, stood at 160 per 100,000 population; roughly one out of every 625 Americans was incarcerated. By 1997, the incarceration rate had skyrocketed to 645 per 100,000. That rate means that in that year one out of every 155 Americans was incarcerated (Mauer 1999). Keep in mind that these numbers are based on the total population, including children and the elderly. If we restricted the population base to those in the peak risk years for going to prison, ages 20 to 40, the rates would be much higher.

The increase in the sheer number of people incarcerated is staggering. In 1971, fewer than 200,000 people were in state and federal prisons. By 1998, the number was approaching 1.3 million, more than a sixfold increase (Austin and Irwin 2001). The size of the American population also rose, but at nowhere near the same rate. Add to the million-plus prison residents another half million held in jails, and you get the total number of people under lock and key—around 1.8 million. Elliott Currie puts that number in perspective by noting that 1.8 million is approximately the size of the population of Houston, Texas, the fourth-largest city in the nation (Currie 1998).

As sobering as these figures are, it is important to remember that they are national averages. In many states the race to incarcerate has been pursued with a vigor that is nothing short of breathtaking. Consider Texas, which has a population of around 18 million. Between 1991 and 1996, the Texas prison population *increased* by 80,000. That *increase* is more than the *total* prison population of France or the United Kingdom. It is about equal to the prison population of Germany, which has a population more than four times the size of Texas. California is another state that has devoted an astonishing amount of resources to imprisoning its citizens. Nearly one in six California state employees works in the prison system (Currie 1998).

The explosion in incarceration has hit African Americans particularly hard. Like every other crime-related risk in America, the risk of incarceration is significantly higher for African Americans than it is for whites. According to the U.S. Bureau of Justice Statistics (BJS), in 1996 the incarceration rate for adult African-American males was 6,607 per 100,000. For adult white males, the rate was 944 per 100,000. African-American males were more than six times as likely as white males to be in jail or prison, or to put it another way, one out of every 15 adult African-American males was incarcerated compared to one out of every 100 adult white males. The disparity in incarceration is just as great for African-American females compared to white females (474 per 100,000 for African-American women versus 73 per 100,000 for white women) (Bureau of Justice Statistics, U.S. Department of Justice 1999).

Another way to look at the risk of imprisonment is to use life table techniques to estimate the lifetime likelihood of going to state or federal prison. Life table techniques are used by demographers and actuaries to summarize observed rates for some event and to project them into the future. Using these techniques, demographers and actuaries can estimate the lifetime rates of familiar life events. For example, based on 1987–88 rates, it is estimated that one out of eight women will develop breast cancer in her lifetime. Thomas P. Bonczar and Allen J. Beck, statisticians for the Bureau of Justice Statistics, used life table techniques to estimate the lifetime likelihood of going to state or federal prison. According to their estimates, if the 1991 incarceration rates remain unchanged in the future, an estimated one of every 20 persons (5.1 percent) will serve time in prison in his or her lifetime. The rate for men (9.0 percent) is much higher than that for women (1.1 percent). But the really stark differences in lifetime probabilities are between men of different races and ethnic groups. For white men, the lifetime likelihood of being admitted to prison is 4.4 percent. For Hispanics, the rate is about four times higher (16 percent). For African Americans, the likelihood that a man will spend time in prison is 28.5 percent. In other words, at 1991 incarceration rates, an African-American male has a greater than one in four chance of going to prison during his lifetime (Bonczar and Beck 1997).

The number of African Americans in prison and jail does not tell the whole story of how the criminal justice system has reached into their lives. In addition to incarceration, there are other ways to be under correctional supervision, such as probation and parole. To fully appreciate how pervasively the criminal justice system penetrates the lives of African Americans, we need to take these forms of correctional supervision into account as well. In 1996, the adult African-

American population was estimated at 23,434,000. The Bureau of Justice Statistics calculates that in that year alone approximately 2,099,500 African Americans were under correctional supervision. That is one out of 11.

Even the figure of one out of 11 does not really convey how difficult it is for some African Americans to avoid the criminal justice system, because this figure is a national average that includes everyone over the age of 18. For young African-American males the risk is much higher. In the mid-1990s, roughly one out of three young African-American men in America was under correctional supervision. In Baltimore, Maryland, the correctional system was supervising in one way or another over half of all young African-American men in the city (Currie 1998). By 1994, in California, 40 percent of African-American men in their twenties were under correctional supervision (Christianson 1998).

Soledad Brother by George Jackson was published in 1970, just before the United States began its now three-decade-long obsession with prisons. It is depressing and sobering to realize how extraordinarily worse things have gotten for African-American men in the United States since Jackson penned the quotation that opened this chapter. Perhaps he saw it coming.

What Jackson may not have seen coming was that growing numbers of women would soon join men behind bars. Between 1983 and 1998, the growth in the number of women incarcerated in state and federal prisons was even larger than it was for men, 344 percent to 207 percent, respectively (Austin and Irwin 2001), and a disproportionate share of female inmates were African Americans. According to Marc Mauer and Tracy Huling of The Sentencing Project, because of the war on drugs "African-American women have experienced the greatest increase in criminal justice supervision" (cited in Austin and Irwin 2001, 59).

The reasons behind the explosive growth in imprisonment that took place in the United States toward the end of the twentieth century are complex. The United States was not the only country that built more prisons in the latter half of the twentieth century. Since the end of World War II, imprisonment rates in other Western nations have also increased (Sutton 2001). In a longitudinal analysis of the United States, Canada, New Zealand, Australia, and Britain, John Sutton found that over the course of thirty years (1955 to 1985) the use of imprisonment in these countries was influenced by the homicide rate, military enlistments, welfare spending, unemployment rates, and "right-wing party dominance." Imprisonment rates increase when homicide and unemployment rates rise, when military enlistments increase, and when right-wing political parties, such as the Republicans in the United States, dominate national politics. The use of incarceration decreases, on the other hand, when countries spend more on welfare. Sutton's analyses shed a great deal of light on the structural causes of variation in imprisonment, and they show that these causes operate in other countries as well as in the United States. Yet, the United States is still unique among nations in its extraordinarily high rate of imprisonment. Particularly since 1972, the growth in imprisonment in the United States has been unmatched in any other country. What accounts for our extraordinary increase in punitiveness?

Certainly, at least part of the increase can be attributed to rising crime rates, especially violent crime rates. Between the mid-1950s and the mid-1970s, the U.S. homicide rate doubled. Rates for other violent crimes, such as rape, robbery, and aggravated assault, grew just as fast or faster. The rising crime rate and the civil disorders of the late 1960s made it appear to many Americans that civil society was falling apart and that they were under siege in their own homes and neighborhoods. They demanded action. Politicians responded with proposals to "crack down" on crime by reforming sentencing policies, building more prisons, and inaugurating a new war on drugs. In the "race to incarcerate," as Marc Mauer of The Sentencing Project calls it, many nonviolent drug offenders were swept into America's new infrastructure of state and federal prisons (Mauer 1999).

The history of American response to drugs is long and confused. Throughout much of the nineteenth century, most of those who used narcotics were members of legitimate society. Narcotics such as morphine, opium, cocaine, and heroin were widely thought to have beneficial health and medical effects. They were available from family physicians, pharmacists, and even grocers (Inciardi 1986). Toward the end of the nineteenth century, the tide of favorable public and medical opinion began to turn. Both the medical and religious communities began to rail against the haphazard and growing use of drugs. The image of the addict as patient began to be replaced in the public eye by the addict as moral derelict and criminal. In 1914, the transformation became official with the passage of the Harrison Act, which made the use of narcotics criminal and in the process created a new class of criminals.

Since the passage of the Harrison Act, crackdowns on drugs have alternated with periods of indifference. The current war on drugs began in the early 1980s with the crack cocaine epidemic. Since that time, federal, state, and local governments have poured an enormous amount of resources into combating drugs. A variety of different policies have been pursued, but they can be grouped into two broad categories: those that focus on supply and those that focus on demand. Supply-side policies are directed toward reducing the supply of illegal drugs available for potential users to purchase. For example, the Drug Enforcement Administration attempts to reduce supply by interdicting illegal drugs as they are being smuggled into the country from foreign nations. Demand policies, on the other hand, try to reduce the number of users either through education or deterrence.

As measured by their effects on individual life courses, deterrence-oriented demand policies are the ones we need to be concerned about. These policies focus on arresting and locking up ordinary users and small-time street level dealers. They have contributed substantially to the dramatic increases in the U.S. prison population witnessed throughout the 1980s and 1990s. Since the mid-1980s, drug offenders have constituted the fastest growing segment of the prison population (Currie 1998). In 1980, just under 100,000 people were in state prisons for property offenses, and less than 20,000 were in prison for drug offenses. By 1996, the number of property offenders in state prison had more than doubled to about 236,000. But the increase in property offenders in prisons pales in comparison to the explosion in incarcerated drug offenders. In 1996, the number of drug offenders in state prisons nearly equaled the number of property offenders at 234,000, which is more than a tenfold increase (Bureau of Justice Statistics, U.S. Department of Justice 1999).

Over the course of a decade and a half, the number of persons sentenced to state prisons for drug offenses grew steadily, so that they accounted for an ever larger percentage of the state prison population. In 1980, drug offenders accounted for less than 10 percent of all persons admitted to state prisons. Violent offenders accounted for almost 50 percent of those admitted. By 1996, the percentage of persons admitted for drug offenses had more than tripled to 30 percent, and the percentage of violent offenders admitted had fallen to 30 percent. During that same year, drug offenders accounted for 60 percent of all inmates in federal correctional institutions. In other words, the most serious offense committed by three out of every five federal inmates is a drug offense (Bureau of Justice Statistics, U.S. Department of Justice 1999).

Overall, because of the get-tough movement, the prison experiment, and the war on drugs, proportionately more Americans than ever before in history are ensnared by the criminal justice system at some point in their lives. The full effects of the increased penetration of the state into the lives of ordinary citizens are not yet completely understood. But it seems likely that sometime in the future life course historians will look back on this period as a major historical event that shaped the structure of the life course. For young African-American males living in urban areas, the effects of the war on drugs and the prison experiment are not unlike those of a real war. As a result of these policies and programs, a substantial percentage of young African-American males were taken away from their homes and families. Like military service, stays in prison interrupted their lives, putting on hold all of the normal routine transitions that precede or accompany entry into adulthood. Changes in criminal justice policy in the last quarter of the twentieth century greatly increased the rate at which people in the United States became ensnared in the machinery of justice. These changes hit African Americans and Hispanics especially hard, particularly those who live in disadvantaged communities.

Public Policy, Globalization, and the Inner City

Because the criminal justice system so directly and obviously affects crime, it is easy to overlook the criminogenic effects of other public policies. Yet, governmental decisions about transportation, housing, and economics also have criminological consequences. Like the war on drugs and the prison experiment, policy shifts in these areas have worked to the detriment of racial and ethnic minorities. In this section, we examine some historical developments in public policy that are not directly related to crime but that nevertheless indirectly affect opportunities and motivations for crime.

In his seminal work, *The Truly Disadvantaged*, William Julius Wilson describes the historical transformation of American inner cities (Wilson 1987). He shows that a large proportion of African Americans who reside in urban areas live in neighborhoods that expose them to criminogenic conditions. These conditions include high rates of poverty, family disruption, and residential instability. Neighborhoods with these structural conditions also tend to have high rates of crime and victimization (Sampson and Wilson 1994). Robert Sampson has shown that African Americans are much more likely than whites to live in such disadvantaged neighborhoods like these. Indeed, racial differences in levels of neighborhood poverty and family disruption are so striking that whites who reside in the "worst" urban contexts for whites live in areas that are better than the average urban context of African Americans (Sampson 1987). In no city over 100,000 in America do African Americans live in ecological equality with whites (Sampson and Wilson 1994). And the situation got worse as the twentieth century drew to a close. The percentage of African Americans who lived in ghetto or extreme poverty areas doubled from 20 percent to 40 percent between 1970 and 1980 (Sampson and Wilson 1994).

The macrostructural factors that combined to concentrate urban African-American poverty and family disruption in inner cities are complex and involve historical changes that have played out over several decades. But it is important to note that these changes resulted in part from deliberate decisions by politicians, bureaucrats, and private individuals that had the effect, unintended or otherwise, of destroying the social fabric of inner-city communities (Skogan 1986). For example, urban-renewal programs disproportionately uprooted urban African-American communities (Skogan 1986). Most notably, in the 1950s the construction of the interstate highway system drove through the hearts of many inner cities and destroyed low-income communities (Sampson and Wilson 1994). Consider the experience of the residents of Atlanta. As part of urban-renewal programs, one of six residents was dislocated, and the great majority of those were poor African Americans. Nationwide, between 1960 and 1970, 20 percent of central-city housing units occupied by African Americans were lost as a result of urban-renewal projects, and this figure does not include displacements brought about by normal market forces, such as evictions, rent increases, and commercial development (Logan and Molotch 1987).

Robert Sampson and William Julius Wilson (1994, 43) note that, for many African Americans, the most pernicious public policies involved housing. Throughout the 1950s and 1960s, de facto federal policy tolerated extensive segregation against African Americans in urban-housing markets. Local governments neglected the rehabilitation of inner-city housing units. Residents of well-to-do urban and suburban neighborhoods resisted efforts to locate public housing for minorities and the disadvantaged in their neighborhoods. All of these forces combined to lead to massive segregated public-housing projects that eventually became ghettos for poor African Americans. Public-housing projects have become a physically permanent institution for the isolation of African-American families by race and social class from mainstream American society (Bickford and Massey 1991, 1035). Within these projects, the problems of gang violence and illegal drugs reached epidemic proportions.

The detrimental effects of urban renewal, public housing, and the placement of infrastructure on inner-city America have been exacerbated by changes in the American economy brought about by globalization. Beginning a few years after the end of World War II, the United States experienced an economic boom that lasted almost a quarter of a century, from 1954 to 1974. During this period, economic growth averaged close to 5 percent a year (Hagan 1997). But after 1974, a period of economic slowdown followed, and economic growth shrunk to half the size it had been previously. Over the course of the next two decades, the American economy was transformed. Secure high-wage manufacturing jobs were lost and only partially replaced by less stable and poorer paying jobs in the service sector (Averitt 1992; Revenga 1992).

It was during the 1980s, as corporations closed their manufacturing plants and left them to rot, that the Midwest became known, appropriately, as the "rust belt." For example, the city of Chicago lost more than one-fifth of its manufacturing jobs between 1980 and 1983 (Skogan 1986). Corporations opened new plants in Mexico or overseas in southeast Asia, where they found cheap labor, lax environmental regulations, few worker protection laws, and no labor unions. From the point of view of capitalist corporations, it made good economic sense to leave the United States and to produce their goods elsewhere. The costs of production were much lower and profits much higher. However, from the point of view of workers, what was good for business was definitely not good for them.

The transformation of the economy hit the poorest members of minority groups the hardest. They experienced actual declines in real income during the 1980s (Hagan 1997). Most devastating for minorities was the loss of core manufacturing jobs, because these jobs offered an opportunity for high-paying employment that did not require advanced education. Furthermore, because they were environmentally undesirable, auto plants, steel mills, and other smoke-belching manufacturing plants were often located in areas where minorities could find housing. Since many whites were not eager to live by the plants, nearby housing was cheaper than in the suburbs and residential segregation was less of a problem for minorities. But as America deindustrialized, jobs shifted from the center city to the suburbs. The locational advantages of inner-city neighborhoods disappeared and so did the economic well-being of the people who lived there (Skogan 1986).

As jobs disappeared from the inner city, a spiral of decline was set in motion. Crime and fear of crime began to rise. Middle-class people and the businesses they supported moved out. Drug addicts, vagrants, the mentally ill, and criminals moved in. Very few people want to live in a decaying area where crime is rising, but not everyone can move. Those who move are different from those who stay. Race and economics dominate the process. An investigation of the Chicago metropolitan area found that "households that left the central city were more affluent, had more education, and more often were intact nuclear families" (Skogan 1986, 208). The households that stayed behind were inhabited disproportionately by African Americans, unmarried adults, and the poor (Skogan and Maxfield 1981). As a result, over time the most disadvantaged people, especially minorities, came to be concentrated in extremely disorganized neighborhoods in inner-city America (Wilson 1987).

From the perspective of life course theory, it is reasonable to conclude that the decline of the inner city profoundly affected trajectories in all domains of life for the young people who suffered the misfortune of having to grow up in these areas. John Hagan (1997) argues that as a result of the loss of capital and legitimate employment opportunities, the residents of inner cities have turned to deviance as a way of recapitalizing and bringing economic resources back into their neighborhoods. In his view, many inner-city ghettos have become deviance service centers, in which access to illegal commodities like drugs and sex is provided. Young people who grow up in these service centers are exposed to strains, temptations, and criminal opportunities on a daily basis. Is it any wonder that the developmental trajectories of so many of them intersect so often and so deeply with crime and the criminal justice system?

Criminologists working in the life course tradition have not yet devoted as much effort to understanding contextual effects on trajectories in crime as they have to studying the parameters of careers at the individual level. Nevertheless, evidence of the powerful effects of neighborhood context on trajectories in a variety of different domains is emerging. Contextual influences are now evident on many types of behavior often thought to be determined solely by individual-level factors and decisions, including such intimate matters as domestic violence, child maltreatment, teenage childbearing, and low IQ (Benson et al. 2000; Sucoff and Upchurch 1998; Brooks-Gunn, Duncan, and Aber 1997a; Coulton et al. 1995; Brooks-Gunn et al. 1993). With respect to trajectories in crime, contextual effects seem to be most pronounced in extremely disadvantaged communities. Rates of crime and victimization are substantially higher in communities that are economically and racially disadvantaged. Since the 1930s and the pioneering work of Shaw and McKay, community-level research has identified a host of structural antecedents to higher crime rates, including poverty, ethnic heterogeneity, urbanization (e.g., population and housing density), residential mobility, opportunity structures for predatory crime (e.g., density of convenience stores), and rates of community change and population turnover (Sampson and Lauritsen 1994).

Although it is well-known and easy to show that disadvantaged communities tend to have high crime rates, it is less easy to explain why this happens. How do the structural or aggregate characteristics of a community affect the behavior of residents? By what intervening mechanisms does community structure affect individual behavior, and to what degree? It is difficult to study the intervening mechanisms that link the social structure of a community to the behavior of residents. Although there is reason to hope that the situation will improve in the future, at present only a handful of studies are available to shed light on this connection.

What research there is suggests that in structurally disadvantaged communities residents behave differently toward one another than they do in more well-off communities. Local friendship networks tend to be sparse, participation in neighborhood organizations is low, and informal social controls are weak (Sampson and Groves 1989; Taylor and Covington 1988). As Robert Sampson and colleagues argue, disadvantaged communities tend to be low in *collective efficacy* (Sampson, Raudenbush, and Earls 1997). Collective efficacy refers to "social cohesion among neighbors combined with their willingness to intervene on behalf of the common good" (Sampson 1997, 918). Sampson and colleagues argue that collective efficacy is the intervening mechanism that links the structural characteristics of neighborhoods to the behavior of residents. They have demonstrated that low levels of collective efficacy are associated with high levels of violent crime independent of the characteristics of the individuals in an area.

The concept of collective efficacy is the most promising development in the effort to understand how community context shapes the life course. Even more important than the finding that collective efficacy influences rates of violent crime in neighborhoods is research on how the structural characteristics of communities affect collective efficacy for children (Sampson, Morenoff, and Earls 1999). The Project on Human Development in Chicago combined census data with a massive survey of over 8,000 Chicago residents located in 342 neighborhoods. The investigators used census data to identify neighborhoods of concentrated disadvantage (i.e., poor) and those of concentrated affluence (i.e., wealthy), as well as neighborhoods in between these extremes. Using census data, the investigators were also able to measure the rate of residential stability in neighborhoods.

The survey of residents revealed several important things about how adults in these different types of neighborhoods relate to one another and to neighborhood children. First, residential stability predicts the level of *reciprocated exchanges* between adults in the neighborhood—that is, the intensity of interfamily interaction and adult interaction about children. Regardless of the level of disadvantage or racial and ethnic composition, stable neighborhoods exhibit higher levels of reciprocated exchange than do unstable neighborhoods. Second, in neighborhoods of concentrated disadvantage, shared expectations for the informal social control of children were significantly lower than in more affluent neighborhoods (Sampson et al. 1999, 656). Taken together, the results indicate that children in stable affluent neighborhoods are exposed to greater amounts of child-centered collective efficacy than children in unstable disadvantaged neighborhoods. The consequences of this variation in exposure to collective efficacy for the development of children are not yet fully understood. Whether and to what degree neighborhood-level collective efficacy for children influences trajectories in crime and delinquency remain important unanswered questions.

A Note on Crime and the Life Course in Other Countries

With only occasional exceptions, we have not paid much attention throughout this book to countries other than the United States. Whereas it is always wise to be sensitive to cross-cultural differences, focusing on the United States probably has not led us to misunderstand how individual-level factors influence behavior. It seems safe to assume that what we have learned about genetics, personality, and families can be generalized elsewhere. The neuropsychological deficits and personality traits that predispose people to troublesome behavior in the United States probably operate in much the same way in other countries (Caspi et al. 1994). Likewise, children born into troubled families, regardless of whether they are located in the United States or elsewhere, appear to be developmentally disadvantaged. But once we move above the level of individuals and families, countries become more important. Their histories, their social structures, their values, all of these macrolevel factors influence how societies manage the life course and how they respond to socially problematic people. History, social structure, and values also influence how people adapt their trajectories in life in response to structural changes in society. We can learn more about the influence of macrolevel factors on crime and the life course by looking at other countries.

Perhaps the most dramatic recent evidence of the connection between crime and social change comes from developments in Russia after the fall of communism. Getting reliable crime statistics in Russia is not easy. The government is not above manipulating numbers to create a positive impression of law and order. But in recent years the United Nations has attempted to get a reliable picture of what is happening in this rapidly changing society. The results have been sobering, though certainly not entirely surprising in light of historical developments. According to a report prepared jointly by the United Nations Interregional Crime and Justice Research Institute and the Research Institute of the Ministry of the Interior of the Russian Federation, between 1988 and 1993 the crime rate in the Russian Federation more than doubled from around 800 to 1,887 per 100,000 (United Nations Interregional Crime and Justice Research Institute 1994). The list of causes cited by the researchers to explain Russia's crime boom reads like a veritable who's who of the macrosociological causes dear to the hearts of criminologists: political instability, plummeting levels of personal income, mass migrations, ethnic conflict, and the rapid divide of society into a wealthy class and a poor class. Exacerbating the effects of these usual suspects has been the transformation of the Russian economy from public to private ownership. According to the United Nation's researchers:

> The development of private business in Moscow instantly resulted in the struggle of certain criminal groups to divide the city into new territories. . . . A new type of crime developed: the extortion of large sums of money from managers of commercial enterprises and state organs for certain services, under the threat of physical violence or damage to private property. (1994, 37)

For a society to double its crime rate in only five years is no mean achievement. Even during the crime boom that began in the United States in 1960, it took over ten years for the property crime rate to double (Bursik 2000). From the perspective of life course theory, the Russian experience points to the profound and sometimes immediate impact that social change can have on involvement in criminal trajectories. Just as the crime boom that hit the United States in the mid-1960s was not caused by any transformation in our genetic code, neither can Russia's current difficulties be traced to changes in individual-level factors. There's more crime in Russia now because people have more opportunity and motivation and fewer constraints. What is happening in Russia unequivocally reiterates the point, if it needs repeating, that crime patterns can never be understood just by looking at individuals. No matter how methodologically sophisticated life course research may become in studying individuals, individual-level studies will at best tell only part of the story.

On the other end of the crime continuum from contemporary Russia (and the United States, for that matter) are countries such as Japan, which have had historically low and falling crime rates. In the decades following World War II, Japan also encountered many of the conditions that criminologists would expect to result in high crime rates. Immediately after the humiliation of being defeated in the war, Japan experienced anomie in the Durkheimian sense of a general breakdown in norms governing behavior (Braithwaite 1989a). Then, with the help of its former enemies, it industrialized at an extraordinarily rapid rate. It is a highly urbanized society, its people densely packed in cities. Social breakdown coupled with rapid industrialization and urbanization is a combination that most criminologists would regard as a recipe for disaster. To be fair, Japan is culturally homogeneous and has had low unemployment rates in the postwar period working in its favor. But still, compared to the United States, it has extraordinarily low crime rates. For example, in 1984, the rate for rape in Japan was 1.6 per 100,000 versus 35.7 in the United States, and the robbery rate was 1.8 per 100,000 versus 205.4 per 100,000 in the United States (Westermann and Burfeind 1991, 3). What accounts for these extraordinary disparities? Are the Japanese an especially nonviolent people? Is their criminal justice system extraordinarily effective at deterring offenders?

The argument that the Japanese have a genetic or cultural legacy of nonviolence is difficult to sustain in light of their competitiveness and their history, which is replete with violent conflict (Westermann 1991, 5). Recall as well the atrocities committed by Japan's armies in World War I and II. The historical evidence does not support the idea that the Japanese are by nature nonaggressive. The Japanese criminal justice system is efficient in the sense of apprehending a high proportion of offenders, but it is also very lenient. Compared to the United States, Japanese offenders are 20 times less likely to be incarcerated after conviction, and when they are imprisoned, they serve shorter sentences (Braithwaite 1989a). Neither genetics nor criminal justice seem to be viable candidates to explain Japan's low-crime rates.

Scholars who have examined the Japanese case suggest that the answer lies primarily in the nature of Japanese society. The Japanese have a fundamentally different conception of how the individual life course relates to families, informal groups, and formal organizations than is found in the United States. It is a society saturated by a sense of group consciousness. In Japan, individuals are socialized to be highly interdependent. They are raised to be dependent on others and to expect that others are dependent on them (Braithwaite 1989, 98–99). Virtually every commentator on Japanese life and culture stresses the centrality of individual connections to groups in determining individual behavior. This sense of group-relatedness does not mean that the Japanese are without their own sense of individuality, but rather that the Japanese sense of self and self-worth derives from being connected to the group, including the family, the work group, and the nation (Westermann and Burfeind 1991). Individual well-being is tightly connected to the well-being of the group.

The process of building in a psychological need for group support starts early. Child-rearing practices are oriented to produce a "physical and psychical dependence for gratification on the mother" that then "grows into psychic dependence for gratification from the warmth and approval of the group" (Reischauer 1988, 144). The need for approval from the group forms the basis for individual achievement motivation, which is very high in Japan. In contrast, in the United States achievement motivation is based on notions of independence and self-reliance (Smith 1983).

High levels of interdependency among individuals produce what John Braithwaite (1989a) calls a high level of communitarianism in Japanese society. In a highly communitarian society, "individuals are densely enmeshed in interdependencies which have the special quali-ties of mutual help and trust" (Braithwaite 1989a, 100). Loyalty to the group takes precedence over individual interests. Connections to others are based on concern for their and the group's well-being, as opposed to being merely relationships of commercial or personal convenience. Thus, in Japan, individuals are enmeshed in mutual networks of moral and social obligations, and society is tightly knit together by these overlapping individual interdependencies.

According to Braithwaite (1989a), the criminological payoff for interdependency and communitarianism is high and multifaceted. Individual interdependency serves as a strong form of informal social control. Individuals who feel connected and responsible to others must always think, before they act, about how their behavior will affect others who are important to them. The prospect of being caught doing something untoward carries with it the risk of ostracism and disapproval from the group. These are powerful disincentives for anyone who cares about group approval.

Interdependency and communitarianism also create opportunities for Japan's criminal justice system to operate differently from the system in the United States (Clifford 1976; Bayley 1976). Japanese society and its criminal justice system can use shaming rather than formal punishment to a much greater degree than is possible in the United States. Indeed, Braithwaite (1989a, 62–64) argues that in Japan the approach taken to criminal offenders is like that of a family toward misbehaving children. The overriding goal is not to punish the offender and thereby secure compliance through fear but rather to shame and then reintegrate offenders into society. Compliance is achieved by resocializing the offender instead of by administering formal punishment.

Judged by official crime and arrest rates, Japan's approach to crime control is spectacularly successful. Compared to the United States, far fewer of its citizens become involved in crime and delinquency. To put it in the jargon of life course theory, far fewer pursue criminal trajectories. Although we have no direct evidence on the parameters of criminal careers in Japan, it seems likely that they are shorter and less serious than in the United States. The Japanese experience confirms the powerful impact of culture on the life course.

Despite their undeniable appeal, Japan's crime control accomplishments may come at a cost that many in the United States would be unwilling to pay. Interdependency, shaming, and communitarianism connote a high level of community involvement in the life course of individuals. Reared on notions of independence, self-reliance, and the right to privacy, Americans dislike and distrust intrusions into their private affairs. There are other differences as well. The average Japanese would find the cultural diversity and ethnic heterogeneity of American society incomprehensible. It is difficult to imagine the circumstances under which the Japanese approach to crime control could be replicated in the United States.

Summary

In the United States, we are accustomed to thinking of life as a possession, as something we can spend or use, within reason of course, more or less as we see fit. The teenager's rebellious yell "It's *my* life!" captures the sentiment. To an extent, of course, this perspective on life is accurate. We all can make decisions, and we all can choose to pursue one path over another. Go to school, or join a gang, or deal drugs. But this freedom of choice always occurs within parameters set by larger social structures. These structures shape and limit our perceptions of the range of options from which choices are made, and they determine how others will respond to our choices. The interaction between individual choice and social response shapes the life course.

All societies develop institutions for managing different stages of the life course. In the United States, families do the early work, followed by schools, the labor market, pension programs, and then hospitals and nursing homes. The central theme of this chapter has been that as these institutions change, as society places more or less emphasis on them, the structure of the life course changes as well. The structure of the life course also varies across cultures and societies.

Historical developments in several major social institutions—the economy, education, and the family—have profoundly altered the structure of the life course, with far-reaching criminological implications. It is not too far-fetched to say that as a recognizable stage in the life course, the modern teenager was created by the rise of the maturity gap. Whatever the second decade of life was like 200 years ago, it is not like that today. The maturity gap is a fundamental cause of youth crime. The transformation of the American family and household is another historical development that has contributed to the growth of youth crime.

Changes in the global economy that began in the 1960s dramatically altered the labor market and contributed to the deterioration of inner cities in the United States. These developments have not had salutary effects on the life chances of African Americans and other minorities. The concentration of poverty and the emergence of hyperghettos in inner cities blunted the life chances of all who live in these devastated communities. Access to good jobs largely disappeared, making it extraordinarily difficult for young people to follow standard occupational trajectories. As job and career opportunities contracted, young people looked elsewhere for ways to spend their time and energy. The end result was burgeoning numbers of minority youths involved in crime, gangs, drugs, and other sectors of the deviance service industry throughout the 1980s and early 1990s.

Finally, in the United States, the modern life course, especially for poor young minority men, is being shaped increasingly by the prison experiment and the war on drugs. Because of our astonishingly high rates of incarceration, a notable proportion of children born today can look forward to spending some part of their life in prison or jail. At today's rates, nearly one out of four African-American males born in the 1990s will be incarcerated sometime during his life (Bonczar and Beck 1997). Many more will have their lives disrupted by the criminal justice system through arrests, probation, deferred sentences, or some other type of legal intervention. In California, close to half of all African-American males are under some form of correctional supervision (Christianson 1998). In the United States, the criminal justice system has become a major institution for managing the life course of young men (and increasingly, young women) from poor, minority backgrounds. ✦

Chapter 7

Crime and the Life Course: Summing Up

Genes plus geography equals destiny.

—Anonymous

Overview

We have covered a lot of ground so far in our foray into the life course perspective on crime. You might say we have gone from genes to geography. The diversity of topics discussed throughout this book reflects both the interdisciplinary nature of the life course perspective and the extraordinary complexity of human behavior. No single discipline can ever hope to fully explain why people do what they do or why they develop in one way rather than another. Genes matter, but so do families, peers, spouses, neighborhoods, labor markets, justice systems, societies, cultures, and historical epochs. One of the great strengths of the life course perspective is its explicit recognition of the multidetermined, historically contingent nature of human behavior and development. The rise of the life course perspective has contributed to the breakdown in disciplinary isolation that has impeded progress in biology, sociology, and all the other sciences that focus on things human.

Although the theoretical diversity encompassed by the life course perspective is, indeed, a welcome development, it has drawbacks as well. It is difficult to summarize the perspective in simple terms. Researchers from a broad array of disciplines have made contributions that appear relevant to our understanding of the life course, but it is not yet clear exactly how they all fit together. The current state of knowledge is a little bit like a very complicated "connect the dots" type of picture. We know that the dot representing biology or genetic endowments connects in some way to the dot representing family. And we know that from this dot, multiple routes can be taken that travel through the points that stand for peers, neighborhoods, societies, and time periods. But exactly how all the dots connect to form individuals' life courses, how many different patterns they may form, and how the set of possible patterns may change over time is not certain. In other words, there is a lot that we do not know yet.

With this caveat in mind, we can, nevertheless, briefly recapitulate the main points, themes, and contributions of the life course perspective on crime.

Genetics, Nature, and Nurture

We all are born with a unique genetic endowment that influences how we think, feel, and perceive. Through the use of twin and adoption studies, geneticists have shown that predispositions to criminality are genetically transmitted from parents to their children. The research suggests that some individuals are born with endowments that predispose them to behave in ways that societies often define as antisocial, deviant, or criminal. These behavioral predispositions may be caused by neuropsychological deficits. The size of the genetic contribution to crime, however, is not known and may not be very large. Some individuals do seem to be at an initial disadvantage for developing prosocial trajectories through life. But it is not clear how large a disadvantage they face.

One thing, though, is becoming increasingly clear, and that is that the debate over whether nature or nurture is more important in determining human behavior is misguided. How individuals develop is ultimately determined by the interaction of genetic endowments and environments. Neither side of the equation can be ignored. In regard to developmental trajectories in crime, an especially potent interaction involves genetically based neuropsychological deficits and a poor quality of family life (Moffitt 1997). One benefit of the emergence of the life course perspective is that this fundamental truth is now out in the open and increasingly acknowledged by those who study crime, regardless of whether their disciplinary background is in biology, psychology, or sociology.

Families

The life course perspective has reinvigorated research on the family as a source of early conduct problems and later delinquency. Children who grow up to become serious juvenile delinquents are often raised in troubled and disadvantaged families. In these families, the parents either ignore their children or treat them with excessive harshness. They provide little in the way of emotional warmth and support for their offspring. In regard to promoting or preventing delinquency, what seems to matter most is not the structure of the family but rather the prevailing emotional climate in the home and the emotional closeness of the parent and child relationship.

Children who start out in troubled families often display conduct problems at a young age. Their behavioral problems are sufficiently outside the norm that they are recognized as troublesome by parents and other early caretakers. As toddlers and preschoolers, they have more temper tantrums and are more aggressive toward their peers than is normal for their age group. Having a difficult temperament as a young child portends trouble in a variety of life domains later in life, such as schooling and delinquency. Children who display early conduct problems are at risk of poor performance in school and early onset of delinquency. Early onset, in turn, is associated with having a lengthy criminal career.

Continuity and Discontinuity

One of the most consistent and well-documented empirical findings to emerge out of the life course perspective has been the discovery of continuity in behavior over time and in different domains of functioning. At every stage of the life course, behavior in the preceding stage is one of the strongest predictors of behavior in the current stage. Children as young as toddlers can be differentiated from one another on the basis of behavioral problems. Those who exhibit above-average levels of temper tantrums or aggressiveness are more likely to display conduct problems as they grow up than are toddlers who are closer to the norm in their behavior. Viewed retrospectively, one finds almost without exception very pronounced signs of trouble in the early personal histories of serious adult criminals. They do not just suddenly emerge fully formed in adulthood; rather, they have long histories of run-ins with the law. They also tend to exhibit less than optimal performance in most other domains of life. Their lives are characterized by poor school performance, unstable employment, and dysfunctional marital relationships.

The discovery of continuity in the life course has helped sensitize researchers to the importance of selection effects. These effects arise when individuals select themselves into different statuses because of underlying differences in temperament or criminal potential. Selection effects contribute to the empirical correlations we observe between crime and other events in the life course. For example, individuals with low self-control are likely to be both unemployed and involved in criminal behavior. In this situation, however, it would be a mistake to assume that the correlation between employment status and crime means that unemployment causes crime. In order to get an accurate picture of the causal effect of unemployment on crime, it is necessary to control for the selection effect, that is, to control for individual differences in self-control or some other construct of criminal potential.

Although retrospective examinations of the life histories of adult criminals always uncover both homotypic and heterotypic continuity, this does not mean that we can tell early on what sort of criminal trajectory a young child will follow through life. Discontinuity is just as much a part of the life course as continuity. Most antisocial children do not grow up to be antisocial adults. In the prospective longitudinal studies conducted to date, researchers have been unable to identify any set of early predictors that can unerringly single out the children who will develop into serious criminals. In most studies, a majority of those who show signs of conduct disorders or antisocial behavior as toddlers or preschoolers do not go on to become serious juvenile delinquents. And most delinquents discontinue their involvement in crime as they enter their twenties. In regard to trajectories in crime, discontinuity appears to be just as much a part of the life course as continuity.

The existence of discontinuity in the life course alerts us to the importance of avoiding the ontogenetic fallacy, that is, the assumption that development takes place entirely through the maturational unfolding of inborn traits. Research documents the importance of many events as potentially consequential turning points in the life course. In terms of redirecting criminal trajectories toward desistance, the most important turning points seem to reside in the development of informal social controls through marriage and employment. Establishing a good relationship with a romantic partner or finding a good job appears to hasten desistance, or if not desistance, then at least a reduction in criminal conduct.

History and Social Change

Continuity and discontinuity in trajectories in crime are linked to the broader social context within which individual life courses develop. It is important to remember that the life course is socially and historically embedded. Community context and historical change affect the life course in myriad ways. Compared to white children raised in affluent neighborhoods, minority children who grow up in severely disadvantaged communities experience much higher risks of a long list of criminogenic events and conditions, including domestic violence, child maltreatment, teenage parenthood, family disruption, poverty, and neighborhood instability (McGee et al. 1991). The criminal trajectories of children raised in these conditions often start early and lead inexorably to criminal embeddedness. Because they are located in areas that are socially isolated, they have fewer chances of experiencing the positive turning points that redirect criminal trajectories. And the life course disadvantages faced by the urban poor got worse after the 1970s, especially for minorities (Sampson and Wilson 1994). The historical causes of the changing context of urban poverty include the deindustrialization of the U.S. economy, residential segregation by race, the flight of minority middle-class families from the inner city, and federal and local government policies (Gephart 1997).

But just as we do not yet clearly understand the individual level causes of continuity or discontinuity in crime, neither do we clearly understand how community context shapes developmental trajectories. Obviously, not everyone who grows up in poverty ends up as a career criminal. People follow different trajectories in poverty-stricken areas just as they do elsewhere, and many people who grow up in disadvantaged circumstances somehow manage to lead conventional law-abiding lives despite the disadvantages. How people get sorted into these different paths is still an open question. There are still relatively few longitudinal studies that have combined individual and contextual-level information in ways that permit the investigation of contextual effects on individual development. This situation may improve dramatically in the not-too-distant future as a result of two major research initiatives that are focusing on the developmental consequences of community context. The Project on Human Development in Chicago has been discussed at several points in this book. In addition to that effort, the Social Science Research Council has established a Working Group on Communities and Neighborhoods, Family Processes, and Individual Development. The Working Group will investigate how neighborhoods and communities influence the development of families and children (Brooks-Gunn, Duncan, and Aber 1997a; 1997b). For now, though, it is probably best to keep an open mind about how community context shapes the life course. We have to be careful to avoid environmental determinism as well as genetic determinism.

A Final Conclusion

If we had to sum up in a sentence or two the main points that have emerged from the life course perspective, we might paraphrase the old newspaper adage that a good news story covers "who, what, where, when, and why." The shape of your life course is determined by *when* you are born, *where* you are born, *who* your parents are, *how* they treat you, and *who* you meet as you age. Or, to put it more analytically, the life course is shaped by history, geography, genes, family environment, and other people. To this list, we should probably add *luck*. Luck is important in the sense that the turning points that criminologists have identified as important routes out of crime are to some degree inherently unpredictable events. Meeting the right person to settle down with or finding a fulfilling job depend in part on circumstances beyond individuals' control. That these turning points happen to some people and not others is partly a matter of chance. ✦

References

Allan, Emilie A. and Darrell Steffensmeier. 1989. "Youth, Underemployment, and Property Crime: Differential Effects of Job Availability and Job Quality on Juvenile and Young Adult Arrest Rates." *American Sociological Review* 54:107–23.

Anderson, Elijah. 1990. *Streetwise: Race, Class and Change in an Urban Community.* Chicago: University of Chicago Press.

Austin, James and John Irwin. 2001. *It's About Time: America's Imprisonment Binge.* Belmont, CA: Wadsworth.

Averitt, Robert. 1992. "The New Structuralism." *Contemporary Sociology* 21:650–53.

Bartusch, Dawn R. J., Donald R. Lynam, Terrie E. Moffitt, and Phil A. Silva. 1997. "Is Age Important? Testing a General Versus a Developmental Theory of Antisocial Behavior." *Criminology* 35(1):13–48.

Bayley, David H. 1976. *Forces of Order: Police Behavior in Japan and the United States.* Berkeley: University of California Press.

Begley, Sharon. 2000. "Getting Inside a Teen Brain." *Newsweek* (February 28), 135:58.

Bennett, William J., John J. Jr. DiIuLio, and John P. Walters. 1996. *Body Count: Moral Poverty—and How to Win America's War Against Crime and Drugs.* New York: Simon Schuster.

Benson, Michael and Elizabeth Moore. 1992. "Are White-Collar and Common Offenders the Same: An Empirical and Theoretical Critique of a Recently Proposed General Theory of Crime." *Journal of Research in Crime and Delinquency* 29(3):251–72.

Benson, Michael L. 1984. "The Fall From Grace: Loss of Occupational Status Among Convicted White Collar Offenders." *Criminology* 22(4):573–93.

——. 1985a. "Denying the Guilty Mind: Accounting for Involvement in a White-Collar Crime." *Criminology* 23(4):583–607.

——. 1985b. "White-Collar Offenders Under Community Supervision." *Justice Quarterly* 2(3):429–38.

——. 1989. "The Influence of Class Position on the Formal and Informal Sanctioning of White-Collar Offenders." *Sociology Quarterly* 30(3):465–80.

Benson, Michael L. and Francis T. Cullen. 1998. *Combating Corporate Crime: Local Prosecutors at Work.* Boston: Northeastern University Press.

Benson, Michael L., Greer L. Fox, Alfred DeMaris, and Judy Van Wyk. 2000. "Violence in Families: The Intersection of Race, Poverty and Community Context." Greer L. Fox and Michael Benson (eds.) in *Families, Crime, and Criminal Justice*, pp. 91–109. New York: Elsevier Science, Inc.

Benson, Michael L. and Kent R. Kerley. 2000. "Life Course Theory and White-Collar Crime." Henry N. Pontell and David Shichor (eds.) in *Contemporary Issues in Crime and Criminal Justice: Essays in Honor of Gilbert Geis*, pp. 121–36. Saddle River, NJ: Prentice Hall.

Benson, Michael L. and Esteban Walker. 1988. "Sentencing the White-Collar Offender." *American Sociological Review* 53:294–302.

Bickford, Adam S. and Douglas S. Massey. 1991. "Segregation in the Second Ghetto: Racial and Ethnic Segregation in American Public Housing, 1977." *Social Forces* 69(4):1011–36.

Blumstein, Alfred and Jacqueline Cohen. 1987. "Characterizing Criminal Careers." *Science* 237(4818):985–91.

Blumstein, Alfred, Jacqueline Cohen, Jeffrey A. Roth, and Christy A. Visher (eds.) 1986. *Criminal Careers and 'Career Criminals.'* Vol. 1. Washington, DC: National Academy Press.

Bonczar, Thomas P. and Allen J. Beck. 1997. *Lifetime Likelihood of Going to State or Federal Prison.* Washington, DC: U.S. Department of Justice.

Braithwaite, John. 1982. "Challenging Just Desserts: Punishing White-Collar Criminals." *Journal of Criminal Law & Criminology* 73(2):723–63.

——. 1989a. *Crime, Shame and Reintegration.* Cambridge, MA: Cambridge University Press.

——. 1989b. "Criminological Theory and Organizational Crime." *Justice Quarterly* 6(3):333–58.

Braithwaite, John and Brent Fisse. 1990. "On the Plausibility of Corporate Crime Control." *Advances in Criminological Theory* 2:15–37.

Brodeur, Paul. 1985. *Outrageous Misconduct.* New York: Pantheon.

Brooks-Gunn, Jeanne, Greg J. Duncan, and Lawrence Aber (Eds.). 1997a. *Neighborhood Poverty: Context and Consequences for Children.* New York: Russell Sage.

——. (Eds.). 1997b. *Neighborhood Poverty: Policy Implications in Studying Neighborhoods.* New York: Russell Sage.

Brooks-Gunn, Jeanne, Greg J. Duncan, Pamela Kato, and Naomi Sealand. 1993. "Do Neighborhoods Influence Child and Adolescent Behavior?" *American Journal of Sociology* 99:353–95.

Browning, Katharine, David Huizinga, Rolf Loeber, and Terence P. Thornberry. 1999. *OJJDP Fact Sheet Report, Number 100.* Washington, DC: Office of Juvenile Justice and Delinquency Prevention.

Brownlee, Shannon, Robert Hotinski, Bellamy Pailthorp, Erin Ragan, and Kathleen Wong. 1999. "Inside the Teenage Brain." *U.S. News and World Report,* (August 9) 127:44.

Buikhuisen, W. 1987. "Cerebral Dysfunctions and Persistent Juvenile Delinquency." In Sarnoff A. Mednick, Terrie E. Moffitt, and Susan A. Stact (eds.), *The Causes of Crime: New Biological Approaches,* pp. 168–84. Cambridge: Cambridge University Press.

Bureau of Justice Statistics, U.S. Department of Justice. 1999. "Trends in U.S. Correctional Populations." *Correctional Populations in the United States, 1996.* Washington, D.C.: Department of Justice.

Bursik, Robert J. 2000. "Property Crime Trends." In Joseph F. Sheley (ed.), *Criminology: A Contemporary Handbook,* pp. 215–32. Belmont, CA: Wadsworth.

Carey, Gregory. 1994. "Genetics and Violence." In Albert J. Reiss, Klaus A. Miczek, and Jeffrey A. Roth (eds.), *Understanding and Preventing Violence,* vol. 2, pp. 21–58. Washington, DC: National Academy Press.

——. 2000. *Human Genetics for the Social Science.* Available: <http:psych.colorado.edu/hgss/>.

Caspi, Avshalom, Glen H. Elder, Jr., and Daryl J. Bem. 1987. "Moving Against the World: Life-Course Patterns of Explosive Children." *Developmental Psychology* 23(2):308–13.

Caspi, Avshalom, Donald Lynam, Terrie E. Moffitt, and Phil A. Silva. 1993. "Unraveling Girls' Delinquency: Biological, Dispositional, and Contextual Contributions to Adolescent Misbehavior." *Developmental Psychology* 29(1):19–30.

Caspi, Avshalom, Terrie E. Moffitt, Phil A. Silva, Magda Stouthamer-Loeber, Robert F. Krueger, and Pamela S. Schmutte. 1994. "Are Some People Crime-Prone? Replications of the Personality-Crime Relationship Across Countries, Genders, Races, and Methods." *Criminology* 32(2):163–94.

Chaiken, Jan M. and M. Chaiken. 1982. *Varieties of Criminal Behavior.* Santa Monica, CA: Rand Corporation.

Chiricos, Theodore. 1987. "Rates of Crime and Unemployment: An Analysis of Aggregate Research Evidence." *Social Problems* 34:187–212.

Christiansen, Karl O. 1977. "A Preliminary Study of Criminality Among Twins." In Sarnoff A. Mednick and Karl O. Christiansen (eds.), *Biosocial Bases of Criminal Behavior*, pp. 89–108. New York: Gardner Press, Inc.

Christianson, Scott. 1998. *With Liberty for Some: 500 Years of Imprisonment in America*. Boston: Northeastern University Press.

Clifford, W. 1976. *Crime Control in Japan*. Lexington, MA: Lexington Books.

Clinard, Marshall B. and Richard Quinney. 1973. *Criminal Behavior Systems: A Typology*. New York: Holt, Rinehart, and Winston.

Clinard, Marshall B. and Peter C. Yeager. 1980. *Corporate Crime*. New York: Free Press.

Coleman, James S. 1988. "Social Capital in the Creation of Human Capital." *American Journal of Sociology* 94 (Supplement):S95–S120.

Coleman, James W. 1987. "Toward An Integrated Theory of White-Collar Crime." *American Journal of Sociology* 93(2):406–39.

—. 1989. *The Criminal Elite*. New York: St. Martin's Press.

—. 1994. *The Criminal Elite: The Sociology of White-Collar Crime*. 3rd ed. New York: St. Martin's Press.

Conklin, John E. 1977. *Illegal But Not Criminal: Business Crime in America*. Englewood Cliffs, CA: Prentice-Hall.

Coulton, C, S. Pandey, and J. Chow. 1990. "Concentration of Poverty and Risk to Children in Urban Neighborhoods: An Analysis of the Cleveland Area." *Social Work Research and Abstracts* 26(4):5–16.

Coulton, Claudia, Jill Korbin, Marilyn Su, and Julian Chow. 1995. "Community Level Factors and Child Maltreatment Rates." *Child Development* 66:1262–76.

Coulton, S. J. and S. Pandey. 1992. "Geographic Concentration of Poverty and Risk to Children in Urban Neighborhoods." *American Behavioral Scientist* 35(3):238–57.

Cressey, Donald. 1953. *Other People's Money*. New York: Free Press.

—. 1989. "The Poverty of Theory in Corporate Crime Research." In William S. Laufer and Freda Adler (eds.), *Advances in Criminological Theory*, vol. 1, pp. 31–55. New Brunswick: Transaction.

Croall, Hazel. 1989. "Who Is the White-Collar Criminal." *British Journal of Criminology* 29(2):157–74.

Crowe, R. R. 1972. "The Adopted Offspring of Women Criminal Offenders: A Study of Their Arrest Records." *General Psychiatry* 27:600–603.

Cullen, Francis T. 1994. "Social Support As an Organizing Concept for Criminology: Presidential Address to the Academy of Criminal Justice Sciences." *Justice Quarterly* 11(4):527–59.

Cullen, Francis T., William J. Maakestad, and Gray Cavendar. 1987. *Corporate Crime Under Attack*. Cincinnati, OH: Anderson .

Currie, Elliot. 1993. *Reckoning: Drugs, the Cities, and the American Future*. New York: Hill and Wang.

——. 1998. *Crime and Punishment in America*. New York: Metropolitan Books.

Daly, Kathleen. 1989. "Gender and Varieties of White-Collar Crime." *Criminology* 27(4):769–94.

Dannefer, Dale. 1984. "Adult Development and Social Theory: A Paradigmatic Reappraisal." *American Sociological Review* 49:100–16.

Edelhertz, Herbert. 1970. *The Nature, Impact and Prosecution of White-Collar Crime*. Washington, DC: Department of Justice.

Eichorn, Dorothy H., John A. Clausen, Norma Haan, Marjorie Honzik, and Paul H. Mussen (Eds.). 1981. *Past and Present in Middle Life*. New York: Academic Press.

Elder, Glen H. Jr. 1974. *Children of the Great Depression: Social Change in Life Experience*. Chicago: University of Chicago Press.

——. 1985. "Perspectives on the Life Course." In Glen H. Elder, Jr. (ed.), *Life Course Dynamics: Trajectories and Transitions, 1968–1980*, 23–49. Ithaca, NY: Cornell University Press.

——. 1994. "Time, Human Agency, and Social Change." *Social Psychology Quarterly* 57(1):4–15.

——. 1995. "The Life Course Paradigm: Social Change and Individual Development." In Phyliss Moen, Glen H. Elder, Jr., and Kurt Luscher (eds.), *Examining Lives in Context: Perspectives on the Ecology of Human Development*, pp. 101–135. Washington, DC: American Psychological Association.

——. 1996. "Human Lives in Changing Societies: Life Course and Developmental Insights." In Robert B. Cairns, Glen H. Jr. Elder, and E. J. Costello (eds.), *Developmental Science*, pp. 31–62. New York: Cambridge.

Elliott, Delbert S. 1994. "Serious Violent Offenders: Onset, Developmental Course and Termination." *Criminology* 32(1):1–22.

Elliott, Delbert S. and David Huizinga. 1983. "Social Class and Delinquent Behavior in a National Youth Panel: 1976–1980." *Criminology* 21:149–77.

Elliott, Delbert, David Huizinga, and Suzanne Ageton. 1985. *Explaining Delinquency and Drug Use*. Beverly Hills, CA: Sage.

Ellis, Lee. 1990. "Conceptualizing Criminal and Related Behavior From a Biosocial Perspective." In Lee Ellis and Harry Hoffman (eds.), *Crime in Biological, Social, and Moral Contexts*, pp. 18–35. New York: Praeger Publishers.

Ermann, M. D. and Richard J. Lundman, Editors. 1992. *Corporate and Governmental Deviance*. 4th ed. New York: Oxford University Press.

Evans, T. David, Francis T. Cullen, Velmer S. Burton, Jr., R. Greg Dunaway, and Michael L. Benson. 1997. "The Social Consequences of Self-Control: Testing the General Theory of Crime." *Criminology* 35(3):475–501.

Farrington, David P. 1977. "The Effects of Public Labelling." *British Journal of Criminology* 17(2):112–25.

——. 1978. "The Family Background of Aggressive Youths." In L. A. Hersov, M. Berger, and D. Shaffer (eds.), *Aggression and Antisocial Behavior in Childhood and Adolescence*, pp. 73–93. Oxford: Pergamon Press.

——. 1979. "Longitudinal Research on Crime and Delinquency." In Norval Morris and Michael Tonry (eds.), *Crime and Justice: An Annual Review of Research*, vol. 1, pp. 289–350. Chicago: University of Chicago Press.

——. 1983. "Offending From 10 to 25 Years of Age." In Katherine T. Van Dusen and Sarnoff A. Mednick (eds.), *Prospective Studies of Crime and Delinquency*, pp. 17–38. Boston: Kluwer-Nijhoff Publishing.

——. 1994. "Human Development and Criminal Careers." In Mike Maguire, Rod Morgan, and Robert Reiner (eds.), in *Oxford Handbook of Criminology*, pp. 511–84. New York: Oxford University Press.

Farrington, David P., Horwar N. Snyder, and Terrence A. Finnegan. 1988. "Specialization in Juvenile Court Careers." *Criminology* 26(3):461–85.

Farrington, David P., Lloyd E. Ohlin, and James Q. Wilson. 1986. *Understanding and Controlling Crime*. New York: Springer-Verlag.

Farrington, David P. and Donald J. West. 1990. "The Cambridge Study in Delinquent Development: A Long-Term Follow-Up of 411 London Males." In H. J. Kerner and G. Kaiser (eds.), *Kriminalitat: Personlichkeit, Legensgeschichte, Und Verhalten*, pp. 115–38. Berlin: Springer-Verlag.

Felson, Marcus. 1994. *Crime and Everyday Life: Insights and Implications for Society*. Thousand Oaks, CA: Pine Forge Press.

——. 1998. *Crime and Everyday Life*. Thousand Oaks, CA: Pine Forge Press.

Fischbein, Siv. 1980. "IQ and Social Class." *Intelligence* 4:51–63.

Frank, Nancy. 1985. *Crimes Against Health and Safety*. New York: Harrow and Heston.

Forst, Brian and William Rhodes. The data utilized in this publication were made available by the Interuniversity Consortium for Political and Social Research. The data for *Sentencing in Eight United States District Courts, 1973–1978* were originally collected by Brian Forst and William Rhodes. Neither the collectors of the original data nor the consortium bear any responsibility for the analyses or interpretations presented here.

Freedman, Deborah, Arland Thornton, Donald Camburn, Duane Alwin, and Linda Young-DeMarco. 1988. "The Life History Calendar: A Technique for Collecting Retrospective Data." *Sociological Methodology* 18:37–68.

Freeman, Richard B. 1987. "The Relation of Criminal Activity to Black Youth Unemployment." *Review of Black Political Economy* 16(1–2):99–107.

——. 1992. "Crime and the Employment of Disadvantaged Youth." In George Peterson and Wayne Vroman (eds.), *Urban Labor Markets and Job Opportunity*, pp. 201–37. Washington, DC: The Urban Institute Press.

——. 1995. "The Labor Market." In James Q. Wilson and Joan Petersilia (eds.), *Crime*, pp. 171–91. San Francisco, CA: Institute for Contemporary Studies.

Freidman, Lawrence M. and Jack Ladinsky. 1967. "Social Change and the Law of Industrial Accidents." *Columbia Law Review* 67(1):50–82.

Furstenberg, Frank F., Jeanne Brooks-Gunn, and S. P. Morgan. 1987. *Adolescent Mothers in Later Life*. New York: Cambridge University Press.

Gabor, Thomas. 1994. *Everybody Does It! Crime by the Public*. Toronto: University of Toronto Press.

Geis, Gilbert. 1988. "From Deuteronomy to Deniability: A Historical Perspective on White-Collar Crime." *Justice Quarterly* 5(1):7–32.

——. 1995. "A Review, Rebuttal, and Reconciliation of Cressey and Braithwaite and Fisse on Criminological Theory and Corporate Crime." *White-Collar Crime: Classic and Contemporary Views*, 3rd ed., pp. 450–476. New York: Free Press.

Gelles, Richard J. 1992. "Poverty and Violence Toward Children." *American Behavioral Scientist* 35(3):258–74.

——. 1950. *Unraveling Juvenile Delinquency*. Cambridge, MA: Harvard University Press.

Gephart, Martha A. 1997. "Neighborhoods and communities as contexts for development." In J. Brooks-Gunn, G. J. Duncan, and J. L. Aber (eds.), *Neighborhood Poverty: Context and Consequences for Children*, pp. 1–43. New York: Russell Sage.

Glueck, Sheldon and Eleanor Glueck. 1952. *Delinquents in the Making: Paths to Prevention*. New York: Harper & Row .

——. 1956. *Physique and Delinquency*. New York: Harper & Brothers.

——. 1968. *Delinquents and Nondelinquents in Perspective*. Cambridge, MA: Harvard University Press.

Gold, Martin. 1966. "Undetected Delinquent Behavior." *Journal of Research in Crime and Delinquency* 3:27–46.

Gottfredson, Michael R. and Travis Hirschi. 1990. *A General Theory of Crime*. Stanford, CA: Stanford University Press.

Gottlieb, Gilbert. 1996. "Developmental Psychobiological Theory." In Robert B. Cairns, Glen H. Elder, Jr., and E. J. Costello (eds.), *Developmental Science: Toward a Unified Framework*, pp. 63–77. Cambridge: Cambridge University Press.

Gould, Stephen J. 1981. *The Mismeasure of Man*. New York: W. W. Norton & Company.

Gouldner, Alvin W. 1970. *The Coming Crisis of Western Sociology*. New York: Basic Books.

Greenberg, David F. 1977. "Delinquency and the Age Structure of Society." *Contemporary Crises* 1:189–223.

Hagan, John. 1991. "Destiny and Drift: Subcultural Preferences, Status Attainment, and the Risks and Rewards of Youth." *American Sociological Review* 56:567–82.

——. 1993. "The Social Embeddedness of Crime and Unemployment." *Criminology* 31(4):465–92.

——. 1994. *Crime and Disrepute*. Thousand Oaks, CA.: Pine Forge.

——. 1997a. "Crime and Capitalization: Toward a Developmental Theory of Street Crime in America." In Terence P. Thornberry (ed.), in *Developmental Theories of Crime and Delinquency*, pp. 287–308. New Brunswick, NJ: Transaction Publishers.

——. 1997b. "Defiance and Despair: Subcultural and Structural Linkages Between Delinquency and Despair in the Life Course." *Social Forces* 76(1):119–34.

Hagan, John and Ronit Dinovitzer. 1999. "Collateral Consequences of Imprisonment for Children, Communities, and Prisoners." In Michael Tonry and Joan Petersilia (eds.), *Crime and Punishment: Prisons*, Vol. 26, pp. 121–62. Chicago: University of Chicago Press.

Hagan, John and Bill McCarthy. 1997. *Mean Streets: Youth Crime and Homelessness*. Cambridge: Cambridge University Press.

Hagan, John, Ilene H. Nagel-Bernstein, and Celesta Albonetti. 1980. "The Differential Sentencing of White Collar Offenders in Ten Federal District Courts." *American Sociological Review* 45:802–20.

Hagan, John and Alberto Palloni. 1988. "Crimes As Social Events in the Life Course: Reconceiving a Criminological Controversy." *Criminology* 26(1):87–100.

Hagedorn, John. 1988. *People and Folks: Gangs, Crime and the Underclass in a Rustbelt City*. Chicago: Lakeview Press.

——. 1994. "Homeboys, Dope Fiends, Legits, and New Jacks." *Criminology* 32(2):197–219.

Harris, Judith R. 1995. "Where Is the Child's Environment? A Group Socialization Theory of Development." *Psychological Review* 102(3):458–89.

Henry, Bill, Avshalom Caspi, Terrie E. Moffitt, and Phil A. Silva. 1996. "Temperamental and Familial Predictors of Violent and Nonviolent Criminal Convictions: Age 3 to Age 18." *Developmental Psychology* 32(4):613–23.

Hills, Stuart L. (ed.). 1987. *Corporate Violence.* Totowa, NJ: Rowman & Littlefield.

Hindelang, Michael. 1973. "Causes of Delinquency: A Partial Replication and Extension." *Social Problems* 20:471–87.

Hirschi, Travis. 1969. *Causes of Delinquency.* Berkeley, CA: University of California Press.

Hirschi, Travis and Michael Gottfredson. 1987. "Causes of White-Collar Crime." *Criminology* 25:949–74.

Hochstedler, Ellen (Ed.). 1984. *Corporations As Criminals.* Beverly Hills, CA: Sage.

Hofferth, Sandra. 1985. "Updating Children's Life Course." *Journal of Marriage and the Family* 47:93–115.

Huesmann, L. R., L. D. Eron, M. M. Lefkowitz, and L. O. Walder. 1984. "Stability of Aggression Over Time and Generations." *Developmental Psychology* 20:1120–34.

Huizinga, David, A. W. Weiher, Scott Menard, R. Espiritu, and Finn Esbensen. 1998. "Some Not So Boring Findings From the Denver Youth Survey." Paper Presented at the American Society of Criminology Meeting, Washington, DC.

Inciardi, James A. 1986. *The War on Drugs: Heroin, Cocaine, Crime and Public Policy.* Palo Alto, CA: Mayfield Publishing Company.

Institute for Social Research. 1996. *Monitoring the Future, 1995.* Ann Arbor, MI: Institute for Social Research.

Janis, Irving L. 1972. *Victims of Groupthink.* Boston: Houghton Mifflin.

Jarrett, Robin L. 1997. "Bringing Families Back In: Neighborhood Effects on Child Development." In Jeanne Brooks-Gunn, Greg J. Duncan, and J. L. Aber (eds.), *Neighborhood Poverty: Policy Implications in Studying Neighborhoods,* Vol. 2, pp. 48–64. New York: Russell Sage Foundation.

Johnston, Denise and Michael Carlin. 1996. "Enduring Trauma Among Children of Criminal Offenders." *Progress: Family Systems Research and Therapy* 5:9–36.

Kempf, Kimberly L. 1987. "Specialization and the Criminal Career." *Criminology* 25(2):399–420.

Klein, Malcom W. 1987. "Watch Out for That Last Variable." In Sarnoff A. Mednick, Terrie E. Moffitt, and Susan A. Stack (eds.), *The Causes of Crime: New Biological Approaches,* pp. 25–41. Cambridge, MA: Cambridge University Press.

Kowalski, Kathiann M. 2000. "What's Inside the Teenage Brain." *Current Health 2,* 27(3):6.

Kramer, Ronald C. 1984. "Corporate Criminality: Development of an Idea." In Ellen Hochstedler (ed.), *Corporations As Criminals*, pp. 13–38. Beverly Hills, CA: Sage Publications.

LaFree, Gary. 1998. *Losing Legitimacy: Street Crime and the Decline of Social Institutions in America.* Boulder, CO: Westview Press.

Lasley, James R. 1988. "Toward a Control Theory of White-Collar Offending." *Journal of Quantitative Criminology* 4(4):347–62.

Laub, John H., Daniel S. Nagin, and Robert J. Sampson. 1998. "Trajectories of Change in Criminal Offending: Good Marriages and the Desistance Process." *American Sociological Review* 63(2):225–38.

Laub, John H. and Robert J. Sampson. 1993. "Turning Points in the Life Course: Why Change Matters to the Study of Crime." *Criminology* 32(3):301–25.

Lerman, Robert I. 1993. "A National Profile of Young Unwed Fathers." In Robert I. Lerman and Theodora J. Ooms (eds.), *Young Unwed Fathers: Changing Roles and Emerging Policies*, pp. 27–51. Philadelphia, PA: Temple University Press.

Levi, Michael. 1987. *Regulating Fraud.* London: Tavistock.

Levinson, Daniel J. 1978. *The Seasons of a Man's Life.* New York: Alfred A. Knopf.

Lin, Nan. 1986. "Conceptualizing Social Support." In Nan Lin, A. Dean, and W. Edsel (eds.), *Social Support, Life Events, and Depression*, pp. 17–30. Orlando, FL: Academic Press.

Loeber, Rolf and T. Dishion. 1983. "Early Predictors of Male Delinquency: A Review." *Psychological Bulletin* 94(1):68–99.

Loeber, Rolf, David P. Farrington, Magda Stouthamer-Loeber, Terrie Moffitt, and Avashalom Caspi. 1998. "The Development of Male Offending: Key Findings From the First Decade of the Pittsburgh Youth Study." *Studies in Crime and Crime Prevention* 7:141–72.

Loeber, Rolf and Dale F. Hay. 1994. "Developmental Approaches to Aggression and Conduct Problems." In Michael Rutter and Dale F. Hay (ed.), *Development Through Life: A Handbook for Clinicians*, pp. 488–516. Oxford, England: Blackwell Scientific Publications.

Loeber, Rolf and Magda Stouthamer-Loeber. 1986. "Family Factors As Correlates and Predictors of Juvenile Conduct Problems and Delinquency." In Michael Tonry and Norval Morris (eds.), *Crime and Justice: An Annual Review of Research*, Vol. 7, pp. 29–149. Chicago: University of Chicago Press.

Loeber, Rolf, Magda Stouthamer-Loeber, and S. M. Green. 1991. "Age at Onset of Problem Behavior in Boys and Later Disruptive and Delinquent Behaviors." *Criminal Behavior and Mental Health* 1:229–46.

Logan, John R. and Harvey L. Molotch. 1987. *Urban Fortunes: The Political Economy of Place.* Berkeley: University of California Press.

Lombroso, Cesare. 1887. *L'Homme Criminel.* Paris: F. Alcan.

Long, Sharon K. and Ann D. Witte. 1981. "Current Economic Trends: Implications for Crime and Criminal Justice." In Kevin N. Wright (ed.), *Crime and Criminal Justice in a Declining Economy,* pp. 69–143. Cambridge, MA: Oelgeschlage, Gunn and Hain.

Lykken, David T. 1995. *The Antisocial Personalities.* Hillsdale, NJ: Lawrence Erlbaum.

MacLeod, Jay. 1987. *Ain't No Making It: Leveled Aspirations in a Low-Income Neighborhood.* Boulder, CO: Westview Press.

Magnusson, David and Robert B. Cairns. 1996. "Developmental Science: Toward a Unified Framework." In Robert B. Cairns, Glen H. Jr. Elder, and E. J. Costello (eds.), *Developmental Science,* pp. 7–30. Cambridge U.K.: Cambridge University Press.

Mann, Kenneth. 1985. *Defending White-Collar Crime: A Portrait of Attorneys at Work.* New Haven, CT: Yale University Press.

Mann, Kenneth, Stanton Wheeler, and Austin Sarat. 1980. "Sentencing the White-Collar Offender." *American Criminal Law Review* 17(4):479–500.

Mannheim, Hermann. 1965. *Comparative Criminology.* Boston: Houghton Mifflin Co.

Mauer, Marc. 1999. *Race to Incarcerate.* New York: New Press.

Mayer, Karl U. and Walter Muller. 1986. "The State and the Structure of the Life Course." In Aage B. Sorensen, Franz E. Weinert, and Lonnie R. Sherrod (eds.), *Human Development and the Life Course: Multidisciplinary Perspectives,* pp. 217–45. Hillsdale, NJ: Lawrence Erlbaum Associates.

McCord, William and Joan McCord with Irving K. Zola. 1959. *Origins of Crime.* New York: Columbia University Press.

McGee, R., R. Partridge, S. M. Williams, and Phil A. Silva. 1991. "A Twelve Year Follow Up of Preschool Hyperactive Children." *Journal of the American Academy of Child and Adolescent Psychiatry* 30:224–32.

Mednick, Sarnoff A., William F. Jr. Gabrielli, and Barry Hutchings. 1987. "Genetic Factors in the Etiology of Criminal Behavior." In Sarnoff A. Mednick, Terrie E. Moffitt, and Susan A. Stack (eds.), *The Causes of Crime: New Biological Approaches,* pp. 74–91. Cambridge U.K.: Cambridge University Press.

Messerschmidt, James W. 1993. *Masculinities and Crime: Critique and Reconceptualization of Theory.* Boston: Rowman & Littlefield.

Messner, Steven and Richard Rosenfeld. 1997. *Crime and the American Dream.* Belmont, CA: Wadsworth.

Mitchell, S. and P. Rosa. 1981. "Boyhood Behavior Problems As Precursors of Criminality: A Fifteen-Year Follow-Up Study." *Journal of Child Psychology and Psychiatry* 22:19–33.

Moffitt, Terrie E. 1990. "Juvenile Delinquency and Attention Deficit Disorder: Boys' Developmental Trajectories From Age 3 to Age 15." *Child Development* 61:893–910.

——. 1993. "Adolescence-Limited and Life-Course Persistent Antisocial Behavior: A Developmental Taxonomy." *Psychological Review* 100:674–701.

——. 1994. "Natural Histories of Delinquency." In Elmar G. M. Weitekamp and Hans-Jurgen Kerner (eds.), *Cross-National Longitudinal Research on Human Development and Criminal Behavior*, pp. 3–61. London: Kluwer Academic Publishers.

——. 1997. "Adolescence-Limited and Life-Course-Persistent Offending: A Complementary Pair of Developmental Theories." In Terence P. Thornberry (ed.), *Developmental Theories of Crime and Delinquency*, pp. 11–54. New Brunswick, NJ: Transaction Publishers.

Moffitt, Terrie E. and Phil A. Silva. 1988. "Neuropsychological Deficit and Self-Reported Delinquency in an Unselected Birth Cohort." *Journal of the American Academy of Child and Adolescent Psychiatry* 27(2):233–40.

Monk-Turner, Elizabeth. 1989. "Effects of High School Delinquency on Educational Attainment and Adult Occupational Status." *Sociological Perspectives* 32(3):413–18.

Moore, Joan. 1991. *Going Down to the Barrio: Homeboys and Homegirls in Change*. Philadelphia: Temple University Press.

Nagin, Daniel S. and Kenneth C. Land. 1993. "Age, Criminal Careers, and Population Heterogeneity: Specification and Estimation of a Nonparametric, Mixed Poisson Model." *Criminology* 31(3):327–62.

Nagin, Daniel S. and Raymond Paternoster. 1991. "On the Relationship of Past to Future Participation in Delinquency." *Criminology* 29(2):163–89.

Newman, Katherine S. 1999. *No Shame in My Game: The Working Poor in the Inner City*. New York: Knopf & Russell Sage Foundation.

O'Connor, Thomas, Kirby Deater-Deckard, David Fulker, Michael Rutter, and Robert Plomin. 1998. "Genotype-Environment Correlations in Late Childhood and Early Adolescence: Antisocial Behavioral Problems and Coercive Parenting." *Developmental Psychology* 34:970–981.

Orland, Leonard. 1980. "Reflections on Corporate Crime: Law in Search of Theory and Scholarship." *American Criminal Law Review* 17:501–20.

Padilla, Felix. 1992. *The Gang As an American Enterprise*. New Brunswick, NJ: Rutgers University Press.

Passas, Nikos. 1990. "Anomie and Corporate Deviance." *Contemporary Crises* 14:157–78.

Paternoster, Raymond and Sally Simpson. 1993. "A Rational Choice Theory of Corporate Crime." In Ronald V. Clarke and Marcus Felson (eds.), *Routine Activity and Rational Choice*, Vol. 5, pp. 37–58. New Brunswick, NJ: Transaction.

Patterson, Gerald R. 1980. "Children Who Steal." In Travis Hirschi and Michael R. Gottfredson (eds.), *Understanding Crime*, pp. 73–90. Beverly Hills, CA: Sage.

Patterson, Gerald R., J. B. Reid, and T. J. Dishion. 1992. *Antisocial Boys*. Eugene, OR: Castalia Publishing.

Peeples, Faith and Rolf Loeber. 1994. "Do Individual Factors and Neighborhood Context Explain Ethnic Differences in Juvenile Delinquency?" *Journal of Quantitative Criminology* 10(2):141–57.

Piehl, Anne M. 1998. "Economic Conditions, Work, and Crime." In Michael Tonry (ed.), *The Handbook of Crime and Punishment*, pp. 302–19. New York: Oxford University Press.

Plomin, R. R., T. T. Foch, and D. Rowe. 1981. "Bobo Clown Aggression in Childhood: Environment not Genes." *Journal of Research in Personality* 15:331–342.

Plomin, Robert, H. M. Chipuer, and J. C. Loehlin. 1990. "Behavioral Genetics and Personality." In L. A. Pervin (ed.), *Handbook of Personality Theory and Research*, pp. 225–43. New York: Guilford Press.

Pontius, A. A. and B. S. Yudowitz. 1980. "Frontal Lobe System Dysfunction in Some Criminal Actions As Shown in the Narratives Test." *Journal of Nervous and Mental Disease* 168(2):111–17.

Powers, Edwin and Helen Witmer. 1951. *An Experiment in the Prevention of Delinquency*. New York: Columbia University Press.

Reasons, Charles, Lee Ross, and C. Paterson. 1981. *Assault on the Worker: Occupational Health and Safety in Canada*. Toronto: Butterworths.

Reischauer, Edwin O. 1988. *The Japanese Today*. Cambridge, MA: Harvard University Press.

Revenga, Ana. 1992. "Exporting Jobs? The Impact of Import Competition on Employment and Wages in U. S. Manufacturing." *Quarterly Journal of Economics* 107(1):255–82.

Riley, Matilda W. 1986. "Overview and Highlights of a Sociological Perspective." In Aage B. Sorensen, Franz E. Weinert, and Lonnie R. Sherrod (eds.), *Human Development and the Life Course: Multidisciplinary Perspectives*, pp. 153–175. Hillsdale, NJ: Lawrence Earlbaum Associates.

Rindfuss, Ronald R., C. G. Swicegood, and Rachel A. Rosenfeld. 1987. "Disorder in the Life Course: How Common and Does It Matter?" *American Sociological Review* 52(December):785–801.

Robins, Lee N. 1966. *Deviant Children Grown Up: A Sociological and Psychiatric Study of Sociopathic Personality.* Baltimore, MD: Williams & Wilkins.

——. 1985. "Epidemiology of Antisocial Personality." In J. O. Cavenar (ed.), *Psychiatry*, Vol. 3, pp. 1–14. Philadelphia: Lippincott.

Ross, Edward A. 1977. "The Criminaloid." In Gilbert Geis and Robert Meier (eds.), *White-Collar Crime*, rev. ed., pp. 29–37. New York: MacMillan.

Rothman, Martin L. and Robert P. Gandossy. 1982. "Sad Tales: The Accounts of White-Collar Defendants and the Decision to Sanction." *Pacific Sociological Review* 25(4):449–73.

Rowe, David. C. 1990. "Inherited Dispositions Toward Learning Delinquent and Criminal Behavior: New Evidence." In Lee Ellis and Harry Hoffman (eds.), *Crime in Biological, Social, and Moral Contexts*, pp. 121–33. New York: Praeger Publishers.

——. 1994. *The Limits of Family Influence: Genes, Experience, and Behavior.* New York: Guilford Press.

Rowe, David C. and David P. Farrington. 1997. "The Familial Transmission of Criminal Convictions." *Criminology* 35(1):177–201.

Rutter, Michael. 1996. "Introduction: Concepts of Antisocial Behavior, of Cause, and of Genetic Influences." In Gregory R. Bock and Jamie A. Goode (eds.), *Genetics of Criminal and Antisocial Behavior*, pp. 1–15. Chichester, UK: John Wiley & Sons.

Ryder, Norman B. 1965. "The Cohort As a Concept in the Study of Social Change." *American Sociological Review* 30:843–61.

Sampson, Robert J. and William J. Wilson. 1995. "Toward a Theory of Race, Crime and Urban Inequality." In John Hagan and Ruth Peterson (eds.), *Crime and Inequality*, pp. 37–54. Stanford, CA: Stanford University Press.

Sampson, Robert J. 1987. "Communities and Crime." In Michael R. Gottfredson and Travis Hirschi (eds.), *Positive Criminology*, pp. 91–114. Newbury Park, NJ: Sage.

——. 1997. "The Embeddedness of Child and Adolescent Development: A Community-Level Perspective on Urban Violence." In Joan McCord (ed.), *Violence and Childhood in the Inner City*, pp. 31–77. New York: Cambridge University Press.

Sampson, Robert J. and W. B. Groves. 1989. "Community Structure and Crime: Testing Social-Disorganization Theory." *American Journal of Sociology* 94(4):774–802.

Sampson, Robert J. and John H. Laub. 1990. "Crime and Deviance Over the Life Course." *American Social Review* 55(5):609–27.

——. 1993. *Crime in the Making: Pathways and Turning Points Through Life.* Cambridge, MA: Harvard University Press.

——. 1997. "A Life-Course Theory of Cumulative Disadvantage and the Stability of Delinquency." In Terence P. Thornberry, (ed.), *Developmental Theories of Crime and Delinquency,* pp. 133–62. New Brunswick, NJ: Transaction Publishers.

Sampson, Robert J. and Janet L. Lauritsen. 1994. "Violent Victimization and Offending: Individual-, Situational- and Community-Level Risk Factors." In Albert J. Reiss, Jr. and Julius A. Roth (eds.), *Understanding and Preventing Violence,* Vol. 3, pp. 1–114. Washington, DC: National Academy Press.

Sampson, Robert J., Jeffrey D. Morenoff, and Felton Earls. 1999. "Beyond Social Capital: Spatial Dynamics of Collective Efficacy for Children." *American Sociological Review* 64(5):633–60.

Sampson, Robert J. and Stephen W. Raudenbush. 1999. "Systematic Social Observation of Public Spaces: A New Look at Disorder in Urban Neighborhoods." *American Journal of Sociology* 105(3):603–51.

Sampson, Robert J., Stephen W. Raudenbush, and Felton Earls. 1997. "Neighborhoods and Violent Crime: A Multilevel Study of Collective Efficacy." *Science* 277:918–24.

Sandifer, Jacquelyn L. and Suzanne M. Kurth. 2000. "The Invisible Children of Incarcerated Mothers." In Greer L. Fox and Michael L. Benson (eds.), *Families, Crime and Criminal Justice,* pp. 361–380. New York: Elsevier Science, Inc.

Scarr-Salapatek, Sandra. 1971. "Race, Social Class, and IQ." *Science* 174:1285–95.

Scarr, Sandra and Kathleen McCartney. 1983. "How People Make Their Own Environments: A Theory of Genotype Environment Effects." *Child Development* 63:1–19.

Shah, S. A. and L. H. Roth. 1974. "Biological and Psychophysiological Factors in Criminality." In Daniel Glaser (ed.), *Handbook of Criminology,* pp. 101–173. Chicago: Rand McNally.

Shannon, Lyle W. 1982. *Assessing the Relationship of Adult Criminal Careers to Juvenile Careers: A Summary.* Washington, DC: Department of Justice.

——. 1988. *Criminal Career Continuity: Its Social Context.* New York: Human Sciences Press.

Shapiro, Susan P. 1984. *Wayward Capitalists.* New Haven: Yale University Press.

——. 1985. "The Road Not Taken: The Elusive Path to Criminal Prosecution for White Collar Offenders." *Law & Society Review* 19(2):179–217.

—. 1990. "Collaring the Crime, Not the Criminal: Reconsidering 'White-Collar Crime'." *American Sociological Review* 55(3):346–65.

Short, James and Ivan F. Nye. 1958. "Extent of Undetected Delinquency, Tentative Conclusions." *Journal of Criminal Law, Criminology, and Police Science* 49:296–302.

Shover, Neal. 1985. *Aging Criminals*. Beverly Hills, CA: Sage Publications.

—. 1996. *Great Pretenders: Pursuits and Careers of Persistent Thieves*. Boulder, CO: Westview Press.

Shover, Neal, Greer L. Fox, and Michael Mills. 1994. "Long-Term Consequences of Victimization by White-Collar Crime." *Justice Quarterly* 11(1):75–94.

Shover, Neal and Carol Y. Thompson. 1992. "Age, Differential Expectations, and Crime Desistance." *Criminology* 30(1):89–104.

Simpson, Sally S. 1987. "Cycles of Illegality: Antitrust Violations in Corporate America." *Social Forces* 65:943–63.

Simpson, Sally S., Raymond Paternoster, and Nicole L. Piquero. 1998. "Exploring the Micro-Macro Link in Corporate Crime Research." *Research in the Sociology of Organizations* 15:35–68.

Skogan, Wesley. 1986. "Fear of Crime and Neighborhood Change." In Albert J. Reiss and Michael Tonry (eds.), *Communities and Crime*, pp. 203–30. Chicago: University of Chicago Press.

Skogan, Wesley G. and Michael G. Maxfield. 1981. *Coping With Crime: Individual and Neighborhood Reactions*. Newbury Park, CA: Sage Publications.

Slavin, S. H. 1978. "Information Processing Defects in Delinquents." In Leonard J. Hippchen (ed.), *Ecologic-Biochemical Approaches to Treatment of Delinquents and Criminals*, pp. 75–104. New York: Van Nostrand Reinhold.

Smith, Carolyn and Terence P. Thornberry. 1995. "The Relationship Between Childhood Maltreatment and Adolescent Involvement in Delinquency." *Criminology* 33(4):451–82.

Smith, Carolyn A., Marvin D. Krohn, Alan J. Lizotte, Cynthia P. McCluskey, Magda Stouthamer-Loeber, and Anne Weiher. 2000. "The Effect of Delinquency and Substance Use on Precocious Transitions to Adulthood Among Adolescent Males." In Greer L. Fox and Michael L. Benson (eds.), *Families, Crime and Criminal Justice*, pp. 233–53. New York: Elsevier Science, Inc.

Smith, Robert J. 1983. *Japanese Society: Tradition, Self, and the Social Order*. New York: Cambridge University Press.

Sommers, Ira, Deborah R. Baskin, and Jeffrey Fagan. 1994. "Getting Out of the Life: Crime Desistance by Female Street Offenders." In Paul Cromwell (ed.), *In Their Own Words*, 2nd ed., pp. 87–96. Los Angeles, CA: Roxbury Publishing.

Sorensen, Aage B., Franz E. Weinert, and Lonnie R. Sherrod. 1986. "Preface." In Aage B. Sorensen, Franz E. Weinert, and Lonnie R. Sherrod (eds.), *Human Development and the Life Course: Multidisciplinary Perspectives*, pp. xv–xxiv. Hillsdale, NJ: Lawrence Erlbaum Associates.

Spencer, John C. 1965. "White-Collar Crime." In Tadeusz Grygier, Howard Jones, and John C. Spencer (eds.), *Criminology in Transition*, pp. 233–66. London: Tavistock Publishers.

Steffensmeier, Darrell and Emilie Allan. 1995. "Age-Inequality and Property Crime: The Effects of Age-Linked Stratification and Status Attainment Processes on Patterns of Criminality Across the Life Course." In John Hagan and Ruth Petersen (eds.), *Crime and Inequality*, pp. 95–115. Stanford, CA: Stanford University Press.

——. 2000. "Looking for Patterns: Gender, Age, and Crime." In Joseph F. Sheley (ed.), *Criminology: A Contemporary Handbook*, 3rd ed., pp. 85–128. Belmont, CA: Wadsworth.

Steffensmeier, Darrell, Emilie Allan, Miles D. Harer, and Cathy Streifel. 1989. "Age and the Distribution of Crime." *American Journal of Sociology* 94(4):803–31.

Steffensmeier, Darrell, Emilie Allan, and Cathy Streifel. 1989. "Development and Female Crime: A Cross-National Test of Alternative Explanations." *Social Forces* 69:869–94.

Sucoff, Clea and Dawn Upchurch. 1998. "Neighborhood Context and the Risk of Childbearing Among Metropolitan-Area Black Adolescents." *American Sociological Review* 63:571–85.

Sullivan, Mercer. 1989. *Getting Paid: Youth Crime and Work in the Inner City*. Ithaca, NY: Cornell University Press.

Sutherland, Edwin H. 1940. "White-Collar Criminality." *American Sociological Review* 5:1–12.

——. 1949. *White-Collar Crime*. New York: Holt, Rinehart and Winston.

Sutton, John R. 2001. "Imprisonment and Social Classification in Five Common-Law Democracies, 1955–1985." *American Journal of Sociology* 106(2):350–386.

Tanner, Julian, Scott Davies, and Bill O'Grady. 1999. "Whatever Happened to Yesterday's Rebels? Longitudinal Effects of Youth Delinquency on Education and Employment." *Social Problems* 46(2):250–274.

Tappan, Paul W. 1947. "Who Is the Criminal." *American Sociological Review* 12:96–102.

Taylor, Ian, Paul Walton, and Jock Young. 1973. *The New Criminology: For a Social Theory of Deviance*. London: Routledge and Kegan Paul.

Taylor, Ralph B. and Jeanette Covington. 1988. "Neighborhood Changes in Ecology and Violence." *Criminology* 26(4):553–89.

Thomas, William. I. and Florian Znaniecki. 1974. *The Polish Peasant in Europe and America.* New York: Octagon.

Thornberry, Terence P. 1987. "Toward an Interactional Theory of Delinquency." *Criminology* 25(4):863–92.

——. 1997. "Introduction: Some Advantages of Developmental and Life-Course Perspectives for the Study of Crime and Delinquency." In Terence P. Thornberry (ed.), *Developmental Theories of Crime and Delinquency,* pp. 1–10. New Brunswick, NJ: Transaction Publishers.

Thornberry, Terence P. and R. L. Christenson. 1984. "Unemployment and Criminal Involvement: An Investigation of Reciprocal Causal Structures." *American Sociological Review* 49:398–411.

Thornberry, Terence P., Marvin D. Krohn, Alan J. Lizotte, Carolyn A. Smith, and P. K. Perter. 1998. "Taking Stock: An Overview of the Findings From the Rochester Youth Development Study." Paper Presented at the American Society of Criminology Meeting, Washington, DC.

Thornberry, Terence P., Evelyn H. Wei, Magda Stouthamer-Loeber, and Joyce Van Dyke. 2000. *Teenage Fatherhood and Delinquent Behavior.* NCJ 178899. Washington, DC: Office of Juvenile Justice and Delinquency Prevention.

Tittle, Charles R. and Raymond Paternoster. 2000. *Social Deviance and Crime: An Organizational and Theoretical Approach.* Los Angeles: Roxbury Publishing.

Tracy, Paul, Marvin Wolfgang, and Robert Figlio. 1990. *Delinquency Careers in Two Birth Cohorts.* New York: Plenum.

Uggen, Christopher. 2000. "Work As a Turning Point in the Life Course of Criminals: A Duration Model of Age, Employment, and Recidivism." *American Sociological Review* 65(4):529–46.

United Nations Interregional Crime & Justice Research Institute. 1994. *Crime and Crime Prevention in Moscow.* Rome/Moscow: United Nations Publications.

Vaux, A. 1988. *Social Support: Theory, Research and Intervention.* New York: Praeger.

Venables, Peter. 1987. "Autonomic Nervous System Factors in Criminal Behavior." In Sarnoff Mednick, Terrie E. Moffitt, and Susan Stack (eds.), *The Causes of Crime: New Biological Approaches,* pp. 110–136. Cambridge, UK: University of Cambridge Press.

Voorhees, J. 1981. "Neuropsychological Differences Between Juvenile Delinquents and Functional Adolescents: A Preliminary Study." *Adolescence* 16(61):57–66.

Wallach, Michael A., Nathan Kogan, and Daryl J. Bem. 1964. "Diffusion of Responsibility and Level of Risk Taking in Groups." *Journal of Abnormal and Social Psychology* 68:263–74.

Walsh, Anthony. 2000. "Behavior Genetics and Anomie/Strain Theory." *Criminology* 38(4):1075–108.

Warr, Mark. 1998. "Life-Course Transitions and Desistance From Crime." *Criminology* 36(2):183–216.

Weisburd, David, Ellen F. Chayet, and Elin J. Waring. 1990. "White-Collar Crime and Criminal Careers: Some Preliminary Findings." *Crime & Delinquency* 36(3):342–55.

Weisburd, David, Elin Waring, and Ellen F. Chayet. 2001. *White-Collar Crime and Criminal Careers*. New York: Cambridge University Press.

Weisburd, David, Stanton Wheeler, Elin Waring, and N. Bode. 1991. *Crimes of the Middle Classes: White-Collar Offenders in the Federal Courts*. New Haven: Yale University Press.

West, Donald J. and David P. Farrington. 1973. *Who Becomes Delinquent?* London: Heinemann.

—. 1977. *The Delinquent Way of Life*. London: Hienemann.

Westermann, Ted D. and James W. Burfeind. 1991. *Crime and Justice in Two Societies: Japan and the United States*. Pacific Grove, CA: Brooks/Cole Publishing.

Wheeler, Stanton, Kenneth Mann, and Austin Sarat. 1988. *Sitting in Judgement: The Sentencing of White-Collar Criminals*. New Haven: Yale University Press.

Wheeler, Stanton and Mitchell L. Rothman. 1980. "The Organization As Weapon in White-Collar Crime." *Michigan Law Review* 80(7):1403–26.

Wheeler, Stanton, David Weisburd, and Nancy Bode. 1982. "Sentencing the White-Collar Offender: Rhetoric and Reality." *American Sociological Review* 47(5):641–59.

Wheeler, Stanton, David Weisburd, Elin Waring, and Nancy Bode. 1988. "White Collar Crime and Criminals." *American Criminal Law Review* 25:331–57.

White, J., Terrie E. Moffitt, Felton Earls, Lee N. Robins, and Phil A. Silva. 1990. "How Early Can We Tell? Preschool Predictors of Boys' Conduct Disorders and Delinquency." *Criminology* 28:507–33.

Wikstrom, Per-Olof H. and Rolf Loeber. 2000. "Do Disadvantaged Neighborhoods Cause Well-Adjusted Children to Become Adolescent Delinquents? A Study of Male Juvenile Serious Offending, Individual Risk and Protective Factors, and Neighborhood Context." *Criminology* 38(4):1109–42.

Wilson, James Q. 1975. *Thinking About Crime*. New York: Basic Books.

Wilson, James Q. and Richard J. Herrnstein. 1985. *Crime and Human Nature.* New York: Simon & Schuster.

Wilson, William J. 1987. *The Truly Disadvantaged.* Chicago: University of Chicago Press.

Wolfgang, Marvin E., Robert M. Figlio, and Thorsten Sellin. 1972. *Delinquency in a Birth Cohort.* Chicago: University of Chicago Press.

Wolfgang, Marvin E., Terence P. Thornberry, and Robert M. Figlio. 1987. *From Boy to Man, From Delinquency to Crime.* Chicago: University of Chicago Press.

Wright, Bradley R. E., Avshalom Caspi, Terrie E. Moffitt, and Phil A. Silva. 1999. "Low Self-Control, Social Bonds, and Crime: Social Causation, Social Selection, or Both?" *Criminology* 37(3):479–514.

—. 2000. "The Effects of Social Ties on Crime Vary by Criminal Propensity: A Life-Course Model of Interdependence." Unpublished manuscript.

Yeager, Peter C. and Gary E. Reed. 1998. "Of Corporate Persons and Straw Men: A Reply to Herbert, Green and Larragoite." *Criminology* 36(4):885–97.

Yeudall, L. T., D. Fromm-Auch, and P. Davies. 1982. "Neuropsychological Impairment of Persistent Delinquency." *Journal of Nervous and Mental Disease* 170(5):257–65.

Zhou, Xueguang and Liren Hou. 1999. "Children of the Cultural Revolution: The State and the Life Course in the People's Republic of China." *American Sociological Review* 64(1):12–36. ✦

Author
and
Subject
Indices

Author Index

Subject Index